Designing and Coding

Reusable C++

Martin D. Carroll

Margaret A. Ellis

AT&T

ADDISON-WESLEY PUBLISHING COMPANY, INC.

Reading, Massachusetts • Menlo Park, California • New York • Don Mills, Ontario
Wokingham, England • Amsterdam • Bonn • Singapore • Tokyo
Madrid • San Juan • Sydney • Milan • Paris

This book was reproduced from PostScript files supplied by the authors. The authors typeset the book using the L^AT_EX document preparation system.

The photograph on the back cover is by Marybeth Williams.

The credits are continued on page 318.

Sponsoring Editor: Thomas Stone
Associate Editor: Deborah Lafferty
Production Supervisor: Juliet Silveri
Production Services: Superscript Editorial Production Services
Cover Design Supervisor: Eileen Hoff
Manufacturing Manager: Roy Logan

Library of Congress Cataloging-in-Publication Data
Carroll, Martin D.
    Designing and coding reusable C++ / Martin D. Carroll,
    Margaret A. Ellis.
            p.   cm.
    includes bibliographical references and index.
    ISBN 0-201-51284-X
    1. C++ (Computer program language)   I. Ellis, Margaret A.
    II. Title.
    QA76.73.C153C39   1995   94-49369
    005.13'3--dc20   CIP

For more information about Addison-Wesley titles, please visit our gopher site via the Internet: gopher aw.com to connect to our on-line book information listing.

1 2 3 4 5 6 7 8 9 10-MA-98979695

To Mom, Dad, Sun, Steve, Eileen, Don, Brian, Janet, Mom, Harold, Kathy, Rick, Jessica, Ginny, Bob, Jennifer, Ben, David, Tamerly, Elizabeth, Marybeth, Michael, Kelsey, Dylan, and Jerry

With love

Preface

> *All things are to be examined and called into question.*
> — Edith Hamilton

The primary goal of this book is to show how to write *reusable* code in the C++ programming language — that is, code that can easily be used with little or no change in five, fifty, or five hundred programs with varying requirements, written by different programmers, and possibly running on different systems. It is *not* a goal of this book to argue that all code should be reusable, nor that making code reusable will solve all programming problems. Making code reusable has costs, and it makes sense to incur those costs for a given piece of code only if it can reasonably be expected that that code will be reused. It *is* a goal of this book to document the costs of reusability so that, faced with the choice of whether to write a given piece of code reusably, you can make an informed decision.

About This Book

This book is intended for C++ programmers who would like to benefit from the many insights about good C++ programming that are contained herein, as well as those who need or want to learn how to write reusable code. We assume throughout that the reader already knows how to write correct C++ code.

The C++ language is not yet standardized. Almost every pair of C++ implementations support (slightly or not so slightly) different languages. As of this writing, no implementations support the entire language as it will be defined in the final ANSI/ISO C++ standard, and one release of a given implementation might implement a different language from the previous release. Trying to write a book for a moving target is difficult. Whenever we discuss or use a language feature that might not yet be implemented or might not be implemented the same way by all major C++ implementations, we point out this possibility.

When we state that or imply that a code example in this book is legal, we mean that it is legal according to the September 1994 ANSI/ISO C++ working paper [ANS94] (sometimes called the "draft standard"). We have, in our code examples, avoided the use of language features that, in our opinion, have a nontrivial probability of being removed or significantly changed before the final ANSI/ISO C++ standard is published.

Several sources are available for following the evolution of the C++ language. The Internet newsgroups `comp.lang.c++` and `comp.std.c++` are devoted to discussions about C++. A home page for C++ on the Worldwide Web is

> `http://info.desy.de/user/projects/C++.html`

Articles of interest to the C++ programmer appear regularly in the *C++ Report*, published by SIGS Publications, New York. Many textbooks are available for learning C++; Lippman's primer [Lip91] and Stroustrup's book [Str91] are highly recommended.

Any thorough discussion of reusability must also discuss other topics related to software development: design of interfaces, efficiency of implementations, portability, and conflict, to name a few. We assume that the reader is familiar with software development, and we focus on these topics *as they apply to reusable code*, not as they apply to software development in general.

A favorite adage of one of our teachers was "Every textbook lies." What she meant was that every textbook, for the sake of instructional clarity, must simplify and thereby might distort the information it presents. Topics must be presented in such a way that the essential information is not lost in a morass of detail. This book is no exception. Readers who already grasp the full scope of a topic are asked to bear with us and forgive an occasional simplification. Life in the software business is more complex than it appears in books.

Tradeoffs and Recommendations

Designing and writing reusable code involves making many tradeoffs, some of them painful. Usually there is no clear-cut right answer — no matter what you do, there will be a price to pay. We discuss the advantages and disadvantages of various alternatives so that prospective authors of reusable code can make informed decisions.

Sometimes, we believe that one style or approach to a given decision is preferable to all others. When we do, we make an explicit recommendation and present evidence supporting our position. Usually, however, only the designer of a C++ library can decide what is the best approach for the users of that library.

A goal of this book is to present thoroughly and clearly the significant tradeoffs involved in writing reusable code. If we have omitted any important tradeoffs, we would like to hear about them.

Many of the discussions of tradeoffs in this book mention efficiency. *We do not believe that efficiency should be the primary goal of all reusable C++ code.* For many libraries, other properties such as extensibility or flexibility will be more important than efficiency. There is a preponderance of text devoted to efficiency because it trades off with almost every other desirable property of reusable C++ code. Our desire to present all the tradeoffs forces us to devote much discussion to efficiency.

Code Examples

It is our intention that this book be useful and that when you have finished reading this book you will know how to program for reusability better than you did before you started. Thus, we use examples extensively. Many of the code examples in this book were taken from real code. Those that were not illustrate problems that arise in real code or techniques that are used in real code.

To save space in the text, the bodies of member functions are often shown in their class declarations, even though they would not be implemented as inline functions in code destined for reuse. For example, the reader should not infer from the following class definition that f should be inlined in real code:

```
class Z {
    void f() {
        // ...
    }
};
```

(How to determine whether a function should be inlined is discussed in Section 4.4.1.)

When referring to template member functions, we often omit the template arguments if there is no resulting loss of clarity. For example, we might refer to the member function f in

```
template<class T>
class X {
    void f();
};
```

as `X::f` rather than `X<T>::f`.

Often, what is shown as a class in an example would be a template in a real library. Again, we are simplifying for easier reading and for a clearer presentation of the topic. Similarly, classes that in a real library would be nested in other classes are not always shown as nested. When we do show a nested class, we do not use forward-declaration syntax. For example, we write

```
class X {
    class Y {
        // ...
    };
    // ...
};
```

rather than

```
class X {
    class Y;
    // ...
};
class X::Y {
    // ...
};
```

Although forward declarations result in more readable code, they are not yet implemented by many C++ compilers.

The new cast syntax is not yet implemented in any of the compilers available to us. It is (as of this writing) very new to C++, and we have no experience with its use; therefore, we have chosen not to use it in this edition.

Terminology

In this text we use the term *library* to mean a collection of reusable code. We often use *library* and *reusable code* interchangeably. When we say *write* a piece of code, we mean "design and implement" that code.

We use *compiler* to mean any program or set of programs that translates source code to an executable form. Translation may include preprocessing

C++ to another language, which is then compiled or assembled into executable code.

For the sake of brevity, we use *base* or *base class* not only to mean a class that is a base class of another class, but also to mean a class that is *intended* to be derived from.

The C++ operators

```
ostream& operator<<(ostream& o, const T& t);
istream& operator>>(istream& i, T& t);
```

(for a given type T) provide stream-insertion and stream-extraction operations for T. Consistent with common usage, we often call them the *output* and *input* operators for T, respectively.

There is some inconsistency in the C++ community regarding terms relating to templates and template instantiation. Different people use each of the terms *template class, class template, instantiation, instance, specialization*, and so on to mean (perhaps slightly) different things. The precise, standard meanings of these terms will eventually be defined by the C++ ANSI/ISO committee. Here is how we use these terms:

> *class template*: A template of the form `template<...>`X, where X is a class definition.
>
> *function template*: A template of the form `template<...>`f, where f is a function definition.
>
> *class template specialization*: The class that results when the parameters of a class template are replaced by actual arguments.
>
> *function template specialization*: The function that results when the parameters of a function template are replaced by actual arguments.
>
> *instantiation*: The process of creating specializations.
>
> *template class*: We do not use this term.
>
> *template function*: We do not use this term.

For example, consider the following class template:

```
template<class T>
class X {
    // ...
};
```

The classes X<int> and X<char> are two specializations of this template. Specializations are usually implicitly defined:

```
template<class T> class X { /* ... */ };
X<int> x;   // X<int> is implicitly defined
```

Occasionally, a specialization is explicitly defined by the C++ programmer:

```
template<class T> class X { /* ... */ };
class X<int> { /* ... */ };   // X<int> is explicitly defined
X<int> x;
```

Many people use the term *specialization* to refer only to explicit specialization. Our definitions of these terms correspond closely, we believe, to how ANSI/ISO will define them.

Often, we use *class* to mean "class template" and *function* to mean "function template" when no confusion would result.

Acknowledgments

Many people supported us, in many ways, in creating this book. We are grateful to all of them.

Our reviewers contributed tremendously to the quality and value of this book. We are especially grateful to those who were hardest on us; they believed we could do better. Many thanks to Tom Allocco, Manuel Bermudez, Steve Buroff, William Bulley, Tom Cargill, Sonia Carroll, Steve Clamage, James Coggins, Keith Gorlen, Tony Hansen, Chris Hornick, Peter Juhl, Brian Kernighan, Andrew Koenig, Eason Kung, Rao Kurmala, Doug Lea, Stan Lippman, Tom Lyon, Glen McCluskey, Barbara Moo, Rob Murray, Jishnu Mukerji, Scott Myers, Steve Pendergrast, Ed Schiebel, Jonathan Schilling, Jonathan Shopiro, Bjarne Stroustrup, Steve Vinoski, Judy Ward, and Clay Wilson.

We also received useful feedback from Dag Brück, Rich Kempinski, Josée LaJoie, Deborah McGuinness, David C. Oliver, Jeffrey Persch, Elia Weixelbaum, and two fellows called Lars and Steve on the Internet.

Many of the ideas in this book were first brought to our attention during the design and implementation of the Standard Components Library for C++, originally developed at AT&T Bell Laboratories. We would like to thank our colleagues on that project for many insightful discussions: John Isner, Andrew Koenig, Dennis Mancl, Rob Murray, Jonathan Shopiro, Alex Stepanov, Terry Weitzen, and Nancy Wilkinson.

This book (and several others) would not exist without C++. Thanks to Bjarne Stroustrup for inventing one of our favorite programming languages. Thanks also to the dedicated members of the joint ANSI/ISO C++ standardization committee for work (often freely donated) that will serve the entire C++ community for years to come.

Thanks to the folks who were our supervisors while we were working on this book — Martha Currie, Barbara Moo, and John Spicer — for their support and encouragement. Thanks to our employers — AT&T Bell Laboratories and Unix System Laboratories (now Novell's Unix System Group) — for allowing this work to go on and for cycles, disk space, printer paper, and so on.

We are grateful for the terrific support we received from Addison-Wesley. The energetic Tom Stone and ever-cheerful Debbie Lafferty were wonderful to work with. Lyn Dupré gave us top-notch editorial guidance. Juliet Silveri was meticulous as book designer. Ann Knight's team did a great job on production; Pat Daly was a thorough copy-editor, and Roberta Clark gave our manuscript an excellent proofreading. We are grateful to John Wait for persisting in asking Martin to write a book on reuse and C++. Jim DeWolf (our first editor) got us off to a good start before leaving Addison-Wesley to publish books on heating and air conditioning that will sell more copies than any C++ book ever will.

Heartfelt thanks to Tom Reinhardt, the world's best physical therapist. Thanks to Paul Lustgarten, friend and former landlord, for allowing us to tie up his telephone line for hours and hours night after night. Thanks to David Wooley for turning Martin on to programming in a high school BASIC course. Sincere thanks to Marybeth Williams for the back cover photo.

Last, but by no means least, we would like to thank our families and friends, who not only suffered with us through the writing of this book but always stood beside us with love and support.

Martin Carroll
Margaret Ellis
March, 1995

Contents

1   Introduction to Reusability

> *The great consulting room of a wise man*
> *is a library.*
>
> — George Dawson

We begin this introduction to reusability with descriptions of reuse and, in particular, of scavenging — a primitive form of reuse. The disadvantages of scavenging motivate our definition of reusable code. We go on to refute some myths that have arisen about reuse and list the major obstacles — both technical and nontechnical — to reuse. Finally, we offer some hope to the aspiring authors of reusable code.

1.1   What Is Reusability?

Many tasks are done by more than one computer program. For example, more than one program

- Sorts an array
- Solves a system of linear equations
- Computes a mapping from X to Y, for two types X and Y
- Parses C++ code
- Retrieves data from a database
- Communicates with other programs

Rather than design and implement code for each of these tasks — and many others — in each program that needs it, we would prefer to design and implement the code for each task once and reuse that code many times. Reusing code that already exists, rather than writing every application from scratch, speeds development and reduces the cost of writing and maintaining an application.

1

Code reuse is not a new concept. Even the early versions of FORTRAN, the first high-level programming language, had an extensive library of input, output, and formatting operations, as well as a math library. *Reuse* was not a buzzword when FORTRAN was new, but these libraries constituted reusable code. Another notable example is the UNIX operating system, which encourages reuse by providing many small, generally useful commands that can be combined easily in novel ways.

1.1.1 Scavenging as Reuse

A primitive form of code reuse is *scavenging* (or *salvaging*) code from other programs. For example, suppose that we are implementing a compiler for some programming language. Somewhere in the implementation of our compiler we shall probably need an efficient hash table for managing symbol tables. Rather than design and implement a hash table from scratch, we might scavenge the code of other compilers and, if we find suitable hash table code, copy it into our program.

Scavenging is common in practice. Unfortunately, there are significant problems associated with scavenging. First, finding the needed code can be difficult. No one can scavenge more than a small fraction of all existing code in the world. Because scavenging in a body of code requires that one have access to and understand that code, programmers usually scavenge only in their own code or in code written by programmers with whom they work. Second, there is usually little assurance that code appearing in another program is correct. Third, anyone who has tried separating a nontrivial piece of code from its containing program knows that that can be difficult because of dependencies connecting the desired code with other code in the program. Fourth, scavenged code often needs nontrivial change to work in a new program. Names used in the scavenged code might conflict with names already used in the new context, the scavenged code might assume things about its execution environment that are not true of the new program's environment, the scavenged code might be optimized for usage patterns that are typical in the original program but are not true in the new one, and so on.

Writing code from scratch is often easier than scavenging — even if we know that the code we need exists in another program and even if we know where to find it.

1.1.2 Essential Properties of Reusable Code

We would not encounter the difficulties of scavenging mentioned in the previous section if we could find a suitable implementation of the functionality we need that has the following properties:

- It is easy to find and to understand.
- There is reasonable assurance that it is correct.
- It requires no separation from any containing code.
- It requires no changes to be used in a new program.

These properties are the minimal properties that any code must have to be reusable. Any particular piece of code might also have to have other properties, including efficiency, extensibility, portability, and many others.

A collection of reusable code is a *library*. In C++, a library is packaged as a collection of (zero or more) public header files, (zero or more) other source files, (zero or more) object files, and (zero or more) files needed for instantiating templates. The object files are themselves usually packaged in one or more containing files, which are called *archives* on some systems and *link libraries* on others. (A *dynamic link library*, or DLL, is a special kind of link library.) Although *link library* is the more common term, we shall use the term *archive* to avoid confusion with other uses of *library*. Users of a library #include the header files, compile the source files, and link with the resulting object files and the archives, using whatever system-specific mechanisms are provided.

1.2 Myths of Reuse

Many myths have arisen about code reuse. This section briefly refutes several of the more popular ones.

Myth: Reuse will resolve the software crisis. The *software crisis* is the current inability of the programming community to build programs that would solve complex problems, to produce those programs quickly, and to build them such that they are correct and can be maintained easily.

There are signs of progress. One such sign is that with passing time the term *complex problems* has come to denote a different set of problems. In the 1960s, writing a compiler for FORTRAN-66 was considered a complex problem; building a correct compiler for FORTRAN-66 was time consuming, and the end product was not as maintainable as present-day compilers. Today, how to write a correct, maintainable compiler for FORTRAN-66 is well understood. Even so, no one considers the ease of writing a FORTRAN-66 compiler as evidence that the software crisis has been solved. Rather, writing a FORTRAN-66 compiler is no longer considered a complex problem.

Because people will continue to identify ever more complex problems that could be solved with appropriate software, the perception that there is a software crisis probably will not change soon. This observation does not imply, however, that reuse has no benefits. As programmers reuse more code, the complexity of their programming tasks shrinks and formerly complex problems become simpler.

Myth: All code should be reusable. As we shall see throughout this book, reusability has costs. It makes no sense to incur these costs if we never plan to reuse the code we are writing. Take heed, however: Often, the opportunity to reuse a piece of code becomes apparent only *after* it has been written. Rewriting code to increase its reusability is usually more difficult than it would have been to write the code for reusability in the first place.

Myth: Reusing code is always preferable to coding from scratch. It is often easier to write correct, maintainable code from scratch than to find a reusable version of that code, especially for small programming tasks. If we needed a C++ function that converts degrees Celsius to degrees Fahrenheit, for example, it would be easier to write one from scratch than to search for a reusable version of such a function, even though one almost certainly exists somewhere in the world.

Myth: Object-oriented languages make writing reusable code easy. Most programmers who have tried code reuse on any nontrivial scale using an object-oriented language would agree that such languages make reuse easier than languages that are not object oriented, but few would go so far as to say that object-oriented languages make reuse easy. Successful reuse requires knowledge, experience, and hard work.

1.3 Obstacles to Reuse

The truth about reuse is that it is difficult — both nontechnical and technical obstacles exist. A nontechnical obstacle to reuse is something about an organizational structure, a social structure, or a programming culture that prevents reuse. A technical obstacle to reuse is something about programming itself that prevents reuse.

1.3.1 Nontechnical Obstacles

To understand the nontechnical obstacles to reuse, consider what must happen for a C++ programmer to reuse, for example, a class `Widget` from some library.

The author of `Widget` must have suspected that a reusable version of `Widget` would be useful. Making code reusable takes time and effort. Most programmers will not bother making something reusable if they believe the effort would be for naught.

The author of `Widget` must have expected to be rewarded for writing `Widget` reusably and making it available. Things that take time and effort usually do not happen unless they are rewarded. Unfortunately, not only is programming reusably not always rewarded, it is often (sometimes unintentionally) discouraged.

Consider two hypothetical programmers, Pat and Chris, who work in some department in some large company. Pat always completes her assignments in record time, but her code is reusable only by her on her projects. Chris, on the other hand, takes more time to complete her tasks because she writes much of her code to be reusable easily by any programmer in the entire company. Indeed, programmers throughout the company have saved time by using Chris's code. Nevertheless, if Pat and Chris's department cares only about completing its own projects on time, Chris will be penalized when raises are awarded.

Someone must maintain `Widget`. The more successful a piece of reusable code is, the more time will have to be spent maintaining it — that is, fixing errors in it and evolving it to meet new needs. If Chris's code is used throughout the company, she will spend a nontrivial amount of her time answering questions about it, distributing it, and evolving it. The total time spent maintaining a successful piece of reusable code can often exceed the time required to write it. If maintenance is not rewarded, reuse will be short lived at best.

The eventual user of `Widget` must suspect that `Widget` exists and must be able to find it. The author of a large program needs many things. Searching the universe for reusable versions of all those things would not be cost effective; programmers must suspect that a search for a reusable version of a particular piece of code will be successful.

Clearly, organizations must advertise their reusable code (either internally or externally, depending on the intended set of users). Libraries must provide enough documentation and tools to make finding them and finding things in them easy.

The eventual user of `Widget` must be able to obtain `Widget`. Obtaining `Widget` might involve simply copying several files electronically, or it might require receiving a CD-ROM containing the source code for `Widget` and then building from that source. Unfortunately, deliveries and builds fail often enough in practice to constitute nontrivial obstacles to reuse.

There must be no legal obstacles to reuse of `Widget`. Some software is freely available for anyone who chooses to use it. Other software is available upon payment of fees and signing of licenses and nondisclosure agreements. Such legal concerns often inhibit reuse.

The user of `Widget` must be rewarded for reusing `Widget`. Some organizations (thankfully few these days) measure programmer productivity as the number of lines of code written per day. Because programmers who reuse heavily write far less code than programmers who do not reuse, such reward systems actively penalize reuse.

The current hype about reuse, although inflating expectations, is increasing awareness in the programming community about the potential benefits of reuse. One can only hope that the desire to realize these benefits will cause organizations to make changes that will promote, rather than discourage, reuse.

1.3.2 Technical Obstacles

There are many technical obstacles to reuse — some major, some minor. The major technical obstacles follow.

Reusable code is used in many contexts. A *context* for a piece of code is

- A program that uses the code
- How the code is used when that program executes
- The platform (machine type, system interface, available resources, and so on) on which the code is built
- The platform on which the containing program is executed

The more successful reusable code is, the more contexts in which it is used.

We almost never know all the contexts. We almost never know everything about the contexts in which our reusable code will be used. We usually cannot inspect our users' programs, so we know little about their execution behavior, and we might have only an approximate idea of what resources will be available when they run their programs using our code.

User requirements often conflict.   Even if we did somehow know all the contexts in which our reusable code will be used, we might still face major design issues because users' requirements often conflict. Library designers are often forced to make a choice that will displease some of their intended users.

We cannot provide everything everyone wants.   If our users have conflicting requirements, why not provide in our reusable code all the functionality that every user could ever want? The answer is simple: The resulting monster body of code would be too expensive to produce and too difficult to use.

The contexts change.   To make matters worse, the contexts in which reusable code is used change with passing time. New users want to use our code in new programs; old users change their programs to do new things. Thus, designers of reusable code must try to predict what the likeliest changes will be and try to produce a design that can evolve to meet those changes without causing problems for users. Predicting the future is usually difficult.

1.4   Is There Any Hope?

After reading about all the obstacles to reuse, you may be wondering whether there is any hope at all. Yes, there is hope. First, the existence and popularity of reusable libraries — some of them commercially available, some of them proprietary — are ample evidence that software reuse is possible. There are several high-quality general-purpose libraries that implement things like linked lists, sets, strings, and so on; there are libraries that support developing graphical user interfaces and windowing applications; there are untold domain-specific libraries that are not commercially available — for example, database libraries, telecommunications libraries, stock market and financial analysis libraries, and physics number-crunching libraries, to name just a few. Programmers who have access to and use these libraries have an easier time producing high-quality software than programmers who do not.

Second, no library must be all things to all users. Consider your intended domain or domains of applications and the requirements of your intended users. You do not have to write code that is reusable in every C++ program ever written if your domain is the ten number-crunching programs that you maintain. Similarly, there is no sense in working hard to provide extensibility and portability if the only thing that matters to your users is efficiency. Third, if you take the time to make the right design decisions, you will greatly increase your chances of successfully producing reusable code. The fundamental library design questions that must be considered include the following:

- How efficient will the library be?
- In what ways will the library be extensible?
- How coupled or decoupled will the parts of the library be?
- How portable will the library be?
- Will the library use any other libraries?

These and a host of other design questions are discussed in this book.

1.5 How This Book Can Help

Writing reusable code that makes it easier to solve complex problems is intrinsically difficult. This book does not and cannot make an intrinsically difficult process easy. This book does not provide a magic wand, algorithm, or recipe that enables a C++ programmer to produce reusable code effortlessly.

Each chapter of this book discusses one or more topics that a C++ programmer who wishes to write reusable code must understand. Understanding each of these topics will not make writing reusable code easy. It will, however, make it possible.

The remainder of this book is organized as follows:

- Most C++ libraries consist primarily of a collection of classes. Therefore, we start by discussing good class design in Chapter 2.
- Many C++ libraries must be extensible in certain ways; we discuss extensibility in Chapter 3.
- In Chapter 4, we present techniques for writing efficient reusable code.
- In Chapter 5, we discuss errors — how to detect (and avoid) errors in your reusable code and what to do when an error occurs.
- In Chapter 6, we explain how to prevent conflicts between reusable code and other code in users' programs.
- Compatibility, in all its flavors, is the topic of Chapter 7.
- The advantages and disadvantages of various inheritance hierarchy designs are discussed in Chapter 8.
- In Chapter 9, we explain how to make reusable code more portable.

- In Chapter 10, we discuss whether a library of reusable code should reuse other libraries.
- We explain how to document a C++ library in Chapter 11.
- Finally, in Chapter 12, we discuss miscellaneous topics such as static initialization and class coupling.

Exercises

Throughout this book, difficult exercises are starred (∗); very difficult exercises are doubly starred (∗∗).

1.1   Suppose that you are implementing a function that searches a given array for a given value.

   a.   For what uses of the function would linear search be a more efficient implementation than binary search?

   b.   How could you implement your function such that it executes the more efficient search algorithm no matter what its context?

   c.   Suppose that, instead of searching for a user-supplied value, your function searches for the first occurrence of 0. Now for what contexts would linear search be more efficient than binary search?

   d.   Suppose that instead of searching for a specific value in a user-supplied array, your function searches for a *user-supplied* value in a *specific* array. In particular, suppose that the function `is_prime` is to search a known array of all prime numbers less than 10,000 to determine whether a given number, less than 10,000, is prime. Now for what contexts would linear search be more efficient than binary search?

1.2   In this and the next few exercises, we illustrate the problems that can arise if a library designer does not decide explicitly at the outset exactly who the intended users of the library are.

   Suppose that we are the authors of a reusable `Path` class. A `Path` represents a path name in our intended user's file system. For example, on a UNIX system typical paths are `dir`, `dir/dir2/tmp`, and `../tmp`; on a Windows system the corresponding paths are written `dir`, `dir\dir2\tmp`, and `..\tmp`; on a VMS system they are `dir`, `[dir.dir2]tmp`, and `[-]tmp`.

   Suppose that when we initially design `Path`, we forget to decide who our intended users are. Being UNIX programmers, we design a `Path` that models only UNIX paths:

```
class Path {
public:
    Path();
    Path(const String& s);
    // ...
private:
    void canonicalize();
};
```

The default constructor creates the empty path. The other constructor creates the canonical form of **s**. In canonical form, . components are removed, .. components are collapsed wherever possible, multiple consecutive /'s are reduced to a single /, and trailing /'s are removed. Thus, for example, the canonical form of

> ../../dir/./dir2//other_dir/../tmp.c/

is

> ../../dir/dir2/tmp.c

   a. (∗) For what UNIX system users will having the **Path** constructor automatically canonicalize the given string cause undesirable behavior? (Hint: When might **dir1/../some_file** and **some_file** denote different files?)
   b. Why will the second **Path** constructor not behave correctly for Windows users?

1.3 Suppose that to accommodate both Windows and UNIX system programmers, we change **Path** to allow the user to specify the path separator character:

```
class Path {
public:
    Path(const String& s, char separator);
    // ...
};
```

Users on UNIX systems must specify '/' for **separator**; Windows users must specify '\\' (that is, an escaped backslash character). What problem will this change create for our current UNIX users? How could you have changed **Path** instead to prevent that problem?

1.4   Suppose that we now wish to offer our `Path` class to VMS users. On VMS, no particular character is considered a path separator character, so, unfortunately, the `Path` interface of Exercise 1.3 is nonintuitive for VMS users. Suppose that to improve the design, we again change `Path`:

```
class Path {
public:
    enum Style { UNIX, Windows, VMS };
    Path(const String& s, Style style = UNIX);
    // ...
};
```

What problem will this change create for our current UNIX and Windows operating system users?

1.5   Show how to design and implement four classes, `Path`, `Unix_path`, `Windows_path`, and `Vms_path`, such that the latter three inherit from the first and users can write the following:

```
Vms_path r("[dir]tmp");
Unix_path p("/dir/tmp");
Windows_path q("\\dir\\tmp");
```

State one advantage and one disadvantage of this design over the design in Exercise 1.4, assuming that there are no users of any earlier version of the Path class.

References and Further Reading

We are not aware of a good programming-language–independent introduction to software reusability, probably because it is difficult to write anything useful or meaningful about reusability without referring to a particular programming language. Cline and Lomow [CL95], Meyers [Mey92b], and Murray's Chapter 9 [Mur93] also discuss some of the topics presented in this book.

Fontana and Neath [FN91] claim that some programmers prefer scavenging even when reusable code is available.

Tracz [Tra88] and Plauger [Pla93] discuss myths of reuse.

The design of C++ libraries is discussed by (among others) Booch and Vilot [BV93], Carroll [Car93], Coggins [Cog90], Lea [Lea93], Keffer [Kef93],

Koenig [Koe91], and Stroustrup [Str93]. Musser and Stepanov [MS94] present an example of a well-designed C++ library. Staringer [Sta94] gives another example of successful reuse.

Nontechnical obstacles to reuse (and other reuse topics) are the theme of volume 32, number 4, of the *IBM Systems Journal* [IBM]. Fafchamps [Faf94] discusses different organizational structures that can encourage or discourage reuse. Lim [Lim94] documents the effect of reuse on an organization's bottom line.

Discussing the legal issues of reuse is beyond the scope of this book; Will, Baldo, and Fife [WBF91] elaborate on them.

2 Class Design

> *I don't believe in class differences, but luckily my butler disagrees with me.*
> — Marc, cartoon in *The Times* (London)

Most C++ libraries consist primarily of a collection of classes (and templates). For a library to be reusable, its classes must be well designed. In this chapter, we cover several topics crucial to the design of reusable classes: abstraction, regular functions, nice classes, consistency of class interfaces, conversions, and use of `const` in class interfaces.

It has been argued that there is a minimal standard interface to which all classes should conform. We refute this notion and, in particular, argue against providing shallow and deep copy operations.

2.1 Abstraction

Every C++ class — whether reusable or not — should represent some abstraction. For example, a class `Rational` might represent the set of rational numbers, a class `Car` might represent cars, and a class `Parser` might represent C++ parsers. When we design a class, the first thing we should do is define the abstraction the class will represent.

Once we define the abstraction, we can typically implement that abstraction in any of several ways. For example, we might implement `Rational` as a pair of integers, with the requirement that the second integer always be nonzero:

```
class Rational {
private:
    int num;
    int denom;
public:
    // ...
};
```

Alternatively, we might represent a rational number by its repeating decimal expansion.

Separating the abstraction of a class from its implementation is useful for two reasons. First, abstractions simplify. When we abstract, we ignore details that are unimportant for the purposes at hand. Suppose that for the purposes of the users of Car, details such as the number of nicks and dents in a car and the presence or absence of a litterbag do not matter. Then a complete description of the Car abstraction would not mention nicks, dents, or litterbags. The user of Car would be free to forget about those things. A class's documented abstraction is part of the contract between the designer and the user of the class. The simpler the abstraction, the more likely it is that all parties will interpret the contract in the same way.

Second, separating abstraction from implementation allows flexibility in how an abstraction can be implemented. For example, a library might provide both of the implementations of Rational that we mentioned. Alternatively, the library might, instead of providing an implementation, simply provide a design for Rational such that users can easily provide their own implementations.

Just as classes should represent abstractions, functions should represent abstract behavior. That is, the semantics of almost every function should be defined solely in terms of the abstract values of the objects involved in the operation. Consider the following function:

```
Rational operator*(const Rational& r, const Rational& s);
```

If this function is intended to implement multiplication, here is how we should define its semantics:

> Returns the product of r and s.

Notice that this definition does not mention whether num and denom in the returned Rational are in reduced form (that is, whether num and denom might be 9 and 3, respectively, as opposed to 3 and 1). The fact that Rational is represented with num and denom is not part of the abstraction.

2.2   Regular Functions

Certain functions should have the same semantics for all classes that provide them. Consider this copy constructor for `Rational`:

```
class Rational {
public:
    Rational(const Rational& r);
    // ...
};
```

This operation should construct a `Rational` whose value is the same as `r`. (When we say *value* we always mean abstract value.) *Every* class's copy constructor should have the semantics that it constructs an object with the same value as its argument. Although C++ does not — and could not — enforce this restriction, all well-designed classes should adhere to it.

A function whose semantics is the same in all well-designed classes is *regular*. The regular functions in C++ are

- The copy constructor
- The destructor
- The principal assignment operator (that is, the assignment operator for a class T whose single parameter has type `const T&` or T)
- The equality and inequality operators

Here is a class T for which the regular functions are declared explicitly:

```
class T {
public:
    T(const T& t);
    ~T();
    const T& operator=(const T& t);
    // ...
};
bool operator==(const T& t1, const T& t2);
bool operator!=(const T& t1, const T& t2);
```

We show the equality and inequality operators as global functions; alternatively, they might be member functions of T. (The type `bool` is a relatively new addition to C++; it represents the values true and false, which are themselves represented by the new keywords `true` and `false`.)

The semantics of the regular functions should always be as follows:

- `T::T(const T& t);`

  Construct a T whose (abstract) value is the same as t.

- `T::~T();`

  Destroy this T.

- `const T& T::operator=(const T& t);`

  Set the value of this object to the value of t, and return a reference to this object.

- `bool operator==(const T& t1, const T& t2);`

  Return true if and only if t1 and t2 have the same value.

- `bool operator!=(const T& t1, const T& t2);`

  Return true if and only if t1 and t2 have different values.

These *regular semantics* are all abstract; the underlying implementation, of course, is free to implement them in any reasonable way. (In practice, one of `operator==` and `operator!=` should be implemented in terms of the other to ensure that they are implemented correctly.) These semantics should hold even if the given function is implicitly generated by the compiler (as a constructor, destructor, or assignment operator might be) or is a member function rather than a global function (as a binary operator might be).

Because the regular functions have the same semantics in all well-designed code, it is, strictly speaking, not necessary to document their semantics. A prudent C++ library designer, however, will document the semantics of the regular functions in at least one place to assure users that regular semantics are adhered to.

2.3 Nice Classes

We say that a class *provides* a certain function if that function is either explicitly declared as public or protected in the class or implicitly generated by the compiler in programs that need it. For example, this class

```
class X {
public:
    X();
    void f();
};
```

provides a default constructor, a function f, a copy constructor, an assignment operator, and a destructor. The last three operations are generated
by the compiler in programs that need them.

Consider the following generally useful function:

```
template<class T>
void swap(T& t1, T& t2){
    T t = t1;
    t1 = t2;
    t2 = t;
}
```

If x1 and x2 are two objects of some class X, we might want to exchange
their values by calling swap:

```
swap(x1, x2);
```

For this code to compile, X must provide a copy constructor, an assignment
operator, and a destructor.

Now consider another generally useful class:

```
template<class T>
class Array {
private:
    T* rep;
public:
    Array(int size) {
        rep = new T[size];
        // ...
    }
    int size() const;
    T operator[](int i) const;
    // ...
};
```

To create an Array array of 20 Xs, we write

```
Array<X> array(20);
```

For this code to compile, X must provide a default constructor — otherwise
the call to new in the Array constructor would be illegal.

Finally, consider this generally useful function:

```
template<class T>
bool linear_search(const Array<T>& a, const T& t) {
    for (int i = 0; i < a.size(); ++i)
        if (a[i] == t)
            return true;
    return false;
}
```

To search `array` for a given value x of type X, we write

```
if (linear_search(array, x))
    // ...
```

For this code to compile, X must provide either an equality operator or a conversion to a type that provides an equality operator.

The following functions are so widely used that a class that provides them all is called *nice*:

- Default constructor
- Copy constructor
- Assignment operator
- Equality operator
- Destructor

A class that is not nice restricts, sometimes severely, what users can do with it. Hence, reusable classes should be nice whenever possible.

2.4   A Minimal Standard Interface?

Some writers (Riel and Carter [RC90], for example) have gone a step further and claimed that *all* classes should provide a certain *minimal standard interface*. Different writers have proposed different minimal standard interfaces. All such proposed interfaces include the nice functions (that is, the functions provided by nice classes). Some other functions that have been proposed include input and output functions, a hash function, a function that returns the name of the class as a string, and shallow and deep copy operations.

Attempts to define a minimal standard interface for all classes, although well motivated, are misguided. *No function* should be provided by every class. The argument in support of this claim works as follows: For each function that might be proposed for the minimal standard interface, it is possible to describe a class that *should not* provide that function.

If a class is a counterexample for a function being in a standard interface, it is usually for one of three reasons: There might be no sensible semantics to give the function, the function might not be worth implementing, or it might, if implemented, do more harm than good.

Space prevents us from showing a counterexample for every function that has ever been proposed for the minimal standard interface. Instead, we shall show a counterexample for each of the nice functions other than the destructor. If it is possible to find counterexamples for these functions, it is reasonable to believe that there are counterexamples for every function other than the destructor.

2.4.1   Default Constructor

Consider the following special-purpose memory allocator:

```
class Pool {
public:
    Pool(size_t n);
    void* alloc();
    void free(void* p);
    // ...
};
```

A Pool(n) efficiently allocates and deallocates blocks of memory of size n. Pool::alloc returns a pointer to a contiguous block of memory containing at least n free bytes. If p is a pointer that has been returned by a call to alloc on some Pool q, then calling q.free(p) returns to q the block pointed to by p. A reasonable implementation of Pool::free would have the precondition that the value of its argument was returned by an earlier call to alloc on the same Pool.

What happens if we try to give Pool a default constructor?

```
class Pool {
public:
    Pool();
    // ...
};
```

The default constructor for Pool must create an object that efficiently allocates and deallocates blocks of memory of size n for some value of n. Because n is not given by the user, we (as the designers of Pool) must decide what size blocks to allocate. What value should we use?

Randomly choosing a value, say 37, is clearly wrong. We might consider choosing 0 or 1. It is unlikely, however, that users will want to allocate blocks of memory of 0 or 1 byte. Indeed, an attempt to create a Pool that allocates blocks of size 0 or 1 is probably a logic error. Providing a default constructor for `Pool` would move to run time errors that would otherwise be detected at compile time. Because users want errors to be detected as early as possible, we should not provide a default constructor for `Pool`. Hence, `Pool` is a counterexample for inclusion of the default constructor in a minimal standard interface.

2.4.2 Assignment Operator

Suppose that we try to give `Pool` an assignment operator:

```
class Pool {
public:
    const Pool& operator=(const Pool& q);
    // ...
};
```

The regular semantics of assignment imply that this function should change the assigned-to `Pool` into a `Pool(n)`, where n is the size of the blocks allocated by q. For example,

```
Pool p(4);   // p allocates blocks of size 4
Pool q(8);   // q allocates blocks of size 8
p = q;       // p now allocates blocks of size 8
```

Consider the following attempt to assign to a `Pool`:

```
Pool p(4);
void* mem = p.alloc();
Pool q(8);
p = q;
```

Here, the user allocates from the `Pool` p, stores the pointer returned from `p.alloc` in mem, and then assigns `Pool` q to p. Pools p and q, however, allocate blocks of different sizes, so when the user eventually tries to free the block pointed to by mem,

```
p.free(mem);
```

chaos is likely to ensue in any real implementation of `Pool`.

We could try to avoid this problem by giving the `Pool` assignment operator the precondition that the assigned-from `Pool` allocate blocks of the same size as the assigned-to `Pool`. Alternatively, we could require that there be no blocks currently allocated from the assigned-to `Pool`. Note, however, that the regular semantics of assignment operators (shown in Section 2.2) impose no such preconditions. Should we decide to, we could check the second precondition easily by comparing the number of calls to `free` with the number of calls to `alloc` for each `Pool`; if the numbers of calls are equal, then there are no currently allocated blocks.

But why bother? A class like `Pool` is in the toolkit of many C++ programmers, and experience shows that programmers do not need an assignment operator for `Pool`. Further, providing `Pool::operator=` would allow errors to occur at run time that would otherwise be detected at compile time. Hence, `Pool` is a counterexample for the assignment operator being in a minimal standard interface.

2.4.3 Copy Constructor

Now consider the copy constructor. Suppose that we are designing a class `Parser` representing a C++ parser. `Parser` will be complex — a `Parser` object will contain symbol tables and any number of nontrivial internal data structures. Implementing a copy constructor with the proper (regular) semantics for such a complicated object would almost certainly be tedious, time consuming, and error prone. Further, users will almost never want to copy `Parser` objects.

It would not make sense to spend valuable time designing, implementing, and testing a copy constructor that no one needs. Hence, `Parser` is a counterexample for inclusion of the copy constructor in a minimal standard interface.

2.4.4 Equality Operator

Now consider the equality operator. It would be difficult to define and implement an equality operator for certain classes. Consider that the (abstract) values for two `Parser` objects might be the same (and thus they should compare equal) even though their underlying representations have different values. Two `Parser` objects with the same (abstract) value might point to different symbol table objects, which point to different symbol objects, which point to different type objects, which point to different type name objects, and so on.

A considerable effort would be required to implement and test an equality operator for `Parser`. Users will rarely, if ever, want to compare `Parser` objects, so it does not make sense to implement an equality operator for `Parser`.

2.4.5   The Destructor

Finally, consider the destructor. Recall that a compiler will generate a
destructor for any class that needs a destructor and does not have one explicitly declared. Thus, a counterexample for the destructor must explicitly
declare the destructor private:

```
class T {
private:
    ~T();
    // ...
};
```

(If the implementation of the class does not need the destructor, it need
not be defined.)

How would a class T with a private destructor behave? Users of T could
not create a T object in static storage or on the stack:

```
T t;        // error: cannot access private T::~T()

void f() {
    T t;  // error: cannot access private T::~T()
    // ...
}
```

Users could create T objects only in the free store; they could never delete
such objects:

```
T* t = new T;
// ...
delete t;  // error: cannot access private T::~T()
```

Classes for which these properties are desirable are rare, but they do
exist. Suppose, for example, that our users' execution environment has
a garbage collector and that for some reason we wish to disable manual
deletion of objects of class type X. As long as our users do not need to
create X objects in static storage or on the stack, we should declare X's
destructor private.

2.5   Shallow and Deep Copy

Two operations require special mention because they have a reputation for being generally useful in spite of their undesirable properties: the shallow and deep copy operations. A *shallow copy* of an object x is another object of the same type as x, each of whose data members has the same value as the corresponding data member of x. A *deep copy* of an object x is another object of the same type as x in which all directly and indirectly pointed-to objects have also been copied and all sharing and cyclic relations have been preserved. Consider the following three classes:

```
class Z {
    // no data members
    // ...
};

class Y {
private:
    Z* z;
    // no other data members
    // ...
};

class X {
private:
    int i;
    Y* y1;
    Y* y2;
    // no other data members
    // ...
};
```

In Figure 2.1, x2 and x3 are shallow and deep copies, respectively, of the instance x1 of X.

A user of a well-designed, properly implemented library (with few exceptions) should be able to ask for a copy of an object — via the copy constructor — and the library should implement the copy appropriately for the type of the object. Except for unusual classes, users should not be concerned with how the copy is done, nor should they specify any particular way of copying an object.

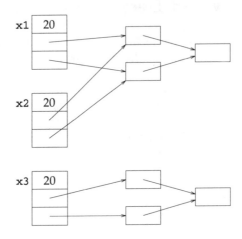

Figure 2.1   Shallow and deep copy. Objects **x2** and **x3** are shallow
and deep copies, respectively, of **x1**.

Rarely, one of the shallow or deep copy operations happens to implement the copy constructor for a given class. For example, suppose that we
implement the `Rational` class of Section 2.1 as follows:

```
class Rational {
private:
    Rational_rep* rep;
    // ...
};
class Rational_rep {
private:
    int num;
    int denom;
    // ...
};
```

Here, we have simply moved `num` and `denom` into a separate class. (As
we shall see in Section 8.2.4, such an implementation helps provide link
compatibility for users of `Rational`.) Here are `Rational` and `Rational_rep`
copy constructors that perform a deep copy:

```
class Rational {
public:
    Rational(const Rational& r) {
        rep = new Rational_rep(*r.rep);
    }
    // ...
};

class Rational_rep {
public:
    Rational_rep(Rational_rep& rep) :
        num(rep.num),
        denom(rep.denom) {
    }
    // ...
};
```

When the appropriate implementation for the copy constructor is a shallow or deep copy, the constructor should, of course, be implemented as such, but the coincidence *should not be advertised* to users. If the implementation of the class ever changes, the copy constructor might no longer implement shallow or deep copy; there should be no commitment to users that it does. Further, this phenomenon — that is, a class's copy constructor being implemented by shallow or deep copy — happens far less often than many programmers believe. For most real classes, neither shallow nor deep copy correctly implements the copy constructor. For nontrivial classes, shallow and deep copy operations usually have an undesirable property: They do not preserve program invariants. For example, suppose that we change the implementation of Rational to share Rational_reps whenever possible:

```
struct Rational_rep {
    int refcnt;
    // ...
};

class Rational {
public:
    Rational(const Rational& r) {
        rep = r.rep;
        ++rep->refcnt;
    }
    // ...
};
```

As usual when we share, we had to add a reference count to enable us to
determine when to delete one of the shared objects. An invariant of any
program that uses this version of Rational is that the reference count in
a Rational_rep is equal to the number of Rationals pointing to it. The
reader can verify that creating a shallow copy of a Rational would break
that invariant.

Nor are problems with Rational limited to shallow copy. Consider the
following conversion, which returns true if the Rational is not zero:

```
class Rational {
public:
    operator bool() const {
        return rep->num != 0;
    }
    // ...
};
```

Suppose that users call this function frequently. To optimize it, let us
change the implementation of Rational such that all Rationals with the
value zero point to the same Rational_rep object:

```
class Rational {
public:
    operator bool() const {
        return rep == rep_of_zero;
    }
    // ...
private:
    static Rational_rep* rep_of_zero;
    // ...
};
```

This implementation of the bool conversion avoids an indirection (admit-
tedly a small gain, but this code is only an example). The reader can verify
that creating a deep copy of a Rational with the value zero breaks the
invariant that all Rationals with the value zero are to point to the same
Rational_rep object.

Of course, if a shallow or deep copy operation potentially breaks an invariant, the class implementor could insert code that restores the invariant.
The ability to restore the invariant, however, does not change the fact that
the shallow or deep copy broke it. Further, in more complicated classes,
the shallow and deep copy operations can break invariants in ways that are
too difficult or even impossible to fix (see Exercise 2.5c).

Suppose that the shallow and deep copy operations for a class X do not break any invariants. Should X then provide these operations? For example,

```
class X {
public:
    X* shallow_copy();   // provide this?
    X* deep_copy();      // provide this?
    // ...
};
```

No, unless X is one those highly unusual classes for which it is appropriate to allow users to specify how copies are to be made. If we were ever to need to change the implementation of X, we might not be able to do so and still provide shallow and deep copy without breaking an invariant. Hence, only rarely should classes provide shallow and deep copy operations (see Exercise 2.5d).

2.6   Interface Consistency

Class interfaces should be as consistent as possible, within and among classes, as well as within and among libraries. Of course, ensuring consistency among libraries is more difficult than ensuring consistency within a library.

Interface consistency is important for several reasons. First, classes with consistent interfaces are easier to learn and remember. For example, suppose that we are designing a container class library. (A *container class* is a class that is designed primarily to hold collections of values or objects.) Here are two classes that we might provide in our library:

```
template<class T>
class Set {
public:
    void insert(const T& t);
    // ...
};

template<class T>
class Bag {
public:
    void insert(const T& t);
    // ...
};
```

A Set<T> is a set of values of type T; a Bag<T> is a bag of values of type
T. (A *bag* differs from a set in that values may appear more than once in
a bag.) Even though inserting a value into a set has a slightly different
meaning from inserting a value into a bag (inserting into a bag creates a
duplicate of the value if the value is already present), we have given both
classes an insertion operation with the same syntactic interface. Learning,
using, and remembering Set and Bag would be more difficult if the insertion
operations had different syntactic interfaces.

   A less important reason for providing interface consistency is to make
it easier for users to change the type of an object in a program. Suppose
that a user has written the following code:

```
Set<int> s;
// ...
s.insert(7);
```

Suppose that after this code has been written the user discovers that Bag
should have been used instead of Set. If Set and Bag have consistent interfaces, only the declaration, not the function call, will have to be changed:

```
Bag<int> s;   // changing Bag to Set here ...
// ...
s.insert(7);  // ... would not require changing this line
```

   Classes with similar interfaces are candidates for derivation from a common base class:

```
template<class T>
class Container {
public:
    virtual void insert(const T& t) = 0;
    // ...
};

template<class T>
class Set : public Container<T> {
public:
    virtual void insert(const T& t);
    // ...
};

// similarly for Bag ...
```

Just because two classes have similar interaces, however, does not imply
that they *should* be derived from a common base class. Suppose that our

users do not need to write functions that can operate polymorphically on either Sets or Bags. If we wish to avoid the overhead of insert being virtual, then we might decide not to derive Set and Bag from Container.

Determining how consistent two interfaces should be can be tricky. Suppose that we also provide a Queue class representing queues. Should Queue also provide an insert operation?

```
template<class T>
class Queue {
public:
    void insert(const T& t);  // provide this function?
    // ...
};
```

If we provide Queue::insert, where should it insert t into the Queue? There are two reasonable places: the head and the tail. Neither choice is preferable. Suppose that we choose the head. We shall also need to provide an operation to insert at the tail. Because we cannot name both operations insert, we would have to call the other operation something else:

```
template<class T>
class Queue {
public:
    void insert(const T& t);
    void insert_tail(const T& t);
    // ...
};
```

This interface, however, would be internally inconsistent. Many users would have trouble remembering whether our Queue class provides an insert/insert_tail pair of operations or an insert/insert_head pair. Some users would call insert, thinking that it does an insertion at the tail.

An internally consistent interface would name these operations insert_head and insert_tail:

```
template<class T>
class Queue {
public:
    void insert_head(const T& t);
    void insert_tail(const T& t);
    // ...
};
```

This `Queue`, however, would be inconsistent with `Set` and `Bag`. To restore consistency, we might try providing all three operations and defining `insert` to be a synonym for `insert_head`:

```
template<class T>
class Queue {
public:
    void insert(const T& t) { insert_head(t); }
    void insert_head(const T& t);
    void insert_tail(const T& t);
    // ...
};
```

Unfortunately, this interface would be larger than the others and thus harder to understand.

It is difficult to make `Queue`'s interface consistent with that of `Set` and `Bag` because, unlike `Set` and `Bag`, `Queue` logically has two insertion operations. Let us consider another class that, like `Set` and `Bag`, provides only one insertion operation. In particular, consider a `Stack` class representing stacks. There is only one way to insert a value into a stack: by pushing it onto the top of the stack. Should we name this operation `insert`, to be consistent with `Set` and `Bag`? Should we name it `push`, because that is what people speak of doing with stacks? Or both? Providing a `push` operation will render `Stack` easier for most users to learn and remember — in particular, those users who are using only `Stack` and are not familiar with the other container classes in our library. Further, it is unlikely that any users would have to change a `Stack` in their program into a `Set` or `Bag`, or the other way around. Hence, the inconsistent interface that provides only `push` is probably preferable.

Interfaces should be as consistent as possible, but they should not be foolishly so. If consistency would force a class's interface to be inappropriate or counterintuitive for that class, then consistency should be sacrificed.

2.7   Conversions

Library designers must pay careful attention to implicit conversions. Recall that there are two ways in C++ to define an implicit conversion from a type `From` to a type `To`. We can define a constructor in `To` that has exactly one parameter (and no additional default parameters):

```
class To {
public:
    To(const From&);   // or To(From)
    // ...
};
```

or we can define a conversion operation in From:

```
class From {
public:
    operator To() const;
    // ...
};
```

If one (and only one) of these functions is present, then when an argument of type From is passed to a parameter of type To (or const To&), the implicit conversion is applied:

```
void f(To);
From from;
f(from);   // implicit conversion applied
```

2.7.1   Multiple Ownership

If both From::operator To and To(const From&) are declared, the call to f is ambiguous:

```
void f(To);
// ...
f(from);        // ambiguous if both conversions defined
f((To)from);    // still ambiguous
```

Adding a cast does not resolve the ambiguity. This *multiple ownership* problem (so named because both From and To "own" the conversion) is easy to prevent. The authors of From and To should be careful not to provide both conversions.

The presence of *symmetric* conversions — that is, one implicit conversion from From to To and one implicit conversion from To to From — does not cause the same ambiguity:

```
void f(To);
void g(From);
To to;
From from;
f(from);  // implicit conversion from From to To applied
g(to);    // implicit conversion from To to From applied
```

Indeed, real classes do provide symmetric conversions. Consider a `Regex` class representing regular expressions [SM77]. Because it makes sense to construct a `Regex` from a string and it also makes sense to interpret a regular expression as a string, a real `Regex` class might provide symmetric conversions with a `String` class:

```
class Regex {
public:
    Regex(const String& s);
    operator String() const;
    // ...
};
```

If we cannot change the definition of `String`, then, of course, both conversions will have to be defined in `Regex`.

2.7.2   Sensible Conversions

An implicit conversion from `From` to `To` is *sensible* if it represents a natural mapping from `From` to `To` and if it is a conversion that users will want to have silently applied. Most conversions should be sensible (we shall discuss exceptions in the next section).

Let us consider some examples of sensibility. Suppose that we are the designers of a mathematical library providing the classes `Rational` and `Complex` representing, respectively, rational and complex numbers. If we consider only the types `int`, `double`, `Rational`, and `Complex`, there are 12 possible implicit conversions. Which of those are sensible?

- `Complex` to `int`. This conversion is clearly not sensible. Although it is possible to define any number of mappings from complex numbers to integers, no such mapping is arguably natural.
- `int` to `Complex`. Here, there is an obvious mapping: The integer x maps to the complex number $x + (0)(\sqrt{-1})$. Further, users will almost certainly want `int`s silently converted to `Complex`es. Hence, this conversion is sensible.

- `Rational` to `double`. Mapping a `Rational` to the value that results from performing the rational division and storing the result in a `double` would result in some loss of accuracy. Although this mapping might be considered natural, many users would not want it silently applied. Hence, this conversion is not sensible.
- `double` to `Rational`. If we consider `double` to represent the set of real numbers, there is no natural mapping. Every `double` in fact represents a terminating decimal, however, and there *is* a natural mapping from terminating decimals to rationals. This conversion is probably sensible.
- `Complex` to `Rational`. There is no natural mapping from `Complex` to `Rational` that users will want to have silently applied. This conversion is not sensible.
- `Rational` to `Complex`. This one is tricky. Every rational number is also complex, so we might claim that there is a natural mapping from `Rational` to `Complex`. If, however, `Complex` can represent only complex numbers of the form $x + (y)(\sqrt{-1})$ where x and y are representable by `double`, then this conversion is not sensible for the same reason the `Rational` to `double` conversion is not sensible.

As this example shows, most implicit conversions, upon close analysis, turn out not to be sensible and thus should not be provided. (Exercise 2.6 asks the reader to determine the sensibility of the remaining conversions.)

Note that what is not sensible as an *implicit* conversion might be useful functionality as an *explicit* conversion. For example, although an implicit conversion of `Rational` to `double` is not sensible, users, knowing that there may be a loss of accuracy, might want to convert explicitly a `Rational` to a `double`. We might provide this function in our mathematical library:

```
class Rational {
public:
    double to_double() const;
    // ...
};
```

2.7.3   Nonsensible Conversions

Recall the `Pool` class of Section 2.4.1. As argued in Section 2.4.1, the `Pool` constructor must take a size argument:

```
Pool::Pool(size_t n) { /* ... */ };
```

Further, there are no other arguments we might pass to it. Hence, we need a single-argument constructor, which constitutes a conversion function. Unfortunately, the conversion from `size_t` to `Pool` is not sensible — almost no users will want a `size_t` silently converted to a `Pool`:

```
void f(const Pool& p);
// ...
f(17);  // legal, but almost certainly a mistake
```

We can deal with this problem in either of two ways. First, we can provide the constructor and impose the responsibility for avoiding the implicit conversion on users. Alternatively, we can define an intermediate class:

```
class Pool {
public:
    class Size {
    public:
        Size(size_t n);
        // ...
    };
    Pool(Size n);
    // ...
};
```

Because C++ will not (implicitly) apply more than one user-defined conversion to an actual argument to a function, this design will cause the erroneous code to be rejected by the compiler:

```
void f(const Pool&);
// ...
f(17);  // error
```

The disadvantage, however, is that `Pool` becomes more difficult to understand and use. To construct a `Pool`, users must now write

```
Pool p(Pool::Size(17));
```

Most users will prefer the simpler, slightly more error-prone interface. Thus, libraries sometimes provide nonsensible conversions.

2.7.4   Fanout

Let us define the *fanout* of a type to be the number of other types to which the given type can be converted implicitly. Large fanouts are undesirable because they are potential causes of ambiguity. For example, suppose that From fans out to two types, To and Another_to. Then the function call in the following code is ambiguous:

```
void f(To);
void f(Another_to);
From from;
f(from);  // ambiguous
```

Supplying a cast resolves the ambiguity:

```
f((To)from);  // ok, conversion from From to To applied
```

C++ libraries should not, if possible, force users to put casts in their code. Hence, C++ libraries should avoid large fanouts. Fortunately, libraries that provide only sensible conversions usually have small fanouts. The only exception are a few built-in types such as int and char*. Because many classes define one-argument constructors from these types, int and char* have large fanout. To avoid ambiguity problems, library users should, whenever possible, avoid relying on implicit conversions from built-in types to library-defined types.

2.8   Use of const

Correct use of const in a library is important. An obstacle to getting the use of const right is that the meaning of const is not always well understood. We shall discuss how const should be interpreted, how it should be applied, and why const should not be reinterpreted even when there is a temptation to do so.

2.8.1   Abstract const versus Bit const

There are several ways to interpret the keyword const. Consider the function sqrt, which computes the square root of a Rational object (where Rational is the rational number class of Section 2.1):

```
Rational sqrt(const Rational& r);
```

Under the *abstract interpretation*, this declaration promises that sqrt will not use r to change the abstract value of the object referenced by r. Under the *bit interpretation*, this declaration promises that sqrt will not use r to write to any of the bits making up the object referenced by r. (Exercise 2.10 discusses other possible interpretations.)

Bit const has one advantage and several disadvantages over abstract const. If bit const is used everywhere, then const objects of types with no constructor and no destructor can safely be placed in read-only memory (ROM). Placing objects in ROM is an important optimization for some applications. Bit const has the disadvantage, however, of being at a lower level of abstraction than abstract const. The lower the level of abstraction of a C++ library's interface, the more difficult the library is to use.

Further, a library interface that uses bit const reveals implementation details of the library. Any time implementation details are revealed, undesirable things happen. For example, suppose that in a later release of our library we decide to optimize sqrt such that we first put r's num and denom data members into reduced form. Under bit const, this change to sqrt's implementation requires us to drop the const from sqrt's declaration. Unfortunately, this change is source incompatible (see Section 7.4) and might therefore break user code.

Hence, library authors should always use abstract const in both the interface and the implementation of a library. Consider the following code:

```
class Rational {
    // ...
private:
    void reduce() const;
    int num;
    int denom;
};
```

The function reduce puts num and denom into reduced form. Because reducing the representation of a rational number does not change its (abstract) value, we declare reduce as const.

Now consider the implementation of reduce:

```
void Rational::reduce() const {
    int gcd = GCD(num, denom);
    num /= gcd;    // error: cannot modify *this
    demon /= gcd;  // error: cannot modify *this
}
```

Here, GCD is a function that returns the greatest common divisor of its two arguments. Unfortunately, the attempts to modify num and denom are illegal. The C++ compiler has no way of knowing that taken together these modifications do not change the value of *this.

We can solve this problem in three ways. First, we can declare num and denom as mutable:

```
class Rational {
private:
    mutable int num;
    mutable int denom;
    // ...
};
```

Now *any* attempt to modify the num and denom members of a const Rational are legal (including attempts to modify one or both such that the value of the Rational object is changed). An alternative technique that allows modification of num and denom only where we specifically request it is to "cast away const":

```
void Rational::reduce() const {
    // ...
    const_cast<int>(num) /= gcd;      // ok
    const_cast<int>(denom) /= gcd;    // ok
}
```

Because mutable and const_cast are relatively new features of C++, not all C++ compilers currently implement them, and hence code that uses them will not be portable for some time. A more portable technique is to use an old-style cast:

```
void Rational::reduce() const {
    // ...
    Rational* let_me_modify = (Rational*)this;
    let_me_modify->num /= gcd;      // ok
    let_me_modify->denom /= gcd;    // ok
}
```

An attempt to use the old-style cast to cast away the const associated with a class type X has defined behavior only if X has at least one explicit constructor. (Most nontrivial classes satisfy this restriction.)

A third way to avoid the compiler error is to add a level of indirection to the variables we wish to modify:

```
class Rational {
public:
    Rational() : num(new int), denom(new int) { /* ... */ }
    // ...
private:
    int* num;
    int* denom;
};
```

Modifying *num and *denom is legal even in a const member function:

```
void Rational::reduce() const {
    // ...
    *num /= gcd;     // ok
    *denom /= gcd;   // ok
}
```

Adding a level of indirection decreases efficiency, however. Unless portability is a major concern, use of mutable is the best way to solve this problem.

2.8.2 Maximal Use of const

Many C++ programmers consider const to be a nuisance that catches few errors. Thus, not all C++ programmers use const thoroughly. The designer of a C++ library, however, has less freedom. *The interface of a C++ library should use the const keyword everywhere it applies* — that is, everywhere that the use of const makes a promise that the library keeps.

Failure to use const maximally can cause problems for library users. Suppose that we wish to provide a library function that takes two arguments — a pointer p to a null-terminated string and an array a of pointers to null-terminated strings — and returns true if the string pointed to by p is equal to one of the strings pointed to by a. We might be tempted to declare this function as follows:

```
// nonmaximal use of const
bool contains(const char** a, const char* p);
```

This interface works fine for the user who writes the following:

```
static const char* keywords[] = {
    "array", "of", "four", "strings"
};
```

```
bool iskeyword(const char* p) {
    return contains(keywords, p);
}
```

This user code, however, fails to compile:

```
bool iskeyword(const char* const* keywords, const char* p)
{
    return contains(keywords, p);  // error
}
```

The error would be our fault because we did not use const everywhere it applies. Here is the correct interface for contains:

```
// maximal use of const
bool contains(const char* const* a, const char* p);
```

Now all user code, both code that uses const thoroughly and code that does not use const at all, compiles (or not) as desired.

There is one exception to the rule that const should be used maximally. Suppose that contains does not change the values of its parameters a and p. We should nevertheless *not* declare contains as follows:

```
// BAD IDEA:
bool contains(const char* const* const a,  // added const
    const char* const p);                  // added const
```

The promises we have added here make no difference to users, who are rarely affected by changes to nonreference parameters. Further, if a future version of contains does for some reason change the value of a or p, the corresponding const will have to be dropped, breaking compatibility. Therefore, const should never modify a nonreference parameter.

2.8.3   Unsafe Interpretations of const

Sometimes, library designers are tempted to use an interpretation of const other than the abstract or bit interpretation. Most alternative interpretations are not type safe. Consider the following class:

```
class Noderef {
public:
    int value() const;
    void setvalue(int val) const;
    const Noderef& operator=(const Noderef& n);
    // ...
};
```

A Noderef is a reference to some underlying node; every underlying node contains a single int value. The function value returns the value stored in the underlying node, and setvalue sets the value in the underlying node to val. Both value and setvalue are const; neither changes the value of the Noderef itself.

Because it is somewhat surprising for a member function named setvalue to be const, the designer of Noderef might be tempted to reinterpret const when applied to Noderefs. For example, the designer might decide to reinterpret all such uses of const as follows:

The value stored in the underlying node does not change.

This reinterpretation of const is unsafe. Here is Noderef under the proposed reinterpretation:

```
// Noderef with unsafe reinterpretation of const
class Noderef {
public:
    int value() const;
    void setvalue(int val);
    const Noderef& operator=(const Noderef& n) const;
    // ...
};
```

Here, setvalue is no longer const, but now the assignment operator is const! (The assignment operator changes the value of the Noderef, but not the value stored in the underlying node.) This interface contains a type hole. Consider the following code:

```
void f(const Noderef& n) {
    Noderef m = n;   // m now references same node as n
    m.setvalue(0);   // oops!
}
```

The declaration of f promises that f will not use n to change the value stored in the node referenced by n. Under our reinterpretation of const, however, the call to `setvalue`, which compiles without error or warning, breaks that promise. The reader can verify that trying to remove this type hole by the simple expedient of removing the final `const` from the declaration of the `Noderef` assignment operator does not succeed.

The temptation to reinterpret `const` should be resisted.

2.9   Summary

The regular functions — the copy constructor, the destructor, the principal assignment operator, and the equality and inequality operators — should implement the same semantics in all classes.

Although there is no minimal standard interface, the nice functions — the default constructor, the copy constructor, the assignment operator, and the equality operator — should be provided by most classes. No function should be provided by all classes. The shallow and deep copy operations should be provided by almost no classes.

Careful thought should be given to uniformity of interface for classes within a library, but consistency should not be so rigidly adhered to that it renders the interface of a class inappropriate or counterintuitive.

When deciding what conversions to provide, library designers should provide sensible conversions while preventing multiple ownership, avoid nonsensible conversions when possible, and limit fanout.

Use of `const` in libraries also requires attention. In general, libraries should implement abstract `const` in their interfaces, and they should use the `const` keyword every place it makes a promise that the library keeps.

Exercises

2.1   Show a counterexample for each of the following proposed minimal standard functions.
   a.   An input operator
   b.   An output operator
   c.   A function that returns the name of its containing class as a string

2.2   Consider a class `WORM_pool` that is like the `Pool` class of Section 2.4.1 except that it allocates memory blocks on a write-once read-many medium. Is `WORM_pool` a counterexample for the destructor? Why or why not?

2.3   Suppose that we provide users a class `Buf` representing a buffer:

```
class Buf {
public:
    Buf(size_t sz);
    // ...
};
```

The constructor for `Buf` creates a buffer of `sz chars`. Suppose further that our users want to pass around pointers to Bufs, and they manipulate so many pointers to Bufs that it is difficult for them to determine when to delete Bufs.

a.   To help our users, we will create an additional class `Bufptr`, representing a smart pointer to a `Buf`:

```
class Bufptr {
public:
    Bufptr(Buf* p);
    Buf* operator->() { return rep; }
    // ...
private:
    Buf* rep;
};
```

The constructor creates a smart pointer to `p`; `operator->` returns that pointer. We also add a reference count to `Buf`:

```
class Buf {
private:
    friend class Bufptr;
    int refcnt;
    // ...
};
```

The value of `refcnt` will always be equal to the number of `Bufptrs` pointing to the `Buf`. The various `Bufptr` member functions will maintain `refcnt`; the `Bufptr` destructor will delete the pointed-to `Buf` when no other `Bufptr` is pointing to it. What user errors would be prevented if we were to declare `Buf`'s destructor private? What are the disadvantages of declaring `Buf`'s destructor private?

b.   Suppose that, instead of providing `Buf` and `Bufptr`, we provide a single class representing a reference to an underlying buffer:

```
class Bufref {
public:
    Bufref(size_t sz);
    Bufref(const Bufref& b);
    // ...
};
```

The constructor creates a reference to a newly allocated underlying buffer of sz chars. The copy constructor (which has regular semantics) creates a new reference to the buffer referenced by b. Bufref provides a destructor that will delete the underlying buffer if no other Bufref is referencing it. What are the advantages of Bufref over Buf and Bufptr?

    c.   Do the Buf and Bufptr classes make a convincing counterexample for the destructor being in a minimal standard interface?

2.4   In Section 2.4, we gave three reasons a class might be a counterexample for a proposed minimal standard function. In this exercise, we show two additional theoretical reasons that do not arise in practice.

    a.   Let Complexity_class be a class modeling complexity classes (see [HU79]).   Suppose that it is possible to create instances of Complexity_class that represent the complexity classes $\mathcal{P}$ and $\mathcal{NP}$. For what proposed standard functions would Complexity_class be a counterexample?

    b.   (∗) Consider two classes — TM representing a Turing machine [DW83] and TMset representing a set of Turing machines. Suppose that it is possible to create an instance of TMset that represents the set of Turing machines that halt when started on blank tape. Suppose further that the following function, which returns the union tms ∪ {tm}, is available:

```
TMset operator+(const TMset& tms, const TM& tm);
```

Show that implementing operator== for TMset would require computing an incomputable function.

2.5   This exercise further investigates shallow and deep copy.

    a.   Show a realistic class for which the shallow copy operation implements the copy constructor.

    b.   (∗) Show a realistic class having at least one pointer data member, whose implementation has no memory leaks, and for which the shallow copy operation implements the copy constructor.

    c.   (∗∗) Show a realistic class for which the shallow copy operation would break an invariant in a way that is impossible to fix. Show a realistic class for which deep copy would break an invariant in a way that is impossible to fix.

d. (∗∗) Give an example of a realistic class for which there is a strong argument for providing the shallow and deep copy operations.

2.6 Which of the following conversions between the `Rational` and `Complex` types of Section 2.7.2 and `int` and `double` are sensible?

- `Rational` to `int`
- `int` to `Rational`
- `Complex` to `double`
- `double` to `Complex`

2.7 Which of the built-in arithmetic conversions in C++ are sensible?

2.8 Writing an `Int` class that acts just like the C++ built-in type `int` is surprisingly difficult.

a. Write the interface for such a class (that is, show the class declaration). Remember to provide the appropriate conversion functions.

b. (∗) How will your class behave differently from the built-in `int` type despite your best efforts?

c. Suppose that you also need to provide `Char`, `Short`, `Long`, `Float`, and `Double`. What additional conversions will your `Int` class need? Which of `Char`, `Short`, `Long`, `Float`, and `Double` should have a conversion to `Int`?

2.9 Kleene's theorem [DW83] states that a language is accepted by a finite state acceptor if and only if that language can be expressed as a regular expression.

a. (∗) Suppose that your library provides a class `FSA` modeling finite state acceptors and a class `Regex` modeling regular expressions. What classes and functions would you provide if you were modeling Kleene's theorem in your library?

b. If your solution to part a uses any implicit conversions, show that you have prevented multiple ownership, provided only sensible conversions, and avoided unnecessary fanout.

c. Suppose that your library provides the `Regex` class but not the `FSA` class and that some of your users also use a library that does provide an `FSA` class. How can you design the library to make it easy for such users to have the same sort of functionality that you provided in part a? What are the disadvantages of your design?

2.10   Consider the `Noderef` class of Section 2.8.3.

   a.   What problems would arise if we were to interpret `const` when applied to `Noderef`s as "neither the value of the `Noderef` nor the value stored in the underlying node changes"?

   b.   Is there any way to design `Noderef` such that its interface prevents users from changing the values stored in the underlying nodes? If so, how?

2.11   Suppose that we wish to provide a function `firstvowel` which returns a pointer to the first vowel in a given null-terminated string, or 0 if there is no vowel. Consider the following proposed interfaces:

```
char* firstvowel(char* s);              // 1
const char* firstvowel(char* s);        // 2
char* firstvowel(const char* s);        // 3
const char* firstvowel(const char* s);  // 4
```

   a.   For each of the interfaces (1) through (4), state what problems would arise if we were to provide our users only that one interface.

   b.   How would you solve the problems that you discovered in part a?

References and Further Reading

Cargill [Car92a], Cline and Lomow [CL95], and Barton and Nackman [BN94] discuss many issues of good class design.

   Liskov and Guttag [LG86] discuss the concept of abstract state as well as other abstraction principles.

   Although the term *regular semantics* is new, the principle it describes has been adhered to by good programmers for some time. The term *nice class* was first used by Lee and Stepanov [LS93], with a slightly different meaning.

   Implementing the assignment operator correctly in the face of inheritance is surprisingly tricky; see Meyers's columns [Mey94c, Mey94a, Mey94b] in the *C++ Report* for more information.

   Meyers [Mey92c] also presents a criticism of proposals for a minimal standard interface.

   The `Pool` class in this chapter is an adaptation of a class [UNI92] originally designed by Koenig.

Doug Lea suggested the garbage collection example in Section 2.4.5.

The shallow and deep copy operations cause problems in every programming language, not just C++. Knight [Kni93] discusses the problems they cause in Smalltalk. Gorlen, Orlow, and Plexico [GOP90] present a technique for implementing shallow and deep copy in a C++ library.

Murray [Mur88] coined the term *multiple ownership problem*.

It is impossible to design a C++ smart pointer class that models precisely the behavior of real C++ pointers; Edelson [Ede92] explains why.

3 Extensibility

> *Say not you know another entirely, till you*
> *have divided an inheritance with him.*
> — Johann Kaspar Lavater

Extensibility is an important property for many C++ libraries. In this chapter, we look at the tradeoffs of providing extensibility. The most common way of extending a C++ library is by inheriting from its classes, yet every useful class necessarily places limits on the classes that can be derived from it. We define the concept of a function's inheritance semantics; defining clearly the inheritance semantics of all functions in a class increases that class's inheritability. Next, we present the most common obstacles to inheritability and give techniques for avoiding them. We also define a problem often encountered in attempts to inherit — the derived assignment problem — and show how libraries can prevent it. Finally, we discuss providing source code to users, which allows them to correct many kinds of obstacles they might encounter in trying to derive from a library's classes.

3.1 Tradeoffs of Extensibility

Something is *extensible* if it can be extended — that is, if its scope, meaning, or application can be increased. For example, the following things are extensible:

- The vocabulary of a living language
- The legal code of France
- The set of types in a C++ program

The vocabulary of a living language can be extended — a word might be adopted from a work of fiction (*robot*), a technological advance could introduce a word into the language (*television*, *camcorder*), new words are created by combining old words (*smog* resulted from combining *smoke* and *fog*; *motel* is a combination of *motor* and *hotel*), and so on. The legal code of France can be extended by a prescribed process. The set of types in a C++ program can be extended with the definition of a new class and its associated operations.

Few things are extensible in every way imaginable. Consider, for example, a builder of music boxes. The artisan might decide to allow listeners to extend the set of songs played by the music boxes. The music boxes might be designed such that a component could be inserted and the box would play a different song for each different component. The music boxes might, however, accept only components from a certain manufacturer.

Designing for extensibility entails tradeoffs. The extensible music boxes would be more difficult to build than boxes that play only Johannes Brahms's "Lullaby," for example. Thus, the extensible music boxes would probably cost more than nonextensible music boxes.

Often, the users of a product do not need it to be extensible, and they are therefore not willing to incur additional costs for extensibility. Suppose, for example, that our music box builder knows in advance that the only song besides the lullaby that people will ever to want to play is "Bicycle Built for Two." Rather than make the music boxes extensible, the artisan can build those two songs into the box and provide a switch for selecting the desired song. The resulting music box will be more expensive than the single-song version, but probably will be less expensive than an extensible music box.

This example shows that sometimes we can avoid the costs associated with making a product extensible. Suppose that only a few extensions to our product will ever be wanted and we know in advance what those extensions are. Then rather than provide an extensible product, we can, and we might prefer to, provide a product that simply includes all the extensions users will ever want.

3.2 Extensibility and Inheritance

The principal mechanism a C++ library uses to provide extensibility is inheritance.[1] Sometimes, inheriting from a class is easy; other times, it is effectively impossible. How difficult a proposed derivation is depends on the class to be derived and on the design and implementation of the intended base class. A class is *inheritable* if it is easy to inherit appropriate

---

1. Some authors use the term *extensibility* to refer to any kind of flexibility that a library might provide its users. Such authors view constructs other than inheritance (templates, for example) as additional extensibility mechanisms.

derived classes. We say *appropriate* because no one would reasonably consider a class `Military_vehicle` lacking in inheritability just because we cannot easily derive a `Washing_machine` class from it; we might consider `Military_vehicle` lacking in inheritability if we cannot easily derive `Jeep` from it.

To understand what qualities or characteristics a class needs to be inheritable, consider the three purposes of inheritance:

- A user might want to inherit an intended base class's interface but not its implementation. Interface classes, which we discuss in Section 3.2.1, allow this kind of inheritance.
- A user might want to inherit a class's implementation but not its interface. Private derivation accomplishes this kind of inheritance.
- A user might want to inherit both a class's interface and its implementation. Public derivation from a noninterface class accomplishes this kind of inheritance.

(You might notice that we do not discuss protected derivation. Whether protected derivation is useful is debatable.)

3.2.1   Inheriting Only Interface

If we wish to allow users to inherit only an interface and no implementation, we can provide an *interface class* — that is, a class containing no data members, all of whose member functions are pure virtual, and all of whose base classes are interface classes.

For example, suppose that we have decided to provide a binary search tree — a tree in which the value stored at each node n is greater than all the values stored at the nodes in n's left subtree and less than all the values stored at the nodes in n's right subtree [CLR90]. We implement our `BSTree` class in the typical way — specifically, each node in the tree is represented by an object, and each node object contains pointers to its left and right children. Suppose further that our user wishes to create a class `Complete_bstree` representing complete binary search trees. (In a complete binary search tree, all levels containing any nodes are completely filled; the level of a node is its distance from the root of the tree.) Rather than implement `Complete_bstree` with nodes connected by child pointers, the user wishes to exploit a compact array representation [CLR90]. Only a reimplementation of `BSTree` will render it inheritable for such a `Complete_bstree`.

To avoid this shortcoming, we can inherit `BSTree` from an interface class `BSTree_int`:

```
template<class T>
class BSTree_int {
public:
    virtual void insert(const T& t) = 0;
    virtual bool contains(const T& t) = 0;
    // ...
    // only pure virtual functions, nothing else
    // ...
};

template<class T>
class BSTree : public virtual BSTree_int<T> {
public:
    void insert(const T& t);
    bool contains(const T& t);
    // ...
};
```

The type argument T to the templates is the type of the value stored in
each node of the tree. We derive virtually from BSTree_int because when
interface classes are used, they frequently are inherited by some descendants
along more than one derivation path.

Because BSTree_int contains no implementation, our user can easily derive Complete_bstree, using a compact array representation, from
BSTree_int:

```
template<class T>
class Complete_bstree : public virtual BSTree_int<T> {
    // ...
};
```

Any function provided by our library that operates on a pointer or reference to a binary search tree should, if possible, take a pointer or reference
to a BSTree_int, not BSTree. This design will allow the user to pass
Complete_bstrees to such functions. The ability to pass a pointer or reference to an object of type X to a function declared to take a pointer or
reference to a type from which X directly or indirectly inherits is called
substitutability.

A class X is *interfaced* if either X is an interface class or each public
member function of X is declared in at least one interface class from which
X directly or indirectly inherits. To increase the extensibility of a library,
we can interface every class provided by the library. This approach, which

we shall discuss further in Section 8.2.2, should be taken by libraries for which extensibility is a primary design goal.

3.2.2   Inheriting Only Implementation

Sometimes, users will want to inherit the implementation of a base class without also making objects of the derived class substitutable for the base class type. Then private inheritance can be used. For example, suppose that our users wish to implement a Map class using BSTree. A Map<X,Y> is a mapping from values of type X to values of type Y. (Maps are sometimes also called *associative arrays* or *dictionaries*.) The interface for a Map class might look like this:

```
template<class X, class Y>
class Map {
public:
    void insert(const X& x, const Y& y);
    void remove(const X& x);
    bool contains(const X& x);
    Y valueat(const X& x);
    // ...
};
```

The function insert adds the pair $\langle x, y \rangle$ to the mapping after first removing any pair whose first value is x; remove removes any pair whose first value is x; contains removes true if the Map contains a pair whose first value is x; valueat returns the second value associated with the given value x.

To allow implementing Map with BSTree, suppose that we provide some virtual functions in BSTree that the implementor of Map can override (see Exercise 3.2). Because a mapping is not a kind of binary search tree, users do not want objects of type Map to be substitutable for objects of type BSTree. Hence, to implement Map with BSTree, they derive privately:

```
template<class X, class Y>
class Map : private BSTree<X> {
    // override the BSTree functions we provided
    // ...
};
```

Exercise 3.3 suggests a slightly more difficult way to implement Map with BSTree without using private inheritance.

3.2.3 Inheriting Interface and Implementation

Users often want to inherit both a base class's implementation and its interface. Suppose that our users wish to create a class AVLTree representing AVL trees (an AVL tree is a binary search trees with the property that, for each node n in the tree, the difference between the number of nodes on the longest path from n to a leaf node in n's left subtree and the number of nodes on the longest path from n to a leaf node in n's right subtree is no more than 1 [AHU83]). Because an AVL tree is a kind of binary search tree, they would like AVLTree to inherit BSTree's interface. Further, because the implementation of an AVLTree is so similar to the implementation of BSTree, these users would like AVLTree to inherit BSTree's implementation. To inherit both interface and implementation, AVLTree publicly derives from the noninterface class BSTree:

```
template<class T>
class AVLTree : public BSTree<T> {
    // ...
};
```

Of course, BSTree must be suitably inheritable for this derivation to work.

3.3 Inheritance Semantics

The *inheritance semantics* of a class is the semantics that that class satisfies and that all publicly derived classes, whether directly or indirectly derived, are expected to satisfy. Suppose that a class D publicly derives directly from a base class B. For this derivation to work as desired, the authors and users of B and D must follow these rules:

- The author of B must document B's inheritance semantics.
- All users of B (including B's author) must assume only the inheritance semantics of B when manipulating pointers or references to B.
- The author of D must ensure that D adheres to the inheritance semantics of B.
- The author of D must define D's inheritance semantics such that any derived class of D that satisfies D's inheritance semantics will also satisfy B's inheritance semantics.

Suppose, for example, that our BSTree class provides a member function insert,

```
template<class T>
class BSTree {
public:
    virtual void insert(const T& t);
    // ...
};
```

and suppose that the BSTree implementation of insert inserts t into the given BSTree using a recursive binary search tree insertion algorithm. We should not wish to constrain derived classes to use this same algorithm for insertion. On the other hand, we do not wish to allow derived classes to redefine insert to do just any old thing. Hence, we might document the semantics of BSTree::insert as follows:

> Inserts the value t in the tree using a recursive binary search tree insertion algorithm. Derived classes may redefine insert to use another insertion algorithm; the derived class algorithm may arbitrarily rearrange the nodes in the tree as long as the resulting tree is a binary search tree.

When manipulating a pointer or reference to B, programmers should rely on only the documented inheritance semantics. Suppose that our library contains this function:

```
void insert_several(BSTree<int>& bst) {
    bst.insert(0);
    bst.insert(1);
    bst.insert(2);
}
```

If the tree referenced by bst is empty when this function is called, and if that tree is an object of type BSTree<int>, then when insert_several returns, the tree will look like this:

We should not assume, however, that the tree will look like this. If insert_several is passed a reference to a class derived from BSTree<int>, a different insertion algorithm might be used. If bst refers to an AVLTree<int>, for example, insert_several will produce a tree that looks like this:

The most that we should assume is that, when `insert_several` returns, the tree referenced by `bst` will be a binary search tree containing the values 0, 1, and 2.

The author of `AVLTree`, publicly derived from `BSTree`, must ensure that `AVLTree::insert` adheres to the inheritance semantics of `BSTree::insert`. Further, the inheritance semantics of `AVLTree::insert` must be defined such that any class derived from `AVLTree` that satisfies the inheritance semantics of `AVLTree::insert` will also satisfy the inheritance semantics of `BSTree::insert`. For example, the author of `AVLTree` might choose the following semantics for `insert`:

> Inserts the value `t` into the tree using the AVL tree insertion algorithm described in [*some reference*]. Derived classes may redefine `insert` to use another insertion algorithm; the derived class's insertion algorithm may arbitrarily rearrange the nodes in the resulting tree, as long as the resulting tree is an AVL tree.

3.4   Obstacles to Inheritability

In this section, we discuss obstacles to a class's inheritability. Except for the presence of member functions that interfere with inheritability, discussed in Section 3.4.7, the obstacles discussed in this section can occur only in noninterface classes. Thus, we see that interface classes are easier to design inheritably than are noninterface classes.

3.4.1   Nonvirtual Member Function

A common obstacle to inheritability is an intended base class having a function that was not declared virtual. If `BSTree::insert` were not declared virtual,

```
template<class T>
class BSTree {
public:
    void insert(const T& t);  // not virtual
    // ...
};
```

then derived classes would not be able to redefine it (and get the desired behavior). To prevent this problem, we might consider declaring all member functions of an intended base class virtual. Doing so, however, would reduce efficiency (as we shall see in Section 4.4.2, virtual functions are less efficient than nonvirtual functions). Hence, we would like to declare virtual only those functions that any derived class ever will need to redefine.

Predicting what functions derived classes will need to redefine can be tricky. Suppose that we implement `BSTree` as follows:

```
template<class T>
class BSTree {
private:
    class Node {
    public:
        T t;
        Node* left;
        Node* right;
        Node(const T& _t) : t(_t) {}
        // ...
    };
    Node* root;
    // ...
};
```

The nested class `Node` represents a node in the tree; `root` is a pointer to the root node, or 0 if the tree is empty. Now suppose that we implement `insert` as follows:

```
template<class T>
class BSTree {
public:
    virtual void insert(const T& t) {
        doinsert(t, root);
    }
    // ...
private:
    void doinsert(const T& t, Node*& n);
    // ...
};
```

The function `insert` calls `doinsert`; the latter is a recursive binary search tree insertion algorithm:

```
template<class T>
void BSTree<T>::doinsert(const T& t, Node*& n) {
    if (n == 0)
        n = new Node(t);
    else {
        if (t < n->t)
            doinsert(t, n->left);
        else
            doinsert(t, n->right);
    }
}
```

Notice that most of the work is done in `doinsert`. With this implementation of `insert`, a derived class that needs to redefine the insertion
operation probably will want to redefine `doinsert`, not `insert`. Hence,
`doinsert` needs to be virtual, and `insert` probably does not. We also
change `doinsert` from private to protected so derived classes can access it:

```
template<class T>
class BSTree {
public:
    void insert(const T& t);
    // ...
protected:
    virtual void doinsert(const T& t, Node*& n);
    // ...
};
```

(Making `doinsert` protected is not necessary — C++ allows a class to
override private virtual member functions of its base classes. We consider
overriding private functions to be ill advised, however.)

The destructor of every class from which a user might inherit should also
be declared virtual (see Exercise 3.5). Thus, we declare `BSTree`'s destructor
virtual:

```
template<class T>
class BSTree {
public:
    virtual ~BSTree();
    // ...
};
```

3.4.2 Overprotection

Another obstacle to inheritability is overprotection of a class member. In the previous section, we declared the nested `Node` class private, but some kinds of binary search trees will need to add extra fields to the nodes. For example, a class `Threaded_bstree`, representing threaded binary search trees will need to add a thread field:

```
template<class T>
class Threaded_bstree : public BSTree<T> {
protected:
    class Node :
       public BSTree<T>::Node {  // error: cannot access
                                 //    BSTree<T>::Node
    public:
        Node* thread;
        // ...
    };
    // ...
};
```

Hence, we must declare `BSTree::Node` protected rather than private:

```
template<class T>
class BSTree {
protected:
    class Node {
        // ...
    };
    // ...
};
```

Making a class inheritable requires that the class designer understand the sorts of classes users will want to inherit.

To prevent overprotection, we might consider declaring all members of our intended base class either public or protected. A protected member, however, unlike a private member, cannot be changed or removed in future releases of the library without breaking source compatibility — thereby possibly breaking users' code (we shall discuss source compatibility in detail in Section 7.4). Hence, we would like to declare protected only those members that derived classes will need to access. In our example, we suspect that derived classes will need access only to `doinsert`, `Node`, and `root`:

```
template<class T>
class BSTree {
protected:
    class Node {
    public:
        virtual ~Node();
        // ...
    };
    Node* root;
    virtual void doinsert(const T& t, Node*& n);
    // ...
};
```

We also made the destructor of Node, from which users might now inherit, virtual.

Predicting what members of a class should be protected can be tricky. For example, if BSTree also contained a data member ninserts counting the number of insertion operations that have been performed on the given tree, would any derived classes need to access it?

3.4.3 Undermodularization

Another obstacle to inheritability is undermodularization. To illustrate this obstacle, let us examine a typical way in which a derived class might need to redefine BSTree::doinsert. Consider the category of binary search trees called *red-black trees* [CLR90]. Every node in a red-black tree contains an additional field indicating whether the node is red or black.[2] This field is used (in ways that need not concern us here) to guarantee that the tree maintains the following balance property: The longest path in the tree from the root node to a leaf node is no more than twice as long as the shortest path from the root to a leaf. After each insertion or deletion operation, a red-black tree performs a rebalancing operation, which restores the balance property.

Here is how a user might try to derive from BSTree a class RBTree representing red-black trees:

---

2. Every node in a red-black tree also contains a pointer to its parent. To simplify our discussion, we disregard pointers to parents.

```
template<class T>
class RBTree : public BSTree<T> {
protected:
    class Node : public BSTree<T>::Node {
    public:
        bool isred;
        Node(const T& t);
    };
    void doinsert(const T& t, BSTree<T>::Node*& n);
    virtual void rebalance(Node* n);
    // ...
};
```

The function `rebalance` performs the rebalancing operation on **n**. Suspecting that further derived classes might need to redefine `rebalance`, the programmer has declared it protected and virtual.

Here is what `doinsert` for `RBTree` looks like:

```
template<class T>
void RBTree<T>::doinsert(const T& t, BSTree<T>::Node*& n) {
    if (n == 0) {
        Node* m = new Node(t);   // line 1
        n = m;
        rebalance(m);
    }
    else {
        if (t < n->t)
            doinsert(t, n->left);
        else
            doinsert(t, n->right);
    }
}
```

There are only two significant differences between this code and the code for the base class version of `doinsert`. First, the node created on line 1 is an object of type `RBTree::Node`, not `BSTree::Node`. Second, `rebalance` is called on the newly inserted node.

Notice that most of the code in `RBTree::doinsert` is identical (syntactically and semantically) to the code in `BSTree::doinsert`. Replicating code is tedious, error prone, and inelegant. It can also complicate maintenance; if replicated code must be changed for some reason, the maintainers must remember to change all copies of that code. A more inheritable `BSTree` would allow the derived class implementor to replicate as little code as possible. If the designers of `BSTree` realize that many binary search trees need to create a different type of node and to perform rebalancing operations, they might have the foresight to design `BSTree` like this:

```
template<class T>
class BSTree {
protected:
    virtual Node* newnode(const T& t) {
        return new Node(t);
    }
    virtual void rebalance(Node* n) {
        // empty for BSTree
    }
    // ...
};
```

```
template<class T>
void BSTree<T>::doinsert(const T& t, Node*& n) {
    if (n == 0) {
        n = newnode(t);
        rebalance(n);
    }
    else {
        if (t < n->t)
            doinsert(t, n->left);
        else
            doinsert(t, n->right);
    }
}
```

In this version of `BSTree::doinsert`, we have replaced the code that derived classes need to change with calls to virtual functions. The derived class can, as usual, redefine those functions:

```
template<class T>
class RBTree : public BSTree<T> {
protected:
    Node* newnode(const T& t) {
        return new Node(t);
    }
    void rebalance(BSTree<T>::Node* n) {
        // ...
    }
    // ...
};
```

With this design, the derived class programmer is not forced to replicate any code.

The function `RBTree::newnode` returns an `RBTree::Node`, whereas `BSTree::newnode` returned a `BSTree::Node`. If a base class's virtual function `f` has a return type that is a pointer (or reference) to some class `X`, then it is legal (and type safe) for a derived class version of `f` to have a return type that is a pointer (or reference) to a derived class of `X`. The ability to change the return type of a virtual function in the way that we have just described is called *function return type covariance* and is a relatively new feature of C++.

We had to change the argument type of `RBTree::rebalance` from `RBTree::Node` to `BSTree::Node`. Unfortunately, this change requires `RBTree::rebalance` to perform a downcast to access the `isred` field of the `RBNode` pointed to by `n`. This disadvantage is probably minor compared to the freedom from having to replicate code.

If we wish to ensure that derived class programmers will never have to replicate code, then we should factor out into a separate virtual function any piece of code that any derived class might need to change. There are two disadvantages to this strategy, however. First, determining the perfect factorization is time consuming and will be impossible if we do not have enough information about the sorts of classes that users will derive from our class. Second, every additional virtual function call reduces the efficiency of both the base and derived classes. For example, the call to the empty function `BSTree::rebalance` in `BSTree::doinsert` is a virtual function call that did not occur in the original `BSTree::doinsert`. Although this single virtual function call probably will have no noticeable effect on the efficiency of `BSTree` and its derived classes, a perfectly factored design might be too slow.

3.4.4   Use of Friend

Relying on friends can reduce the inheritability of a class. To show this, we
shall change our BSTree to use friendship. In Sections 3.4.1 through 3.4.3,
we nested the class Node within the class BSTree. An alternative design
is to make Node a separate class (and in the process change its name to
BSNode):

```
template<class T> class BSTree;

template<class T>
class BSNode {
protected:
    T t;
    BSNode(const T& t);
    friend class BSTree<T>;
};

template<class T>
class BSTree {
    // no nested Node
    // ...
};
```

Because BSNode is an implementation detail of BSTree, we have declared the
members of BSNode protected to prevent users other than derived classes
from accessing their members accidentally, and we have made BSTree a
friend.

The implementor of RBTree (derived, as in previous sections, from
BSTree) will also derive an RBNode class from BSNode. The implementation of RBTree needs access to the members of the base node class BSNode.
Friendship, however, is not inherited — that is, although BSTree is a friend
of BSNode, derived classes of BSTree are not thereby friends of BSNode. To
solve this problem, either we must declare the members of BSNode public
— thereby sacrificing protection and making the friendship pointless — or
the user must add access functions to RBNode:

```
template<class T>
class RBNode : public BSNode<T> {
protected:
    T& tval() { return t; }
    // ...
};
```

The design in previous sections, which did not use friendship, did not require users to implement access functions.

3.4.5   Excess Data Members

An obstacle to inheritability that happens only rarely in practice is the presence of too many data members in the intended base class. Suppose that the nodes in BSTree contain, in addition to pointers to the left and right children, a pointer to the parent:

```
template<class T>
class BSTree {
protected:
    class Node {
    public:
        Node* parent;
        Node* left;
        Node* right;
        // ...
    };
    // ...
};
```

Now suppose that some user wishes to implement a binary search tree Compact_bstree that is more efficient in its use of space. In Compact_bstree, each node stores only two pointers (to its left and right children) instead of three. Unfortunately, a space-efficient binary search tree cannot be derived from this BSTree because a derived class cannot remove an offending data member inherited from one of its base classes.

To prevent this problem, designers of intended base classes should avoid defining data members that derived classes will find unacceptable. Unfortunately, determining the set of acceptable data members can be difficult, and sometimes this set is empty.

If we interface the class BSTree (see Section 3.2.1), then the author of Compact_bstree can derive Compact_bstree from BSTree's interface class. Compact_bstree, however, will then inherit none of the implementation of BSTree and will have to be implemented from scratch.

3.4.6   Nonvirtual Derivation

Suppose that we decide to provide both BSTree and RBTree in our library. Consider the user who attempts to derive the classes Threaded_bstree and Threaded_rbtree as follows:

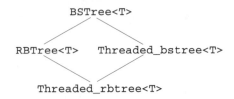

Unfortunately, even though a `Threaded_bstree` is a kind of `BSTree` and a `Threaded_rbtree` is a kind of `RBTree`, this design will not work. Because `RBTree`, as shown in the previous sections, derives nonvirtually from `BSTree`, `Threaded_bstree` will contain two `BSTree` subobjects, which is not what the user wants. This user needs `RBTree` (and `Threaded_bstree`) to derive virtually from `BSTree`.

Virtual derivation has two disadvantages, however. First, if a class B has no virtual member functions and inherits no virtual member functions, it is impossible to downcast from B to a virtually derived class D. Downcasting is sometimes necessary. Second, on most systems, virtual derivation from a noninterface class is less efficient than nonvirtual derivation from a noninterface class.

Hence, we would like to declare virtual only those derivations that would create problems for users if they were nonvirtual. Predicting what derivations should be virtual can be tricky. In our example, if a multiple derivation (either direct or indirect) from `BSTree` through `RBTree` is unlikely, and we desire maximum efficiency then we should leave the derivation of `RBTree` from `BSTree` nonvirtual.

3.4.7   Inheritance-Preventing Member Function

Sometimes, the mere presence of a member function that seems perfectly reasonable for a class nevertheless reduces that class's inheritability. Suppose that our library provides a class `Graph` (a graph is a set of nodes and edges connecting pairs of nodes):

```
template<class T>
class Graph {
public:
    class Node { /* ... */ };
    // ...
};
```

Unlike the `Node` class for `BSTree`, we have decided to declare the `Node` class for `Graph` public because we want users to be able to manipulate `Graph` nodes directly.

A function that we might reasonably choose to provide is one that adds a new node to a `Graph`:

```
template<class T>
class Graph {
public:
    virtual void addnode(Node* n);
    // ...
};
```

Calling `addnode` adds the node pointed to by `n` to the given graph; we declare `addnode` virtual to increase the inheritability of `Graph`. Other functions in `Graph` would allow users to add edges between nodes. Suppose that we define the inheritance semantics of `addnode` as follows:

> Adds the node pointed to by `n` to the given graph.

Suppose further that our user wishes to implement a class `Tree` representing trees. A tree is a kind of graph, so the user would like to inherit `Tree` publicly from `Graph`. Unfortunately, that is not possible. Because adding a node with no incoming or outgoing edges to a graph that is a tree produces a graph that is no longer a tree, `Tree` cannot satisfy the inheritance semantics of `addnode`.

One way to make `Tree` inheritable from `Graph` is to loosen the inheritance semantics of `addnode`, as follows:

> Adds the node pointed to by `n` to the given graph, or does nothing.

`Tree` can satisfy these semantics by redefining `addnode` to be the empty function. The problem with this solution is that if `addnode` is called on a pointer or reference to a `Graph`, the caller will have no guarantee that the node was added:

```
Graph<T>* g;
// ...
g->addnode(n);  // will n be added or not?
```

Here, `g` might point to an object of a type derived from `Graph` for which `addnode` has been redefined to do nothing. Such an interface would be counterintuitive and error prone.

A better way to make `Tree` inheritable from `Graph` is to remove `addnode` from `Graph`:

```
template<class T>
class Graph {
    // no addnode
    // ...
};

template<class T>
class Tree : public Graph<T> {
    // no addnode
    // ...
};
```

We can, of course, introduce `addnode` in a class derived from `Graph`:

```
template<class T>
class Graph_with_addnode : public Graph<T> {
    void addnode(Node* n);
    // ...
};
```

More generally, if a class X has three member functions f, g, and h, each of which decreases the inheritability of X, we can restore inheritability by refining the inheritance graph as shown in Figure 3.1. Classes that satisfy both f and g's inheritance semantics can derive from X_with_f_and_g; classes that satisfy only f's inheritance semantics can derive from X_with_f; and so on.

Although they increase inheritability, such *fine-grained inheritance hierarchies* have the disadvantage of quickly becoming too complex. The number of classes in a maximally fine-grained inheritance hierarchy is exponential in the number of member functions whose mere presence decreases inheritability. To reduce the number of classes, the designer should find the coarsest refinement that provides enough inheritability. For example, suppose we know that any derived class of X that can satisfy the inheritance semantics of either f or g can also satisfy the other and that no user needs a version of X that provides all three functions. Then we can get away with the significantly simpler hierarchy shown in Figure 3.2.

3.5   The Derived Assignment Problem

Recall that an abstract class is one that has at least one pure virtual function, which it may have inherited. An abstract class can be used only as a base class. A class is concrete if it is not abstract.

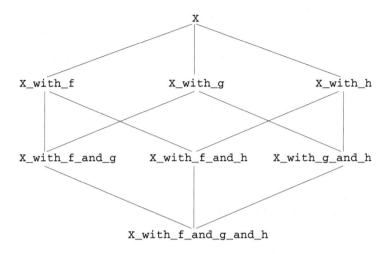

Figure 3.1   A fine-grained inheritance hierarchy.

Figure 3.2   A less fine-grained inheritance hierarchy.

In Sections 3.4.3 through 3.4.6, we derived the concrete class RBTree from the concrete class BSTree. Deriving concrete classes from each other leads to a problem we shall call the *derived assignment* problem.[3]   To understand this problem, suppose that we wish BSTree to be nice (see Section 2.3). Recall that every nice class provides a principal assignment operator:

---

3. Actually, the derived assignment problem is an instance of the more general problem that the designers of derived classes sometimes want covariance on argument types, which C++ disallows. The problem occurs most often in connection with assignment operators, however.

```
template<class T>
class BSTree {
public:
    const BSTree<T>& operator=(const BSTree<T>& t);
    // ...
};
```

Similarly, suppose that the designer of RBTree wants niceness and therefore provides a principal assignment operator:

```
template<class T>
class RBTree : public BSTree<T> {
public:
    const RBTree<T>& operator=(const RBTree<T>& t);
    // ...
};
```

Now consider the following code:

```
void buggy_func() {
    RBTree<int> r, s;
    BSTree<int> b;
    BSTree<int>* p = &r;
    *p = b;  // line 1
    *p = s;  // line 2
}
```

The assignment operations on lines 1 and 2 both call BSTree::operator=, not RBTree::operator=. Hence, on line 1 the BSTree object b will be assigned to the BSTree part of r, and on line 2 the BSTree part of s will be assigned to the BSTree part of r. This behavior is almost certainly not what anyone wants.

We might attempt to solve this problem by declaring the BSTree assignment operator virtual. If we do that, we must also change the argument type of the derived class assignment operator to match exactly:

```
template<class T>
class RBTree : public BSTree<T> {
public:
    // make assignment operator take BSTree:
    const RBTree<T>& operator=(const BSTree<T>& t);
    // ...
};
```

Unfortunately, this operator is no longer the principal assignment operator. More importantly, defining the semantics of this operation is infeasible. What does it mean, for example, to assign a `Threaded_bstree` to an `RBTree` given that a `Threaded_bstree` is not necessarily a kind of `RBTree`?

To solve this problem, we might consider giving `RBTree::operator=` the precondition that the type of the object referred to by `t` be a descendant of `RBTree`. Should we check this precondition? If we do not, then we shall have succeeded only in converting the assignment operations in `buggy_func` from having undesirable behavior to having undefined behavior, which is also undesirable. On the other hand, to check the precondition we would have to add `dynamic_casts` to the implementation of `RBTree::operator=`. Such an implementation is inelegant. Further, it succeeds only in converting the assignment operations in `buggy_func` to run-time errors. We would prefer a design in which those assignments are compile-time errors.

A better solution to the derived assignment problem is not to derive concrete classes publicly from concrete classes. In our example, we can use interface classes to transform our inheritance hierarchy into the one shown in Figure 3.3. Because the derivation of `RBTree` from `BSTree` is now private, the assignment operations in `buggy_func` now generate compile-time errors. The disadvantage of this approach is that it requires more classes and more derivation and is thus more difficult to understand and use. In practice, most library designers use the simpler design and do not worry about the derived assignment problem.

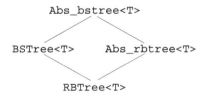

Figure 3.3   Transformed hierarchy that does not have the derived assignment problem. `RBTree` derives privately from `BSTree`.

3.6   Allowing Invasive Inheritance

Some of the obstacles to inheritability can be solved easily by users of a class if they have access to the source code for that class. For example, users who have access to source can add a virtual specifier if they need to redefine a function in a derived class that was not declared virtual in the library, or they can change the protection of members declared private in the library if they need to access those members in a derived class. Changing the code of a base class to enable inheritance from it is sometimes called *invasive inheritance*. Of course, a programmer who inherits invasively risks introducing error in the implementation of the base class. Further, inheriting invasively complicates upgrading to a new release of the library containing the invaded base class.

Because it is difficult to write inheritable classes and because some of the obstacles to inheritability are corrected easily by users when they have library source, you might want to consider distributing source code for all or part of your library. Of course, distributing source comes with its own set of disadvantages (see Exercise 3.11).

3.7 Summary

There are costs associated with providing extensibility. Occasionally, a reasonable alternative to designing a C++ library extensibly is to provide all the functionality users will ever want so that they do not need to extend the library's classes.

More often, users will want extensibility. Extensibility in C++ is provided primarily through inheritance. Properly defining the inheritance semantics of a class and assuming only those semantics throughout the library are essential to writing an extensible class. The burden for successful inheritance rests partly on the user — inheritance will not be successful if a publicly derived type does not adhere to the inheritance semantics of its intended base classes.

It can be difficult to derive from classes not written carefully to allow inheritance. The obstacles to inheritability are as follows:

- Nonvirtual member functions
- Overprotection of data and function members
- Undermodularization of member functions
- Use of friends
- Excess data members
- Nonvirtual derivations
- Inheritance-preventing member functions

Because most of the obstacles to inheritability cannot occur in interface classes, libraries for which extensibility is important should interface all the classes whose interfaces users might wish to inherit.

Exercises

3.1   Which of the following are extensible?
  a.   The collection of books in a library
  b.   The collection of books in the Bible
  c.   The vocabulary of Latin
  d.   The set of all electronic mail addresses on the Internet

3.2   Show how to implement the `Map` class of Section 3.2.2 by overriding the `BSTree::newnode` function shown in Section 3.4.3.

3.3   Explain how to rewrite any private derivation (like the derivation of `BSTree` in `Map` of Section 3.2.2, for example) with a single instance of public derivation and a single instance of embedding one object within another.

3.4   What problems would arise if a class inherited an interface class `X` along more than one derivation path and if along one or more of those paths `X` is inherited nonvirtually?

3.5   Explain why the destructor of every class from which a user might inherit should be declared virtual.

3.6   Use the versions of `BSTree` and `RBTree` from Section 3.4.3 for this and the following exercises.
  a.   Implement the function `BSTree::contains`, returning a `bool` indicating whether its argument (of type `const T&`) is present in the `Tree`.
  b.   Implement `RBTree::contains`. Was `BSTree` inheritable?
  c.   Implement `BSTree::remove`, which removes a given value, if present, from a `BSTree`. `BSTree::remove` should return a `bool` indicating whether the value was present.
  d.   ($*$) Implement `RBTree::remove`. Remember that the remove operation for a red-black tree must rebalance the tree. Was your `BSTree` inheritable?

3.7   For this exercise, recall the `Map` class of Section 3.2.2.
  a.   Implement `Map` with `RBTree`.
  b.   In your solution to part a, did you have to inherit a class from `RBTree`? If so, how inheritable was `RBTree`?

3.8   In this chapter, we have seen how inheritance is used to make a C++ library extensible. Inheritance can also be used to make a library easier to use. Suppose that the chemists in the ShinyBrite toothpaste company want to manipulate `Toothpaste` objects in a toothpaste simulation program. They want to be able to construct a `Toothpaste` by specifying the amounts of the substances that make up the toothpaste.

a.   Explain why the constructor in the following version of `Toothpaste` (where `Quantity` is some class that represents the quantity of an ingredient) would be difficult to use and error prone:

```
class Toothpaste {
public:
    Toothpaste(
        Quantity fluoride,
        Quantity oil_of_peppermint,
        Quantity saccharin,
        Quantity red_dye7,
        Quantity blue_dye10,
        /* several score more parameters */);
    // ...
};
```

b.   Some writers use the expression *feature filtering* to refer to the use of a derived class to provide a simpler interface to a complex base class. Suppose that every variation of ShinyBrite children's toothpaste contains the same amounts of fluoride, saccharin, and blue dye number 10. Show how a feature-filtering class `Childrens_toothpaste` derived from `Toothpaste` could make this library easier to use. (This problem is discussed further in Exercise 8.8.)

3.9   Consider the class `Compact_bstree` discussed at the end of Section 3.4.5. Show how to design `BSTree` and its containing inheritance hierarchy such that the implementor of `Compact_bstree` can reuse as much of the implementation of `BSTree` as possible.

3.10   Suppose that you have a class `Polygon` from which you wish to derive a class `Rectangle`.

a.   Suppose that `Polygon` has a member function `add_vertex` that adds a vertex to the polygon on which it is called. What problem does this cause for inheriting `Rectangle` from `Polygon`?

b. Show an inheritance hierarchy that would allow successful derivation of `Rectangle` from `Polygon` (or some class you design to replace `Polygon`).

3.11 What are the disadvantages of distributing source code for a library?

References and Further Reading

Halbert and O'Brien [HO87] elaborate on the uses of inheritance. Martin [Mar91], Nackman and Barton [NB94], and Linton and Pan [LP94] discuss the use of interface classes in a C++ library, as well as the associated inefficiencies.

Although they do not use the term *undermodularization*, Kiczales and Lamping [KL92] and Weide, Ogden, and Sitaraman [WOS94] present good examples of that phenomenon. The derived assignment problem was first explicated by Meyers [Mey94a, Mey94b]. Fine-grained inheritance is discussed in detail by Johnson and Rees [JR92].

Schwarz [Sch90] discusses shortcomings of C++ as an object-oriented language, including the derived assignment problem.

The concept of substitutability and the problem of inheritance-preventing member functions are fascinating topics. Much more can be said about them than we have space for in this chapter. Interested readers should see Chapters 10 and 11 of Cline and Lomow's book [CL95], Baclawski and Indurkhya's short but excellent discussion [BI94], and the works cited by the latter.

Carroll [Car92b] coined the term *invasive inheritance* and gives a detailed example of the phenomenon.

4 Efficiency

> *More computing sins are committed in the name of efficiency (without necessarily achieving it) than for any other single reason — including blind stupidity.*
>
> — Wm. A. Wulf

Efficiency is an essential property of reusable code. In this chapter, we consider how to design and implement reusable code to use the following resources efficiently: program build time (which includes compile time, link time, and instantiation time), code size, run time, and memory.

4.1 Efficiency and Reusability

Most programmers consider efficiency an essential property of reusability. No matter how conceptually elegant a library might be, it will not be reused if it degrades a program's efficiency significantly. Even if using a library will increase compile time by only a small fraction, the development team with several thousand source files, which take days to build, cannot afford the extra time. The real-time application programmer cannot use a library that causes the application not to meet its timing constraints. The programmer of an embedded system (an automated teller machine, for example) cannot use a library that would make the executable occupy more bytes than are available on the target machine.

Ideally, developers want reusable code to be as fast and as small as their own hand-crafted code would be. Unfortunately, that ideal is rarely achievable. Reusable code must work well in many contexts (see Section 1.3.2); maximally optimizing it for a specific context often renders it unusable in other intended contexts. Luckily, reusable code rarely has to be as efficient as hand-crafted code to be successful. Consider run time. A commonly quoted rule of thumb is that 90 percent of a program's run time is spent in 10 percent of the code (or you may have heard it said that 80 percent of the time is spent in 20 percent of the code). If a piece of reusable code is *not* used in the hot 10 or 20 (or whatever) percent, then that code does need not to be maximally optimized. Analogous 90/10 or 80/20 rules probably hold for most other measures of efficiency. Furthermore, programmers realize other benefits from using reusable code (they do not have to write it themselves, it should have been well tested and thus should be reliable and robust, it should be well documented, and so on) that often make up for a loss of efficiency — provided, of course, that not *too much* efficiency is sacrificed.

Reusable C++ code should consume as little as possible of these resources: build time, code size, run time, free-store space, and stack space. We discuss each of these in the following sections.

4.2   Build Time

The code that results from running the macro preprocessor on a given source file is a *translation unit*. The time required to build a C++ program consists of the time required to compile all its translation units plus the time required to link the translation units into an executable program. Included in the compilation and link time is the time needed to instantiate all the templates used by the program. In this section, we show some techniques a library implementor can use to decrease the build time of users' programs.

4.2.1   Compile Time

One simple technique for decreasing the compile time of programs that use a library is to minimize the code that those programs #include. Suppose, for example, that our library provides an interface to our users' window system and that that interface is defined in a library header file *Window_system.h*:

Window_system.h:

```
class Widget {
    // ...
};

class Button : public Widget {
    // ...
};

// tons more stuff ...
```

Suppose that this header file, like most real window system header files, includes much code (directly and indirectly). Suppose further that we wish to use `Button` in one of our own library header files:

Ourlib.h:

```
#include <Window_system.h>

class Our_window {
private:
    Button button1;
    Button button2;
    // ...
};
```

Unfortunately, if we implement our library this way, all translation units that include *Ourlib.h* — even ones that never use the window system — would include *Window_system.h*. We can speed our users' compilation times by declaring only the names of the classes we need instead of including the header file:

Ourlib.h:

```
class Button;      // instead of #include <Window_system.h>

class Our_window {
private:
    Button* button1;
    Button* button2;
    // ...
};
```

We must also change the type of `button1` and `button2` from `Button` to `Button*`. All access to the button objects will now go through a level of indirection. Hence, this technique trades off compile time against run time.

Sometimes, we might be tempted to generalize this technique and declare something directly other than a class. For example, suppose that *Window_system.h* contains the following declaration of the function `create_buttons`, which returns a pointer to a newly created array of n Buttons:

```
Button* create_buttons(size_t n);
```

If we call `create_buttons` somewhere in *Ourlib.h*, we might try to declare `create_buttons` in *Ourlib.h* to avoid including *Window_system.h*:

Ourlib.h:

```
// instead of #include <Window_system.h>
class Button;
Button* create_buttons(size_t n);

class Our_window {
public:
    Our_window() {
        button1 = create_buttons(1);
        // ...
    }
    // ...
private:
    Button* button1;
    // ...
};
```

This code looks innocent enough, but it might contain an error. The literal 1, passed to `create_buttons`, is of type `int`, not `size_t`. If *Window_system.h* also contains the declaration

```
Button* create_buttons(int n);
```

then our call to `create_buttons` will resolve to the wrong version of that function. Even if *Window_system.h* does not overload `create_buttons`, it might do so in a future release; our code would compile without error with the new release, but it would probably no longer work as intended. To avoid such problems, programmers should declare directly only class names — never functions — instead of including header files.

4.2.2   Instantiation Time

As templates become more widely used, C++ programs will spend more build time instantiating templates. Template instantiation time is already an issue for some C++ users. Development teams are particularly sensitive to build time because they typically compile, run a few tests, debug, apply a few changes, and then compile again. Hence, minimizing template instantiation time for users is an important goal for reusable code.

Simple Techniques

There are two simple techniques for reducing instantiation time: A library can preinstantiate templates (and might have to preinstantiate certain ones), and it can define function templates inline. Preinstantiating templates in the library's archive is the most obvious way to reduce a library user's instantiation time. Suppose, for example, that we are providing the binary search tree template of Section 3.2.1:

```
template<class T>
class BSTree {
    // ...
};
```

If somewhere in the implementation of our library we use, say, BSTree<String>, or if we discover that many of our users typically create a BSTree<String>, then we should preinstantiate BSTree<String> and place the resulting object files into the library archive. The mechanisms for preinstantiating templates are highly system dependent; we discuss them further in Section 9.7.

Some templates *must* be preinstantiated by a library. Suppose that somewhere in the implementation of our library we use a BSTree<Private>, where Private is a type used only within the implementation of the library and not provided in any of the library's public header files. When the user builds a program that uses the library, the instantiator will not be able to find the implementation of Private. Because users cannot instantiate BSTree<Private>, the library must preinstantiate it.

Another technique that reduces the user's instantiation time on most systems is to define function templates inline:

```
template<class T>
class BSTree {
    int _size;
public:
    int size() const { return _size; }
    // ...
};
```

Here, the function size returns the number of nodes in the tree, the value of which is stored in _size. Because size is inline, it will effectively be instantiated at every call site during compilation, which on most systems is the fastest way to instantiate a function. Of course, this technique applies only to functions that are candidates for inlining.

Any programming technique that reduces the amount of code that must be instantiated will also reduce instantiation time. Two such techniques are *hoisting* and using pointer containers.

Hoisting

Suppose, for the sake of argument, that BSTree::size is *not* defined inline:

```
template<class T>
class BSTree {
public:
    int size() const;
    // ...
};

template<class T>
int BSTree<T>::size() const {
    return _size;
}
```

The implementation of size does not depend on the parameters to BSTree. Theoretically, a C++ compilation system could discover that the object code for all specializations of size will be the same and instantiate only one specialization of size. Few (if any) current compilation systems perform this optimization. We can effectively perform it ourselves, however, by hoisting the definition of size to a nontemplate base class we create for that purpose:

```
class BSTreebase {  // nontemplate class for hoisting
public:
    int size() const;
protected:
    int _size;
};

int BSTreebase::size() const {
    return _size;
}

template<class T>
class BSTree: public BSTreebase {
    // size() now inherited
    // ...
};
```

We must also hoist the data member `_size`. Further, we declare `_size` protected because the derived class template `BSTree` will need to access it.

Sometimes, a member function of a class template can be hoisted even though it depends on the template parameters. Suppose that we represent the nodes in a `BSTree` with the following separate class:

```
template<class T>
class Node {
    T t;
    Node* preorder_successor;
    // ...
};
```

We wish to provide a function `BSTree::thread` that threads the given tree in preorder — specifically, when `BSTree::thread` returns, the `preorder_successor` field of every node in the tree points to its preorder successor. Here is pseudocode for `BSTree::thread`:

```
template<class T>
void BSTree<T>::thread() {
    Node<T>* prev = 0;
    Node<T>* n = 0;
    for (each node n in this tree in preorder) {
        if (prev)
            prev->preorder_successor = n;
        prev = n;
    }
    if (n)
        n->preorder_successor = 0;
}
```

The actual implementation of `thread` would probably use a recursive preorder traversal of the tree rather than a `for` loop. Notice that the body of `thread` depends on the template argument T (in the declarations of `prev` and n). Conceptually, however, threading a tree does not depend on the values stored at the nodes in the tree. Hence, with a little effort we should be able to hoist `thread`. First, let us derive the class template `Node` from a nontemplate base class:

```
class Nodebase {  // nontemplate class created for hoisting
protected:
    Nodebase* preorder_successor;
};
```

```
template<class T>
class Node : public Nodebase {
    T t;
    // ...
};
```

We also hoist `preorder_successor`. Now we can rewrite `thread` in terms of `Nodebase`, hoisting `thread` in the process:

```
class BSTreebase {
public:
    void thread();
    // ...
};

void BSTreebase::thread() {
    Nodebase* prev = 0;
    Nodebase* n = 0;
    // rest same as previously shown for BSTree::thread
    // ...
}
```

Pointer Containers

Another technique for reducing the amount of code that must be instantiated is to provide pointer containers. Suppose that our library provides a List template:

```
template<class T>
class List {
public:
    T head() const;
    List<T> tail() const;
    void insert(const T& t);
    // ...
};
```

A List<T> is a list of values of type T. The function **head** returns the first value on the List and has the precondition that the List not be empty; the function **tail**, with the same precondition, returns a List that is equal to the given List except that the first value is removed; the function **insert** inserts the value t at the beginning of the List.

If, for example, a user creates a `List<int>`, a `List<String>`, a `List<Widget*>`, and `List<Blidget*>` (where `Widget` and `Blidget` are user-defined classes) and calls `head`, `tail`, and `insert` on all four objects, then each of these functions will be instantiated four times. A widely useful class such as `List` might be instantiated in user programs with many different types, causing many functions to be instantiated. A significant amount of code might be generated for `List`'s member functions.

We can reduce the amount of code that users need to instantiate if we provide, in addition to a regular `List` template, a version of `List` for pointers:

```
template<class T>
class Plist {
public:
    T* head() const;
    Plist<T> tail() const;
    void insert(T* t);
    // ...
};
```

A `Plist<T>` represents a list of values of type `T*`. Notice that `Plist::head` returns `T*`, not `T`; similarly, `insert` takes a `T*`. Instead of creating a `List<Widget*>`, users can create a `Plist<Widget>`. The implementation of `Plist` uses a `List<void*>`, and each member function of `Plist` calls the corresponding functions of `List` on `rep`:

```
template<class T>
class Plist {
public:
    T* head() const { return (T*)rep.head(); }
    void insert(T* t) { rep.insert(t); }
private:
    List<void*> rep;
    // ...
};
```

If converting a value of type `T*` to `void*` and back again is guaranteed to recover the original value, then this code behaves as desired. Although there are some types `T` for which this property does not hold (for example, pointer-to-member types), it does hold for most types that typical users will want to insert into a container. (The types for which `Plist` works as intended should be documented clearly.)

To implement `tail`, we use a private constructor in `Plist`:

```
template<class T>
class Plist {
private:
    Plist(const List<void*>& r): rep(r) {}
    // ...
};

template<class T>
Plist<T> Plist<T>::tail() const {
    return Plist<T>(rep.tail());
}
```

The bodies of the member functions of Plist are simple; indeed, they are all candidates for inlining, which (as discussed on page 79) is usually the fastest way to instantiate a function. Further, we can preinstantiate List<void*>. Hence, the programmer who uses Plist<Widget> and Plist<Blidget> needs to instantiate less code than the programmer who uses List<Widget*> and List<Blidget*>; the Plist user will see build time reduced.

Although they reduce instantiation time, pointer containers have one notable disadvantage: A container class and its pointer version, although conceptually related, are *not* related in the C++ type system. Suppose that the user of List and Plist writes the following function:

```
template<class T>
void insert_twice(const T& t, List<T>& l) {
    l.insert(t);
    l.insert(t);
}
```

Although this function can be called for every type of List, it cannot be called for any type of Plist. To provide the same functionality for Plist, another function is needed:

```
template<class T>
void insert_twice(const T& t, Plist<T>& l) {
    l.insert(t);
    l.insert(t);
}
```

Some library designers try to solve this problem by relating a class and its pointer version by inheritance:

```
// poor design using inheritance
template<class T>
class Plist: public List<void*> {
public:
    T* head() const { return (T*)List<void*>::head(); }
    // ...
};
```

Unfortunately, this design is not type safe. Consider the following user code, in which X and Y are unrelated classes:

```
void insert_y(List<void*>& l) {
    l.insert(new Y);
}

int main() {
    Plist<X> l;
    insert_y(l);        // insert a Y* into List l
    X* x = l.head();    // oops!  retrieve an X*
    // ...
}
```

This code has neither compile-time nor build-time errors; nevertheless, it converts a value of type Y* to type X*, which is not guaranteed to be a safe conversion.

4.3 Code Size

The *code size* of a program is the number of bytes in all the object files of all the translation units in the program. If a program has large code size, its executable might require much disk space to store and much main memory to execute. (We say "might" because how much space a program actually requires depends on many system-dependent factors, such as whether the program uses dynamic link libraries, the actual values of the bytes in the executable file, and how files are represented on disk and in memory.)

If a C++ library causes user programs to have large code size, then programmers with insufficient disk and memory will be unable to use the library. To increase the reusability of their code, C++ library implementors should try to minimize the library's code size.

4.3.1   Source-File Partitioning

One well-known technique for reducing code size is never to put the definitions of two large functions in the same library implementation file if it is possible for a program to need one but not the other of them. We shall call this technique *source-file partitioning*. (A smart compilation system would obviate the need for source-file partitioning, but few current compilation systems do.) Consider the class BSTreebase shown in Section 4.2.2:

```
class BSTreebase {
public:
    int size() const;
    void thread();
    // ...
};
```

Suppose for the sake of argument that both these functions are large (in reality, size would usually be small). Suppose further that it is possible for a program to need one of these member functions without also needing the other. Then source-file partitioning would dictate that we put their definitions in separate files. On the other hand, if thread were to call some private member function dothread that is called only by thread, source-file partitioning would allow placing dothread and thread in the same file.

When we consider templates, things get a bit trickier. Suppose that the template BSTree of Section 4.2.2 does not inherit from BSTreebase:

```
template<class T>
class BSTree {
public:
    int size() const;
    void thread();
    // ...
};
```

When we write the definitions of BSTree's template member functions, we must typically put them in public header files so that users' instantiators can access them. Our users' instantiators might place requirements on how our template source code is organized (we shall elaborate on requirements of instantiators in Section 9.7). Thus, we might not have a choice about how the object code for the definitions of these functions will be divided among source files.

Source-file partitioning, if aggressively applied to a large library, can create problems. First, many existing programs for creating and manipulating object code archives cannot handle an archive consisting of, say, several hundred files. To solve this problem, some existing C++ libraries provide several smaller archives rather than one large archive. This solution should be used with caution, however, because it requires users to remember to link with all the archives in the right order.

A second problem is that if we are building the debugging variant (see Section 5.3.1) of a library, then typically many library object files will contain duplicate information. If a programmer then uses the debugging variant of our library to build the debugging variant of a program, the program's code size will be huge, defeating the purpose of partitioning.

To solve both these problems, we can relax our source-file partitioning, putting collections of functions that are *likely* to be used in the same program in the same file. Of course, truly minimal pull-in at link time will then no longer be guaranteed.

4.3.2 Outlined Inlines

Library designers who wish to reduce users' code size should be careful to prevent outlined inlines. Recall that the `inline` keyword is only a hint to the C++ compiler. All current C++ compilers have limits on the functions they can inline. For example, a given compiler might be unable to inline any function containing a `goto` statement or might not inline a function more than say fifteen statements long. Some function calls cannot be inlined — it might not be possible to inline all calls to a function that calls itself, for example. As we shall see in Section 4.4.2, most compilers cannot inline even the simplest virtual function when it is difficult to determine statically the type of the object for which the function is being called.

If a function `f` that is declared inline is not inline expanded at one or more call sites in a translation unit, then many compilers will generate in that translation unit an out-of-line copy of `f` with internal linkage. If such a copy is generated in n translation units, the executable file will contain n copies of `f`. The amount of code devoted to outlined inlines can be significant if programmers are not careful about which functions they declare inline.

Paradoxically, with some of the better optimizing compilers it can be difficult to tell whether a nontrivial function will be inlined. Really good optimizers consider the context of the call site — not just the complexity of the function — in determining whether to inline a given function call.

A safe approach library implementors can use is not to declare a function `f` inline if there is a chance that any of the library users' compilers will outline that function at typical call sites. Documentation accompanying a good C++ implementation will say under what conditions the compiler will not inline a function.

4.3.3   Template Specialization Size

Often, the best way for a C++ library to reduce its contribution to users'
code size is to reduce the total size needed for specializations of library
templates in users' programs. The techniques of hoisting and using pointer
containers, described in Section 4.2.2 as ways to reduce build time, also
reduce code size.

Libraries should also use as few templates as possible. Consider the
template BSTree described in Section 4.2.2. Rather than use BSTree<int>,
BSTree<char>, and BSTree<long> in its implementation, a library could
use just BSTree<long> and thereby save code space. A tradeoff is that the
implementation would become more difficult to understand.

Similarly, suppose that over the course of its development, the implementation of a library has acquired a List template, a Sequence template,
and a Linked_list template, all representing slightly different flavors of
lists and all instantiated somewhere in the library with the same argument,
say List<String>, Sequence<String>, and Linked_list<String>. Such
duplication should be eliminated in favor of one of these templates or perhaps a new template that captures the best aspects of all three.

4.4   Run Time

It is probably safe to say that most programmers consider run time to be
the most important measure of efficiency. A program that is too big or
takes too long to build or consumes too much memory will be tolerated
long after an excessively slow program has been abandoned.

The most effective way to minimize run time is to use the most efficient algorithms possible. If, for example, we are implementing a sorting
function for large lists, we should probably use one of several known variants of quicksort [Baa88, CLR90] or the variant of heapsort described
by Wegener [Weg93].

There are many ways of measuring the run-time efficiency of algorithms.
One can consider the worst case, the average case, or the amortized case,
to name a few. One can look at the number of I/O operations, the number
of floating point operations, or any of several other measures.

Once we have identified the best algorithm for our task — according to
whatever measure we have selected — we must implement that algorithm as
efficiently as possible. A thorough discussion of techniques for implementing
algorithms efficiently is beyond the scope of this book (see [Ben82], for
example); here we discuss several techniques that are particularly important
for C++ code.

4.4.1   Inlining

The run time saved by inlining appropriately chosen functions can be significant. Choosing the right functions to inline, however, is more complex than many people realize.

Myths of Inlining

Programmers tend to think that inlining speeds execution at a cost in code size. It often does, but not always. Code size can in fact be reduced by inlining. Suppose that the body of a function is so small that the inline expansion takes less space in the generated code than the code to set up a call and return would require. The more places this function is inline expanded rather than called out of line, the smaller the containing programmer will be.

Further, inlining can slow execution. Suppose that a large function or several small or medium-sized functions are inlined in a loop. If the inline expansions cause the body of the loop to increase such that it no longer fits in an instruction cache (on a machine that has instruction caches), then the inlining might cause execution to be slower than it otherwise would have been. Other idiosyncrasies of various machines can also interact adversely with inlining.

Programmers also tend to think that only small or perhaps medium-sized functions are candidates for inlining. The truth is that any function — no matter what size — can be a candidate for inlining. Consider that if a function is inlined at a given call site, the time that would have been spent pushing and popping argument values had the call not been inlined is saved. Now suppose that a large function is called at only one place in the program, in a frequently executed section of code (and that instruction caching is not an issue on the target hardware). Inlining that function would not increase code size and probably would improve run time.

Tradeoffs of Inlining

The run time saved by inlining is not merely the time that otherwise would have been spent pushing and popping (and possibly copying) argument and return values and calling and returning from the function. Inlining often creates opportunities for optimizers. For one thing, inlining creates larger basic blocks. (For a definition of *basic block* and the other optimization terms used here, see [ASU86].) If calls with constant arguments are inlined, there will be opportunities for constant propagation. Common subexpressions computed in the context of the call might be eliminated in the inlined function body. Registers might be allocated more effectively in the function containing the inline expansion.

Inlining has two potential disadvantages. First, if any function whose inline expansion takes more space in the generated code than the call and return requires is inlined at more than one call site, the code size of the program increases. The increase in code size depends on the number of call sites in the program and the code size of the function itself. The code size of a function cannot necessarily be determined by examining only the function's definition. Consider this function:

```
void f() {
    g();
    h();
}
```

This function looks small, but its effective code size might be large if either or both of g and h are inlined. For another example, consider the following class:

```
class D : public B {
public:
    inline D() {}
    // ...
};
```

Here, D's constructor is empty, but it contains an implicit call to B's default constructor. If B's constructor is inlined, then the size of D's constructor is at least as large as B's constructor. Further, some compilers will add other overhead to D's destructor, such as a call to malloc.

Another potential disadvantage of inlining is that changes to the implementation of an inline function are usually link incompatible — that is, such changes require users to recompile their code. (We shall discuss link compatibility further in Section 7.5.)

When to Inline

Clearly, if we need to maintain forward link compatibility for a function (more than we need execution speed), then we should not define that function as inline. As discussed in Section 4.3.2, many compilers will refuse to inline certain functions or will not inline certain functions in certain contexts. Thus, declaring a function inline might do more harm than good if out-of-line copies are laid down in multiple translation units. Further, most compilers are unable to inline calls to virtual functions when it is difficult to determine statically the type of the object for which the function is being called (we shall elaborate on this issue in Section 4.4.2), so declaring a virtual function inline might bloat code size. What about functions for which link compatibility is not an issue and that most compilers are able to inline? Whether we should define such a function as inline depends on the effects of inlining that function on code size and run time (Table 4.1).

Table 4.1   Whether a function should be inlined.

Effect of Inlining on Run Time	Effect of Inlining on Code Size		
	Decrease	Minimal	Increase
Decrease	yes	yes	maybe
Minimal	yes	probably	no
Increase	maybe	no	no

Although we might not always know what effect inlining a function will have on the size and execution speed of our users' programs without profiling those programs on the systems on which users will run them, often we know enough about typical uses and about the systems our users will run on to make good judgments.

- If inlining f would reduce both user's code size and run time, then certainly we should inline it. Similarly, if inlining f would reduce either code size or run time and would have no significant effect on the other, then we should inline it.
- If inlining f would affect both code size and run time adversely, or if it would increase one and have no significant effect on the other, then it should not be inlined.
- If inlining f would reduce run time and increase code size or would reduce code size and increase run time, then whether f should be inlined depends on the magnitude of each effect and on which resource concerns our users more.
- If the effect on both code size and run time would be negligible, then the balance tips slightly in favor of inlining f to enable opportunities for further optimization.

4.4.2   Virtual Functions

Virtual functions have two costs. First, a call to an out-of-line virtual function typically takes a few extra machine instructions compared to a call to an out-of-line nonvirtual function. This cost is not significant except for *extremely* frequently called functions. Second, and more important, current compilers cannot inline virtual functions in most contexts. Consider the function `BSTree::size` shown at the beginning of Section 4.2.2, which we now declare virtual:

```
template<class T>
class BSTree {
public:
    virtual inline int size() const {
        return _size;
    }
    // ...
};
```

In contexts in which it is easy to determine statically that `BSTree::size` is being called on a `BSTree` object (and not on an object of a derived class), `BSTree::size` will be inlined by most compilers:

```
BSTree<int> b;
// ...
int sz = b.size();  // most compilers will inline
```

On the other hand, if it is difficult to determine statically whether `BSTree::size` is being called on a `BSTree` object, most existing compilers will not inline `BSTree::size`:

```
void f(const BSTree<int>& b) {
    int sz = b.size();  // most compilers will not inline
    // ...
}
```

Thus, with current compiler technology, when we make a function virtual, we give up the ability to inline that function in most contexts. Whether to declare a member function `f` inline or virtual is summarized in Table 4.2.

- If inlining a member function f is crucial and users need to override f, see if some redesign can resolve the conflict. Fortunately, this conflict rarely occurs in practice.
- If inlining a member function f is crucial and users do not need to override f, then f should be nonvirtual and inline.
- If inlining is not crucial and users need to override it, then f should be declared virtual and not inline.
- Finally, if neither inlining nor overriding is important, then f should probably be nonvirtual just to avoid the overhead of calling virtual functions.

Table 4.2   Whether a member function should be virtual or inline.

Users Need to Override	Inlining Crucial	
	Yes	No
Yes	redesign library	virtual, noninline
No	nonvirtual, inline	nonvirtual, see Table 4.1

It can, of course, be difficult to know in advance which functions users will ever need to override (see Section 3.4.1). When there is any doubt, the function should be virtual; otherwise the user who needs to override it will be stuck (unless the source code for the library is distributed; see Section 3.6).

Almost no functions should be declared both virtual and inline. An out-of-line copy of such a function probably will be generated in each translation unit in which a call cannot be inlined (recall Sections 4.3.2 and 4.4.2).

4.4.3   Returning References

One technique often advocated for reducing run time is to return references instead of values that might require expensive copying. Consider the List::head() function shown on page 82. All callers of head — including callers who want only to examine the value at the head of the list — incur the cost of copying that value out of the list:

```
List<Widget> l;
// ...
cout << "first widget is " << l.head();  // copies Widget
```

To avoid the overhead of copying in such uses, we can change **head** to return a reference to the internally stored copy of the value at the head of the list:

```
template<class T>
class List {
public:
    const T& head() const;  // returns reference
    // ...
};
```

With **List** defined this way, the user code shown would not copy a **Widget**. We declare **head** to return a **const** reference; returning a nonconst reference would allow the user to change the value of a **const List** without using a cast to remove the **const**:

```
void whoops(const List<Widget>& l) {
    Widget newvalue;
    // ...
    l.head() = newvalue;  // uh-oh!  legal if head returns
                          // nonconst, but not a good idea
    // ...
}
```

For any library function that returns a reference, the library documentation should state how long that reference remains valid. For example, we might document **head** as follows:

> The reference returned by **head** remains valid until the value to which it refers is removed from the given **List**.

Returning references has two disadvantages. First, it makes user code more error prone. Recall from page 82 that **insert** inserts at the head of the **List** and that **tail** returns the tail of the given **List**. Consider the following code:

```
List<int> l;
l.insert(0);
const int& i = l.head();
l.insert(1);    // i still valid
l = l.tail();   // i still valid
l = l.tail();   // i invalid
```

Any attempt to use the reference i after it is invalid has undefined behavior. Such undefined behavior would not be possible with the version of head that returns T rather than const T&.

The second disadvantage of returning references is that it restricts the ways we can implement the given class. For example, suppose that we determine that most user code would be faster if we implement List with sharing. Specifically, consider the List<int> x whose underlying implementation is represented by the following figure:

If the user writes

```
List<int> y = x;
```

then the implementation of y shares nodes with x:

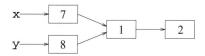

If the user inserts a 7 into x and an 8 into y, the implementation will look like this:

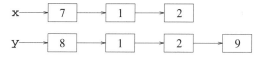

Finally, if the user appends the value 9 to y, then x and y no longer share a suffix, so we make copies of all the shared nodes and append 9 to the resulting list:

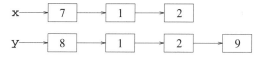

Now suppose that the function remove_all removes all the values from a list, and the function append appends a given value to a list. Consider the following code:

```
List<int> x;
x.insert(0);
List<int> y = x;
const int& i = y.head();
```

Here is what we have at this point:

If we now append to y:

```
y.append(1);     // i still valid
```

x and y will no longer have a common suffix, so y's List will be copied. (An implementation could append to y, leaving y in place and making x point to a copy, but that approach would just move the problem, not solve it — suppose that there is a reference to x.head().) Now we have this:

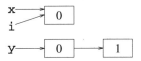

Suppose that x is now changed:

```
x.remove_all();  // i valid?
```

Because there are no other List objects in the program that share nodes with x, the remove_all operation deletes all the nodes in x. Graphically, here is what we have:

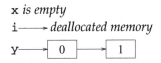

After the call to remove_all, the reference i is probably invalid. Hence, with this implementation of List, we could not (unless we were very clever) guarantee that a reference returned by head remains valid until the value to which it refers is removed from the given List (the List for which head was called, that is).

A guarantee that this implementation of List *can* make is the following:

> The reference returned by head remains valid until a nonconst operation is performed on *any* List<T>.

Unfortunately, with this guarantee, the odds are high that user programs will accidentally manipulate invalid references. Attempting to strengthen the guarantee to prevent that possibility would almost certainly require changes to the implementation of List that reduce its efficiency.

Returning references improves efficiency, but it can make user code more error prone and it can limit the ways a class can be implemented. If references are returned, the library must document how long each such reference will be valid. Care must be exercised to ensure that the guarantees about references are correct.

4.5 Free-Store and Stack Space

The memory of an executing C++ program is conceptually partitioned into three areas:

- The *static storage* holds the program's text and static data.
- The *free store* is the memory that can be acquired by calling `operator new`, the function `malloc`, and other system-specific functions. The amount of free-store space in use can (and usually does) vary over the course of program execution.
- Finally, the *stack* is the memory that can hold automatic variables and function arguments. The amount of stack space in use usually varies during program execution.

In Section 4.3, we discussed ways to reduce the code size of a program and, hence, its static storage. In the following sections, we consider ways to reduce use of free-store and stack space.

4.5.1 Using Efficient Algorithms

The most effective way to minimize the use of free-store space is to employ algorithms that use space efficiently. Suppose that we are implementing a library intended for building C++ programming environments. We might want to provide a function that compiles a given piece of C++ code:

```
bool compile(istream& i, const List<String>& incldirs,
    ostream& o);
```

This function reads the text in i and attempts to compile it, using `incldirs` as the list of directories in which to search for files to be `#included`. If there are no errors, `compile` writes the resulting object code to o and returns `true`; otherwise `compile` returns `false`.

We might consider implementing `compile` in two phases: First, preprocess the code and store the resulting macro-expanded text in the free store, then compile that text. Unfortunately, this algorithm uses on the order of

s bytes of free store, where s is the size of the macro-expanded text. For
real programs, s can easily be 500K bytes or more. If any of our users do
not have enough free-store space to accommodate this implementation of
compile, then we must use a different implementation.

Instead of writing the macro-expanded text into memory, let us write it
to a file. Suppose that we implement the following two functions:

```
bool preprocess(istream& i, const List<String>& incldirs,
    ostream& o);
bool compile_preprocessed(istream& i, ostream& o);
```

The first function preprocesses the text in i. If there are no errors,
preprocess writes the macro-expanded result to o and returns true; otherwise it returns false. The second function compiles the code in i, which is
assumed to be preprocessed. If there are no errors, compile_preprocessed
writes the resulting object code to o and returns true; otherwise it returns
false.

With these functions, we can implement compile as follows:

```
#include <fstream.h>

bool compile(istream& i, const List<String>& incldirs,
    ostream& o) {
    ofstream otmp("tmpfile");
    if (preprocess(i, incldirs, otmp)) {
        otmp.flush();
        ifstream itmp("tmpfile");
        return compile_preprocessed(itmp, o);
    }
    return false;
}
```

This implementation of compile uses file system space, not free-store space,
to store the macro-expanded text; file system space is plentiful on most systems. This implementation, however, requires the entire macro-expanded
text to be written to a file and read back in; file I/O is typically much
slower than writing and reading data in memory.

To make compile efficient in both space and time, we must preprocess
the given text a constant-sized chunk at a time, in memory. To this end,
suppose that we write the following class:

```
class Preprocessor {
public:
    Preprocessor(istream& i, const List<String>& incldirs);
    bool nextchunk(String& s);
    // ...
};
```

The constructor creates a `Preprocessor` on the text in the stream i. As long as preprocessing is not finished, a call to `nextchunk` will set s to the next chunk of macro-expanded text and return `true`; when there is no more text, it will return `false`. The size of each chunk is no greater than some appropriately chosen constant.

We next change the interface of `compile_preprocessed` to take a `Preprocessor` rather than an `istream&`:

```
bool compile_preprocessed(Preprocessor& p, ostream& o);
```

The implementation of this version of `compile_preprocessed` calls `Preprocessor::chunk` whenever it needs more text. We can now implement `compile` as follows:

```
bool compile(istream& i, const List<String>& incldirs,
    ostream& o) {
    Preprocessor p(i, incldirs);
    return compile_preprocessed(p, o);
}
```

This implementation of `compile` uses a constant amount of free-store space to hold the translation unit, no matter how large the input. Further, because it avoids using the file system, it is fast. The tradeoff is that it is more difficult to implement than the other implementations of `compile`.

4.5.2   Freeing Resources ASAP

C++ libraries should generally free resources that they have acquired as soon as possible. Consider `compile_preprocessed`. As code is compiled, there must be symbol table entries for each scope; the symbol table for a scope contains information about the names declared in that scope. The symbol tables will, of course, be allocated in the free store. When is the earliest that the library can delete each symbol table? The answer varies depending on the kind of scope. The symbol table for a function scope can be deleted immediately after the code for that function has been compiled because the meaning of program text following the definition of a function cannot depend on names declared in that function:

```
void f() {
    int i;
    // ...
}
// meaning of code here unaffected by existence of i in f
```

On the other hand, the symbol table for a class scope cannot be deleted until `compile_preprocessed` finishes compiling all the code to be compiled:

```
class T {
public:
    void f();
};

int main() {
    T t;
    t.f();  // uses name declared in T's scope
}
```

It can be difficult to determine the earliest time that a resource can be freed safely. The general solution is to use garbage collection, but ANSI/ISO C++ does not require C++ implementations to provide a garbage collector. (Some C++ implementations do provide a garbage collector, but most do not. Thus, relying on the presence of a garbage collector will limit the portability of your code.)

4.5.3 Static Objects

If the implementation of a library defines any static objects, then the implementor needs to be careful about the free-store space used by those objects. Consider the function `preprocess` discussed in Section 4.5.1. Suppose that for some reason `preprocess` uses a static variable to hold the current line of input text:

```
bool preprocess(istream& i, const List<String>& incldirs,
        ostream& o) {
    static String curline;
    while (more text in i) {
        curline = next line of text in i;
        // ...
    }
    // ...
    return true;
}
```

As the pseudocode shows, each time `preprocess` reads a line of text, `preprocess` assigns it to `curline`. The implementation of `String` then stores that line of text in the free store. The problem arises when `preprocess` returns: `curline` will still store the last line of text. The free-store space used to store it will be wasted until the next call of `preprocess` or the end of program execution, whichever occurs first. There is no bound on the length of an input line and hence no bound on the amount of free-store space that `preprocess` wastes.

To solve this problem, we remember to free the free-store space used by our static object before we return from the library function:

```
bool preprocess(istream& i, const List<String>& incldirs,
    ostream& o) {
    // ...
    curline = "";   // free space used by curline
    return true;
}
```

Assigning the empty string to `curline` frees all but a small constant amount of the free-store space used by `curline`. Naturally, the means by which the space used by an object can be freed depends on the type of the object.

4.5.4 Large Objects

Now let us consider stack space. On many systems, the stack space that is available to a program is significantly less than the free-store space available (which in turn is significantly less than the space available in the file system).

The stack space used by a program at any given time is larger than the sum of all the sizes of all objects then on the stack. (When we say *size of an object*, we mean the `sizeof` that object). If a program runs out of stack space, it is usually for one of two reasons: an error that causes an infinite recursion or the creation of one or more huge objects on the stack. Concerning huge objects, consider the following class:

```
class Huge {
    char buf[1024 * 1024];   // 1 megabyte
    // ...
};
```

If a program creates a `Huge` on the stack, the odds are high that it will run out of stack space. Luckily, the temptation to create a huge class is rare. If we are so tempted and if it is possible that a user program might create an object of that class on the stack, then we should instead allocate the needed memory from the free store:

```
class Huge_in_freestore {
private:
    char* buf;
public:
    Huge_in_freestore() : buf(new char[1024 * 1024]) {
        // ...
    }
    ~Huge_in_freestore() {
        delete[] buf;
    }
    // ...
};
```

As discussed in Section 4.5.2, we must remember to delete objects allocated from the free store as soon as possible. Here, we delete `Huge_in_freestore::buf` in the class's destructor.

4.6 Tradeoffs of Efficiency

Efficiency trades off with almost every other desirable property of a C++ library. In particular, designing a library to be efficient in every possible way usually renders that library both more difficult to implement and more difficult to use.

Suppose that we are the designers of a `Graph` class representing graphs and that we wish `Graph` to be as efficient as possible. Whatever interface we choose to give `Graph`, we shall need classes representing nodes and edges:

```
template<class T>
class Node {
private:
    T t;
    // ...
};
```

```
template<class T>
class Edge {
public:
    Edge(Node<T>* m, Node<T>* n);
    // ...
};
```

T is the type of value stored at each node. The `Edge` constructor takes
pointers to the two nodes to be connected by the edge to be constructed.
(In a real library, we would probably nest `Node` and `Edge` in `Graph`.)

Suppose that we need to store at each node in a `Graph` the set of edges
that are incident on that node, and suppose that we have available the
following general-purpose `Set` class:

```
template<class T>
class Set {
public:
    void insert(const T& t);
    bool is_empty() const;
    // ...
};
```

The function `insert` inserts t into the set; `is_empty` returns `true` if the
set is empty. We can use `Set` to represent `Node`'s incident edge sets:

```
template<class T>
class Node {
private:
    Set<Edge<T>*> incedges;
    // ...
};
```

To allow users to traverse the graphs they create, we will provide a function
that returns the set of edges incident on a node:

```
template<class T>
class Node {
public:
    Set<Edge<T>*> incident_edges() const {
        return incedges;
    }
    // ...
};
```

Unfortunately, this elegant design might not be efficient enough. Set is a general-purpose class and therefore cannot be maximally efficient in all its many intended contexts. Suppose that it turns out that Set is not efficient enough for the incident edges of a Node. To make Graph more efficient, we will design a special-purpose class, Incedges, which will represent the set of edges incident on a node:

```
template<class T>
class Incedges {
public:
    void insert(Edge<T>* e);
    bool contains(Edge<T>* e) const;
    int size() const;
    // ...
};
```

The function insert adds an edge to the set, contains returns true if the given edge is in the set, and size returns the number of edges in the set.

We use Incedges as follows:

```
template<class T>
class Node {
private:
    Incedges<T> incedges;
    // ...
};
```

If we have done our job correctly, then using Incedges instead of Set in Node will produce a more efficient implementation of our library. Unfortunately, this more efficient design renders our library more difficult to implement and to use, as we show in the following sections.

4.6.1   More Difficult to Implement

Efficiency often trades off with ease of implementation. The more efficient implementation of Graph requires that we first design, implement, and test Incedges — additional work we would not have to do if we were to use Set. Furthermore, using Incedges instead of Set to implement Node interferes with implementing the rest of our library. Suppose that we provide the following function:

```
template<class T>
class Node {
public:
    bool is_adjacent(Node<T>* n) const;
    // ...
};
```

If n and the given node are adjacent (that is, connected by an edge), then is_adjacent returns true.

In the version of Node that is implemented with Set, implementing is_adjacent is easy. If operator* is the Set intersection operator, we can write the following one-line function:

```
template<class T>
bool Node<T>::is_adjacent(Node<T>* n) const {
    return !(incedges * n->incedges).is_empty();
}
```

This code simply tests whether the intersection of the two sets is empty.

Suppose that Incedges does not provide any set intersection operator. Then with the version of Node that uses Incedges, implementing is_adjacent is more difficult. Here is a first cut, partly in pseudocode:

```
template<class T>
bool Node<T>::is_adjacent(Node<T>* n) const {
    for (Edgebase* e in incedges)
        if (e connects n and this node)
            return true;
    return false;
}
```

In this implementation, we must iterate through the list of incident edges, checking whether n is on any of the edges. (In real code, iteration would be done using some iterator class, which we have not shown, for Incedges.) Further, although this pseudocode is correct, it is probably not as efficient as it could be. Instead of looping through this node's edge list, it would be faster to loop through the *shorter* of the edge lists for this node and node n:

```
template<class T>
bool Node<T>::is_adjacent(Node<T>* n) const {
    Node<T>* sparser_node = this;
    if (n->incedges.size() < incedges.size())
        sparser_node = n;
```

```
    for (Edgebase* e in sparser_node->incedges)
        if (e connects n and this node)
            return true;
    return false;
}
```

This version of `is_adjacent` is clearly not as easy to implement and understand as the one-line version using `Set`.

4.6.2   More Difficult to Use

Efficiency also often trades off with ease of use. Suppose that the users of our library need a function that returns the set of edges incident on a given node. The most elegant interface would return a `Set` of `Edges`:

```
template<class T>
class Node {
public:
    Set<Edge<T>*> incident_edges() const;
    // ...
};
```

If `Node` is implemented with `Incedges`, then the implementation of `incident_edges` must do a conversion:

```
template<class T>
Set<Edge<T>*> Node<T>::incident_edges() const {
    // convert incedges to a Set
    // ...
};
```

No such conversion is needed if `Node` is implemented with `Set`.

Alternatively, we can eliminate the overhead of the run-time conversion by moving our class `Incedges` to the interface of the library and having `Node::incident_edges` return an `Incedges` instead of a `Set`:

```
template<class T>
class Node {
public:
    Incedges<T> incident_edges() const {
        return incedges;
    }
private:
    Incedges<T> incedges;
    // ...
};
```

Unfortunately, our library is now more difficult to use. Users must learn the special-purpose class Incedges. Further, user code will become more difficult to write, just as the function is_adjacent shown in the previous section became more difficult for us to write.

4.7   Summary

Efficiency is a crucial property for reusable code.

Build time is particularly important for development teams. Minimizing the amount of code that a library includes, preinstantiating templates, defining function templates inline, hoisting template code, and using pointer containers can help keep down build times.

Library implementors can reduce users' code size by partitioning the library's source files and by ensuring that functions declared inline are not laid down out of line. The library implementation itself should use as few templates as possible.

To many users, the most important measure of efficiency is run time. Run time can often be improved significantly through appropriate inlining. It is not always obvious, however, which functions to inline. Returning references is a technique for improving run time, but it can make user code more error prone and limit the ways a class can be implemented.

Free-store and stack space must also be used efficiently. Being careful to use efficient algorithms and freeing resources as soon as possible are two of the best ways to minimize use of space. Large objects usually should be created in the free store rather than on the stack.

Unfortunately, efficiency trades off with almost every other desirable property of a C++ library. In particular, designing a library to be as efficient as possible usually renders that library more difficult to implement and to use.

Exercises

4.1   If we are developing a library including the `BSTree` class of Section 4.2.2, should we also provide a pointer container version of `BSTree`? (Argue whether in practice users would otherwise frequently instantiate `BSTree` with pointer types.)

4.2   Suppose that the designer of a library divides the library's inline functions into two groups: those for which inlining would probably make user code run faster without causing a significant increase in code size, and those for which inlining would probably make user code faster but might also increase code size significantly. Design a scheme that enables users to select at compile time neither, one, or both of these groups for inlining.

4.3   Suppose that a function `f` with code size s has c call sites in a program. Suppose further that the size of the code needed to perform an out-of-line call to `f` is o. Assume that no out-of-line copies of `f` are laid down when `f` is inlined and that exactly one copy of `f` is laid down when `f` is not inlined.

   a.   What is the total code size attributable to `f` if all calls to `f` are inlined?

   b.   What is the total code size attributable to `f` if `f` is never inlined?

   c.   What is the change in total code size when all calls to `f` are inlined as opposed to when `f` is called out of line?

   d.   Under what conditions (expressed in terms of c, s, and o) does the size of a program decrease when all calls to `f` are inlined?

4.4   In the `Map` class defined in Section 3.2.2, suppose that we provide the following operation:

```
template<class X, class Y>
class Map {
public:
    Y& operator[](const X& x);
    // ...
};
```

Calling `operator[]` returns a reference to the internally stored copy of the value to which `x` maps. A precondition of `operator[]` is that the value `x` is in the domain of the `Map`.

a. Suppose that the user creates a nested mapping m of type Map<String, Map<String, String> >. Show the code that the user would write to add the pair ⟨"three", ⟨"blind", "mice"⟩⟩ to m.

b. As explained in Section 4.4.3, returning a reference has disadvantages. Explain how to replace operator[] with two functions, neither of which returns a reference, that allow the user to examine and set the Y value to which a given value of type X maps.

c. Show the code that the user would write to add the pair ⟨"three", ⟨"blind", "mice"⟩⟩ to a Map with the interface you defined in part b. Which version of Map is easier to use?

4.5 Suppose that we overload the List::head function shown in Section 4.4.3 as follows:

```
template<class T>
class List {
public:
    const T& head() const;
    T& head();
    // ...
};
```

Is this design a good idea? Why or why not?

4.6 Another resource that a C++ library should use efficiently is the maximum number of files that a program can have open simultaneously.

a. Suppose that a system allows programs to have 64 files open at once. Explain why a library function that needs to open only five files might nevertheless not be able to open all the files it needs.

b. Can you write a portable function that returns the number of files that a program currently has open?

c. Suppose that a library function needs to read from file *a*, then from file *b*, then from file *a*. If we open both *a* and *b* before reading and close them after reading, we shall have two files open at once. Describe an alternative strategy that never has more than one file open at once. What is the disadvantage of this strategy?

4.7 In the Node class shown on page 103, we stored in Node the set of edges incident at that node. Suppose that users of Graph want to be able to have a given Node present in more than one Graph. Different sets of edges will be incident on a given Node in the different Graphs in which that Node appears. Hence, storing a single incident edge set at each node does not support the desired functionality.

a.   Show how the Map class of Section 3.2.2 can be used with Set, Edge, and Node of Section 4.6 to represent an arbitrary collection of nodes, edges, and graphs. (Keep in mind that users will want to be able to perform the customary graph operations on your Graphs, such as traversing, finding connected subgraphs, and depth-first searching.)

b.   Give an example of a possible use of your Graph class that is rendered easier by your having reused Set and Map.

c.   (∗) How will your uses of Set and Map in your Graph, Node, and Edge classes affect the efficiency of user programs? Consider compile time, instantiation time, code size, memory use, and run time.

d.   Does your design in part a localize costs — that is, are user programs that do not need to have Nodes in multiple Graphs as efficient as they would be in a design that does not permit Nodes to be in multiple Graphs?

e.   Would you reuse Set and Map if you were writing a reusable Graph class?

References and Further Reading

Cohen and colleagues [CHS91] analyze some of the issues discussed in this chapter.

There are a number of good texts on efficient algorithms — good examples are works by Aho, Hopcroft, and Ullman [AHU83], Baase [Baa88], and Cormen, Leiserson, and Rivest [CLR90]. Bentley [Ben82] discusses the art of tuning Pascal code; tuning C++ requires all the techniques he shows, and more.

Koenig [Koe93a] discusses the reasons for and pitfalls of returning a reference from a function.

Meyers [Mey93a, Mey93b] and Sprowl [Spr93] discuss efficient use of the free store. Stroustrup's Section 10.7 [Str94a] discusses the advantages and disadvantages of providing a garbage collector in a C++ execution environment.

The running example in Section 4.6 was inspired by a discussion with Jonathan Shopiro.

5 Errors

There is a good deal to be said for blushing,
if one can do it at the proper moment.

— Oscar Wilde

The occurrence of errors during the execution of library code is inevitable. To be reusable, a library must deal with errors reasonably. In this chapter, we discuss how to detect errors and what to do when they occur. There are many different kinds of errors, so no single detection or handling strategy is best for all errors. A special class of errors is resource-limit errors. These errors occur when some resource is exhausted, often through no fault of either the library or the user. We discuss the ways a library might respond to resource-limit errors. Finally, we present the important notion of *exception safety* — special effort is often required to ensure that reusable code behaves correctly when an exception is thrown.

5.1 Errors in Reusable Code

There are three kinds of errors that library designers must deal with. *Library errors* are errors in the implementation of the library. Of course, a library provider would like to detect and correct as many errors as possible before the library is released, but any nontrivial library is bound to have errors when released.

User errors are errors in how the library is used. Suppose, for example, that our library provides a `Stack` class:

```
template<class T>
class Stack {
public:
    void push(const T& t);
    T pop();
    int size() const;
    // ...
};
```

If we require that the Stack for which pop is called be nonempty, then calling pop on an empty Stack is a user error.

System errors arise from interactions between the user's program and the system on which it is executing. Some of these errors are the fault of the system, others are the fault of the user, and still others are no one's fault. For example, suppose that somewhere in the implementation of our library we try to create a Stack in the free store:

```
Stack<int>* s = new Stack<int>;
```

If there is not enough free-store space left, this operation will fail.

For each possible error that might occur during the execution of a library, the library designer should decide whether to detect the error and how the user program should behave when the error occurs. We shall discuss these issues in Sections 5.2 and 5.3.

5.2   Error Detection

Because there are so many different kinds of errors, no single strategy will detect them all. One strategy, however, that detects many errors is invariant checking. An *invariant* is a property that should always be true. Suppose, for example, that we are about to index an array:

```
char* p = "some nifty string";
int i;
// ...
char c = p[i];
```

Presumably, an invariant of this code is that immediately before the indexing operation i is nonnegative and less than the length of the array pointed to by p,

```
char* p = "some nifty string";
int i;
// ...
if (i < 0 || i >= strlen(p)) {
    // invariant failed - error!
    // ...
}
char c = p[i];
```

Depending on the rest of the code in the program, this error might be a library error, user error, or system error. Notice, incidentally, that the addition of the test to detect the error increases the running time of this code from a constant to linear in the length of the array. Error detection frequently trades off with run time.

In practice, checking two kinds of invariants, function preconditions and representation invariants, can detect many errors.

5.2.1   Function Preconditions

A *function precondition* is an invariant that should be true when a function is entered. We gave an example of a function precondition in `Stack::pop` in Section 5.1 — we required that the `Stack` for which `pop` is called be nonempty. For another example, consider the following `Date` class:

```
class Date {
public:
    Date(const char* datestring);
    // ...
};
```

A `Date` object represents a specific date in a specific year. The constructor creates a `Date` from a character string:

```
Date birthday("April 22, 1870");
Date berlin_wall("9 Nov 1989");
```

Not every null-terminated string can be interpreted sensibly as a date:

```
Date oops("Stardate 3134.0");
```

Thus, the library designer might have the `Date` constructor impose the precondition that the given string is valid. Here is how we might check that precondition:

```
Date::Date(const char* s) {
    if (!valid_date_string(s)) {
        // precondition failed - error!
        // ...
    }
    // ...
}
```

Here, `valid_date_string` is a function that returns `true` if the given string can be interpreted sensibly as a date. Checking all preconditions of all functions is an effective way to detect many errors.

5.2.2   Representation Invariants

Another kind of invariant that catches many errors is a *representation invariant*. A representation invariant of a class is a property that is true of every legitimate or sane object of that class. For example, suppose that our `Date` class is implemented with the following two data members:

```
class Date {
private:
    int jdn;   // Julian day number
    int dow;   // day of week
public:
    // ...
};
```

The member `jdn` is the Julian day number — that is, the number of days that have elapsed since November 24, −4711 on the Gregorian calendar.[1] The member `dow` is a value in the range of 0 to 6, representing the day of the week. Although the day of the week can be computed from the Julian day number, the computation is complex, so we decide to store `dow` for run-time efficiency. A representation invariant of `Date` is that `dow` is indeed the day of week corresponding to `jdn`.

---

1. Use of the modifiers B.C. and A.D. with Gregorian dates is unclear because the Gregorian (new style) calendar did not exist before the sixteenth century and the Julian (old style) calendar, which did exist before the sixteenth century, had no year 0. Gregorian year −4711 is the year on which that number falls if the Gregorian calendar is extrapolated backward and we assume the existence of a Gregorian year 0.

Some library designers give every class a function that checks one or more representation invariants of that class:

```
class Date {
public:
    bool ok() const {
        return dow == jdn2dow(jdn);
    }
    // ...
};
```

Here, `jdn2dow` is a function that does the complex calculation to return the day of week corresponding to the given Julian day number.

Contrary to a common misconception, an invariant of a class is not necessarily a precondition of every member function of that class. Suppose that `Date` has the following two operations:

```
class Date {
private:
    void incr_dow();
public:
    void operator++();
    // ..
};
```

The function `incr_dow` logically increments the day of the week:

```
void Date::incr_dow() {
    dow = (dow + 1) % 7;
}
```

The function `operator++` increments the date:

```
void Date::operator++() {
    ++jdn;
    incr_dow();
}
```

Notice that when `incr_dow` is called by `operator++`, the invariant checked by `ok` is not satisfied. That invariant is not a precondition of `incr_dow`. (If we were to have `operator++` call `incr_dow` *before* incrementing `jdn`, the invariant in `ok` would be satisfied on entry to `incr_dow`.)

It *is* true that when a member function is called by the *user* of a class, all representation invariants should be true. Hence, we would like to write the following:

```
void Date::incr_dow() {
    if (called_by_user_of_Date() && !ok()) {
        // error!
        // ...
    }
    // ...
}
```

It is not practical to try to determine, however, on entry to a member function, who is calling it (see Exercise 5.1). Thus, each member function should impose the strongest preconditions that should hold no matter who calls it.

5.3   Handling Errors

Suppose that we have determined that we should check for a particular error in our our library code. Next, we must determine what the library should do when the error occurs. No single approach is appropriate for all possible errors. The best way to handle an error depends on what the error is and what the code was trying to do when the error occurred. Further, different variants of a library might handle a given error differently. In this section, we discuss the most common behaviors libraries exhibit in response to errors.

5.3.1   Library Variants

Libraries can be executed at different times and by different individuals for different purposes. A library developer, for example, might execute the library to test its functionality or to measure its performance. Library users execute the library while developing their code as well as when they and their users run their applications.

To meet these varying needs, many libraries come in several *variants*. The *development* variant is used for developing and debugging the library itself; the *debugging* variant is used for developing and debugging user code; and the *optimized* variant is used for executing efficiently.

The variants of a library need not all behave the same way. In particular, they need not behave the same way when a given error occurs. In the development and debugging variants, as many errors as possible should be detected, and they should be detected as early as possible. In the optimized variant, error detection is often forsaken for speed.

In practice, the behaviors of the development and debugging variants of a library are often identical because the implementors and users of a library typically want the same set of checks performed while they develop and debug their respective code.

5.3.2   Correct the Problem

Sometimes, when an error occurs, we can correct the problem and continue executing as if the error had not occurred. Consider the implementation of Date shown in Section 5.2.2. If in Date::ok we discover that the invariant is false, we can restore it:

```
bool Date::ok() {
    int correct_dow = jdn2dow(jdn);
    if (dow != correct_dow) {
        dow = correct_dow;
        return false;
    }
    return true;
}
```

(Note that if we use this approach, the function ok can no longer be const because it potentially changes the value of the object.) Of course, restoring the invariant does not fix the ultimate cause of the error, but it might cause the program to behave more robustly.

5.3.3   Exit or Abort

The most drastic thing a library can do when an error occurs is to exit or abort the program. Consider the Date constructor:

```
Date::Date(const char* s) {
    if (!valid_date_string(s)) {
        cerr << "Date: invalid date string, aborting\n";
        abort();
    }
    // ...
}
```

Aborting or exiting, however, is often unacceptable to users. Many C++ programmers require that the libraries they use never exit or abort.

5.3.4   Throw Exception

An elegant way to handle many errors is to throw an exception:

```
class Date {
public:
    class Invalid {};
    // ...
};

Date::Date(const char* s) {
    if (!valid_date_string(s))
        throw Date::Invalid();
    // ...
}
```

Invalid is an empty class defined solely for the purpose of being thrown by the Date constructor. Users can check the validity of a date string by catching the exception:

```
void usedate(const char* s) {
    try {
        Date date(s);
        // ...
    }
    catch (Date::Invalid) {
        cerr << s << " is not a valid date\n";
        // ...
    }
    // ...
}
```

There are several possible drawbacks to throwing an exception. First, not all C++ compilers support exception handling as of this writing. Any library that throws exceptions will not be portable to systems for which no C++ implementation supporting exceptions handling exists. Second, throwing an exception is, on some systems, a slow operation. Further, some C++ compilers that support exceptions produce object code that is bigger or slower — even if an exception is never thrown — than object code produced by compilers that do not support exceptions. To avoid this overhead, some C++ programmers use only code that does not use exceptions.

Some C++ implementations provide a compile-time option to turn off support for exception handling, but this option cannot be relied on to offset the performance problem. Suppose that a library uses exceptions and thus is compiled with support for exceptions turned on. You might think that users who do not intend to catch exceptions could compile with exception handling turned off, to avoid the overhead for exception handling in their own code. The behavior of a program in which only some translation units support exception handling, however, is undefined. Such a program might fail to link, or it might link and execute correctly as long as no exception is thrown; when an exception is thrown, the `terminate` function might be called, the program might abort, or some other behavior might result. The only certainty is that no user-provided handler will be invoked.

Another drawback of exceptions is that they introduce nonlocal flow of control into programs. We shall discuss the problems that the possibility of nonlocal flow of control creates for writers of reusable code in Section 5.5.

5.3.5   Return Error Value

Before exceptions were added to C++, a common way to handle errors was to return an error value. For example, suppose that `Date` has an `incr_year` function to increment a `Date`'s year. We could declare it as follows:

```
class Date {
public:
    bool incr_year();
    // ...
};
```

For any `Date` other than one representing February 29 of some year, `incr_year` increments that `Date`'s year and returns `true`; otherwise `incr_year` returns the error value `false`.

Returning an error value has several drawbacks. First, some functions (specifically, constructors and destructors) cannot return an error value. Other functions cannot return an error value conveniently. For example, suppose that `Date` has a `next_year` function that returns the date one year from the given `Date`:

```
class Date {
public:
    Date next_year() const;
    // ...
};
```

There is no date that can be interpreted reasonably as an error value. Therefore, to return an error value from `next_year`, we would have to change its argument and return types:

```
class Date {
public:
    bool next_year(Date& d) const;
    // ...
};
```

This version of `next_year` sets d to the next year's date and returns an error code. Its interface, however, would be less elegant than the first. (Alternatively, `next_year` could return a `Date` with a nil value; we shall describe this technique in the next section.)

The second drawback of returning error values is that users might fail to check them. Forgetting to check error values is a common source of errors. Libraries should avoid error-prone interfaces.

Further, if many functions in a program return an error value, then users who do remember to check all the values will be forced to write code in which the main flow of control is buried in the mass of code required for checking and propagating error values.

The disadvantages of returning error codes motivated the addition of exceptions to C++. Using exceptions instead of returning error values allows the programmer to check errors only where appropriate and to eliminate almost all code devoted to propagating error values.

5.3.6   Create Nil Value

If an error occurs during the execution of a constructor, then instead of exiting, aborting, or throwing an exception, we might create a *nil value*:

```
class Date {
private:
    bool _is_nil;
    // ...
};

Date::Date(const char* s) {
    _is_nil = !valid_date_string(s);
    // ...
}
```

Of course, users need a way to determine whether a given object is nil:

```
class Date {
public:
    bool is_nil() const {
        return _is_nil;
    }
    // ...
};
```

In this design, the Date constructor does not impose the precondition that the given string is valid.

When we add nil to a class's abstraction, we must remember to specify the behavior of each library function involving any objects of that class when one or more of those objects are nil. Suppose that Date has a dayno function that returns the number of days since the most recent January 1:

```
class Date {
public:
    int dayno() const;
    // ...
};
```

We must specify the behavior of dayno when the given Date is nil. The possible behaviors are those described in Sections 5.3.2 through 5.3.8. For example, dayno could throw an exception.

5.3.7   Interpret Invalid Data as Valid

Library designers sometimes deal with errors by interpreting invalid data as some other valid data. For example, we might have the Date constructor interpret invalid date strings as, say, January 1, 1970:

```
Date::Date(const char* s) {
    if (!valid_date_string(s))
        // set date to January 1, 1970
    // ...
}
```

Such a design is error prone, however. Consider a function compute_interest that computes the interest due with a loan payment. Suppose that a typographical error occurs in the input, like this:

```
July 21, 19992
```

The effect of this error will be that the start date of the period for which interest is computed defaults to a date more than 22 years earlier than the correct date. Unless someone catches this error before the statements are sent out, the borrower is going to have quite a shock. Debugging this error would be easier if the `Date` constructor exited, aborted, threw an exception, or created a nil `Date`.

5.3.8   Allow Undefined Behavior

Sometimes, detecting a particular error is prohibitively inefficient. Suppose for the moment that we do detect violations of the precondition of the `Stack::pop` function discussed in Section 5.1:

```
template<class T>
T Stack<T>::pop() {
    if (size() == 0) {
        // error!
        // ...
    }
    // ...
}
```

Now consider the following user code:

```
Stack<int> s;
// ...
assert(s.size() > 10000);
for (int i = 0; i < 10000; ++i) {
    int nextval = s.pop();
    // ...
}
```

Every call to `pop` will spend time checking `pop`'s precondition. The user, however, knows that the precondition is always true in this loop. To enable users to write efficient code, we might decide to check this precondition (or perhaps all preconditions) only in the debugging variant of our library. If the precondition is violated in any other variant, the error will be undetected, and the user's program will have undefined behavior.

Sometimes, detecting a given error is too difficult or is impossible. Suppose that our library provides alternative versions of the global operators `new` and `delete`. A precondition of `delete` is that the value of `p` was obtained by an earlier call to `new`. Detecting violations of that precondition both portably and efficiently is possible but not easy to implement (see Exercise 5.2). Hence, we might choose not to detect that error in any variant of the library, and allow user programs that contain such an error to have undefined behavior.

5.4 Resource-Limit Errors

In Chapter 4, we discussed many of the resources that a library designer must be concerned about and ways of minimizing the use of these resources. In this section, we discuss how a library might handle (or not handle) errors that arise when, in spite of a designer's best efforts, a finite resource is consumed and an attempt to acquire more of it fails.

5.4.1 Stack Overflow

A program that overflows its stack has undefined behavior. Suppose, for example, that there are only 100 bytes available for the stack to grow when the following function is called:

```
void f() {
    T t;
    // ...
}
```

If `sizeof(T)` is greater than 100, the call to f has undefined behavior; it will abort on most systems. Because there is no portable way to determine whether the stack is in imminent danger of overflowing, there is little hope of detecting this problem or of recovering if it occurs. As mentioned in Section 4.5.4, the risk of stack overflow will be reduced if large objects are allocated from the free store.

5.4.2 Free-Store Exhaustion

If there are only 100 bytes available in the free store and if `sizeof(T)` is greater than 100, then a call to `new T` will return 0 in a C++ implementation that predates the ANSI/ISO standard or throw an exception in ANSI/ISO C++ (when the default `new_handler` is called).

Like stack overflow, there is no portable way to determine whether the free store is nearly exhausted (but see Exercise 5.3). For example, an implementation of `new` (actually, `new_handler`) may abort if not enough memory is available. If `new` returns control to the invoking program, a free-store overflow can sometimes be handled robustly.

One way to recover from free-store overflow is to try allocating something smaller. If, for example, an attempt to allocate a large hash table fails, we might halve the size of the table and try again. Using a C++ implementation predating the ANSI/ISO standard, we would write the code as follows:

```
int min_size = 1024;
int size = 1024 * 32;   // first try 32K

Table_entry* table = new Table_entry[size];
while (table == 0 && size >= min_size) {
    size /= 2;
    table = new Table_entry[size];
}
```

Here, we keep halving the table's size and trying again until it becomes too small to be useful — less than some value `min_size`.

Another way to handle free-store overflow robustly is to delete something and try again:

```
T* t = new T;
while (t == 0) {
    delete something;
    t = new T;
}
```

Of course, if the library implementor has followed the advice of Section 4.5.2 and deleted unneeded objects as soon as possible, it might be difficult to find something to delete. One common candidate for deletion is something in a cache. Suppose, for example, that for efficiency our library is caching in memory the contents of a certain file. If the free store overflows, we could delete that cache and try again.

Often, the most reasonable thing a library can do when the free store overflows is to throw an exception. If our users' C++ implementations do not support exceptions, then terminating the program is probably the only remaining recourse:

```
T* t = new T;
if (t == 0) {
    cerr << "Library Q: out of memory\n";
    abort();
}
```

Note, however, that if the execution of the stream insertion requires allocating memory and the memory needed is more than is available, then we are in trouble. One way to prevent this problem would be to reserve a chunk of memory, `reserved_for_new_failure`, large enough to allow us to do whatever our cleanup requires. When we find the free store exhausted, we would free `reserved_for_new_failure` and then proceed with our error handling. The drawback of this approach is that if every library were to reserve a chunk of memory for error handling, then a program that uses several libraries could have a significant amount of memory tied up solely for defending against unlikely events.

In these examples we show the library code checking the return value of each call to `new` rather than calling `set_new_handler`. (As we shall explain in Section 6.5, C++ libraries should not call `set_new_handler`.) In ANSI/ISO C++, checking each call to `new` will be unnecessary. If we want a failed `new` to throw an exception (which we probably almost always will want), then we simply should not catch the exception that `new` will throw:

```
T* t = new T;    // throws exception under ANSI/ISO C++
                 // if free store overflows
// code here can assume that t != 0
```

If we want to do something more robust, we can catch the exception:

```
T* t = 0;
try {
    t = new T;
}
catch (bad_alloc) {
    delete something;
}
```

The exception caught by this `catch` might have been thrown by a `new` called indirectly by the constructor for T. Library implementors should ensure that their code works correctly no matter which `new` threw the exception.

5.4.3   File System Limits

If the user's machine has a file system and if the file system runs out of space, then any attempts to grow any of its files will fail. For example,

```
ofstream f("tmp");
f << "Make it so!";
if (!f) {
    cerr << "write to file tmp failed\n";
}
```

It is impossible to tell, however, from within the program whether the output failure was caused by a file system overflow or by some other problem (a network failure, for example). Not knowing why an output operation failed makes robust recovery difficult. We might try removing a file to free some space and then try the write again, but that will work only if the failure was caused by an overflow. Thus, usually the most reasonable approach will be to throw an exception, exit, or abort.

Most systems limit the number of files that a program may have open at any given time; limits of 32 or 64 are typical. If a program has the maximum number of files open, then an attempt to open another will fail:

```
ofstream f("tmp");
if (!f) {
    // open failed
}
```

It is not possible to determine through the `iostream` interface whether an attempted open failed because too many files are open. Although most systems provide system calls that can be used to find out, the cause of a failed open usually will not matter — all the library will be able to do sensibly is throw an exception, exit, or abort.

5.5   Exception Safety

With the introduction of exception handling to the C++ language, writers of reusable code must ensure that their code is exception safe — in other words, that it behaves correctly even when an exception is thrown. Existing code that has worked as intended when run in an environment that does not throw exceptions might have to be modified to work correctly when exceptions are possible.

The problem arises because exceptions introduce the possibility of non-local flow of control. When an exception is thrown, the stack is unwound until a handler for the exception is found. Thus, when a function calls another function, control might never return to the calling function. It is not necessarily safe for a function f to call a function g that has an empty throw specification:

```
void g() throw();
```

An exception might propagate to g, resulting in control passing to the **unexpected** function and never returning to f.

Nor are explicit function calls the only possible sources of exceptions. Code that the compiler generates to implement some C++ expression might call some function (notably a constructor, destructor, `new`, or `delete`) that throws an exception. Under ANSI/ISO C++, the `new_handler` may throw an exception if `new` fails.

Any number of things can go wrong in code that is not exception safe. Sections 5.5.1 and 5.5.2 discuss two such potential problems.

5.5.1   Inconsistent States

Often, the implementation of a member function puts the object on which it is called temporarily into an inconsistent state. We saw an example of this in Section 5.2.2, in the implementation of the function `Date::operator++`:

```
void Date::operator++() {
    ++jdn;          // line 1
    incr_dow();     // line 2
}
```

If `*this` is consistent when `operator++` is called, then `*this` will be inconsistent after line 1 executes and consistent once again after line 2.

Suppose that while `*this` is inconsistent, a function is called that might (directly or indirectly) throw an exception:

```
void Date::operator++() {
    ++jdn;
    might_throw_exception();
    incr_dow();
}
```

If `might_throw_exception` does throw an exception, `*this` is left inconsistent. Even the user of `Date` who catches and handles the thrown exception will be left with an inconsistent object. Consider the following user code:

```
void f(Date& d) {
    try {
        // ...
        ++d;
        // ...
    }
    catch (Some_exception e) {
        // ...
    }
```

If the call of `might_throw_exception` in `Date::operator++` throws a value of type `Some_exception`, then when `f` returns the object referred to by `d` will be inconsistent.

A class `X` is *exception safe* if it is impossible for an exception thrown during the execution of any of `X`'s member functions to cause the user of `X` to be left with an inconsistent `X` object. Reusable classes should be as exception safe as possible. To increase the exception safety of `Date`, we can move the call to `might_throw_exception` to a point at which `*this` is consistent:

```
void Date::operator++() {
    ++jdn;
    incr_dow();
    might_throw_exception();
}
```

Of course, whether this transformation preserves the correctness of `Date` depends on the intended behavior of the various functions involved.

In practice, almost all functions potentially throw an exception. Moving the calls to all such functions to a point at which `*this` is consistent is often difficult to do and, even more often, difficult to do efficiently. Suppose that we cannot move the call to `might_throw_exception` to where `*this` is consistent. Then to keep `Date` exception safe, we must write `operator++` like this:

```
void Date::operator++() {
    ++jdn;
    try {
        might_throw_exception();
    }
    catch (...) {
        --jdn;
        throw;  // rethrow exception
    }
    incr_dow();
}
```

This code begins to be difficult to implement and understand. Implementing a real class such that it is exception safe can be challenging; it is sometimes infeasible.

If a member function is not exception safe, the documentation of that function and the corresponding class should state so:

> This function [or class] is not exception safe.

Because exceptions are a relatively new feature in C++ and because implementing classes to be both efficient and exception safe is difficult, many classes currently in use are not exception safe. Further, most exception-unsafe classes are currently not documented as such.

5.5.2   Resource Leaks

A traditional coding style in C and C++ is to allocate or lock some resource, do some computation using that resource, and then free that resource. Unfortunately, this coding style is not exception safe. Consider the following function, for example:

```
void f() {
    Widget* w = new Widget;
    g(w);
    delete w;
}
```

If an exception is thrown from g, the allocated object pointed to by w will never be freed.

There are two ways to prevent such resource leaks and increase the exception safety of code. First, we can use a try block and a catch clause every time a resource must be freed and any exception might be thrown:

```
void f() {
    Widget* w = new Widget;
    try {
        g(w);
    }
    catch (...) {
        delete w;
        throw;  // rethrow exception
    }
    delete w;
}
```

The drawback of this coding style is that applying it thoroughly to real functions can lead to an unreadable web of try blocks. A cleaner solution is to allocate the resource in a constructor and release it in a destructor — the well-known "resource acquisition is initialization" technique [ES90, Str91]. To apply this technique to free-store objects, we might write the following class:

```
template<class T>
class New {
public:
    New() : t(new T) {}
    ~New() { delete t; }
    operator T*() { return t; }
private:
    T* t;

    // hide these
    New(const New& n);
    const New& operator=(const New& n);
};
```

We purposely hide the copy constructor and assignment operator of New because defining their semantics would be difficult and because we do not need them (see Section 2.4).

Using New, we can write our function without a try block:

```
void f() {
    New<Widget> w;
    g(w);
}
```

The allocated object will be freed when w is destroyed, regardless of whether g throws an exception.

5.6 Summary

Code intended for reuse must consider whether to detect and how to handle any error that might arise. Invariants can be used to detect many kinds of errors. Libraries should make good use of function preconditions and representation invariants.

Different variants of a library may handle errors differently. Here are the most common ways to handle an error:

- Correct the problem and continue execution.
- Exit or abort (not acceptable for many libraries).
- Throw an exception.
- Create a nil value.
- Interpret invalid data as valid.
- Do not detect the error (and therefore have undefined behavior).

Among the errors that library designers must consider is exhaustion of system resources. The stack might overflow, the free store might be exhausted, or some file system limit might be reached, to name three possibilities.

With the introduction of exceptions to the C++ language, special care must be taken to ensure that reusable code is exception safe. Classes must be designed so objects are not rendered inconsistent when an exception is thrown. Libraries must be designed to avoid other ill effects from nonlocal flow of control when an exception is thrown.

Exercises

5.1 In Section 5.2.2, we said that an invariant of a class is not necessarily a precondition of every member function of that class. An invariant should always be true, however, when the member function is called by a user of the class. Suppose that to determine whether a member function of a class X has been called by a user of the class (as opposed to having been called by another member function of X), we have each member function test a counter on entry. Each member function would increment the counter after testing it and decrement it before returning. The intention of this scheme would be to allow functions to check invariants when they are called by users but not when they are called by other member functions.

  a. Would this scheme work correctly for virtual functions? For static member functions? For classes with static data members?

  b. How would you extend this scheme so that X's member functions checked their invariants when called by functions that are not members of X even when those functions have been called by members of X?

  c. Is this scheme exception safe?

  d. Would you consider it worthwhile to implement such a scheme to allow checking of invariants?

5.2 In Section 5.3.8, we said that delete has the precondition that the value of its argument must have been obtained by an earlier call to new.

  a. (∗) Show how to implement portable versions of new and delete such that delete checks for violations of its precondition.

  b. Discuss the efficiency of your solution to part a.

5.3 In Section 5.4.2, we stated that there is no completely portable way to determine whether the free store is nearly exhausted. Impending free-store exhaustion can be detected on some systems, however.

 a. Write a function `freestore_avail` for use on systems that return zero when the user requests more memory than is available. Your function should return the largest power of 2 less than or equal to the number of bytes available in the free store, or zero if no bytes are available. (For example, if 250 bytes are available, `freestore_avail` should return the value 128.)

 b. Suppose that a call to `freestore_avail` indicates that the amount of memory you need is available and you attempt to allocate the memory. Why might your attempted allocation fail nevertheless?

5.4 Suppose that you are designing a `Compact_tree` class that represents trees stored in compact form. Rather than use pointers, which take up space, you decide to represent a `Compact_tree` with an array consisting of the nodes of the tree in preorder:

```
class Compact_tree {
private:
    Node* array_of_nodes_in_preorder;
    // ...
};
```

You represent a `Node` by its depth-first search number in its containing tree:

```
class Node {
private:
    int dfsnum;
    // ...
};
```

Suppose that one of the member functions of `Compact_tree` is advance:

```
class Compact_tree {
public:
    bool advance(Node& n);
    // ...
};
```

If n has a preorder successor, `advance` sets n to that successor and returns `true`; otherwise `advance` returns `false` without affecting n.

 a. A precondition of `advance` is that n refers to a node in the `Compact_tree` on which `advance` was called. What data member must you add to `Node` to enable `advance` to check this precondition?

b. Suppose that you need the data member you just added only when the macro NDEBUG is not defined. To keep Node objects as small as possible, you might declare your data member conditionally, like this:

```
class Node {
private:
#ifndef NDEBUG
    // your data member goes here
#endif
    // ...
};
```

If you declare your data member conditionally, what will happen to a user who accidentally tries to link code compiled with NDEBUG defined and code with NDEBUG not defined?

c. Considering that compilation systems are not required to detect violations of C++'s "One-Definition Rule," do you think that checking advance's precondition is a good idea?

5.5 Consider this code:

```
clock_t clock1 = clock();
time_consuming_computation();
clock_t clock2 = clock();
cout << "time_consuming_computation took approximately" <<
    (clock2 - clock1)/CLK_TCK << " seconds to complete\n";
```

The intention here is to report how long the time-consuming computation takes, but there is an error: If for any reason a call to clock() cannot get the elapsed processor time, it will return -1.

a. Change this code so that it does not report erroneous results when clock() fails.

b. Suppose that clock_t is implemented in 32 bits and that CLK_TCK is 1000000. Then the time returned by clock wraps around in about 36 minutes (as pointed out by Harbison and Steele [HS91]). Rewrite the preceding code so that it does not give erroneous results when clock wraps around.

c. (∗∗) Your solution for part b probably would not yield correct results when clock wraps around more than once. Can you think of a way to write the code such that it always reports correctly how long time_consuming_computation takes, no matter how long that might be?

d. Your solutions to parts b and c probably assume that whenever the second call to clock() returns a smaller value than the value returned by the first call to clock(), it was because the clock has wrapped around. Suppose that between your two calls to clock() someone somehow reset the processor clock. How difficult would it be to differentiate between the clock having been reset and having wrapped around? How likely is it that the clock will have been reset? Should a library attempt to detect this error?

5.6 Sometimes, people talk about code being maximally robust. Maximally robust code should detect and handle all possible errors. Consider the following (not maximally robust) code:

```
ofstream f("tmp");
f.write("hello", 5);
f.flush();
ifstream g("tmp");
char buf[5];
g.read(buf, 5);
```

This code first opens a file named "tmp", creating it if it did not already exist. The stream f is opened for writing and positioned initially at the beginning of the file. The code then writes five characters to the file and flushes the stream to ensure that the characters actually are written. Next, it opens the same file for reading and reads the five characters just written.

  a. What system errors might cause this code to fail?

  b. Show how this code would have to be rewritten to be maximally robust. (You need not show what action you would take for each possible error.)

  c. For many software development projects, checking the success of every operation that could ever fail will not be worth the effort. Further, determining what to do for each possible failure can be difficult. If you were writing reusable code that included the preceding fragment, which operations would you test for possible failure and which would you not check?

5.7 In Chapter 4, we discussed minimizing program build time, run time, code size, and memory use. These are not the only resources a library must use efficiently, however. As discussed in Section 5.4.3, most systems limit the number of files that a program may have open at any given time; thus, files must be opened sparingly.

  Consider handling #include statements in the function preprocess of Section 4.5.1. When preprocess encounters an #include statement in the text it is preprocessing, it will need to open the referenced file and preprocess the contents.

    a. A naive strategy for implementing `preprocess` would be to keep a stack of nested `#includes` and keep all files in the stack open. Suppose that a user's system allows 32 files to be open at a time and that this user has 31 files open before calling `preprocess` to preprocess code that has `#includes` nested three levels deep. What will happen if `preprocess` does not detect the resulting error? Can you think of any way `preprocess` can handle this error that will make the user happy?

    b. How can you make `preprocess` handle nested `#includes` to whatever depth the user's system supports, even if `preprocess` is called when the user already has files open?

5.8   Give two reasons why `*this` might not be consistent when `Date::operator++` in Section 5.5.1 is called.

References and Further Reading

Good introductions to the theory of program correctness can be found in Stanat and McAllister's Chapter 1 [SM77] and in Meyer's Chapter 7 [Mey88]. Liskov and Guttag [LG86] and Meyer's Chapter 9 [Mey92a] discuss invariants and preconditions.

    Dershowitz and Reingold [DR90] and Reingold, Dershowitz, and Clamen [RDC93] discuss Julian day numbers, the Gregorian calendar, and other fascinating aspects of calendrical systems.

    Writing robust code that interacts with the file system is notoriously difficult; C++ programmers interested in using the `iostream` library robustly should read Teale's book [Tea93] or Plauger's book [Pla95].

    Cargill [Car94] discusses the difficulty of writing exception-safe classes.

    Several commercial products exist for detecting resource leaks in C++ programs.

    The `Compact_tree` and `Node` classes of Exercise 5.4 were inspired by Koenig's description [Koe92c] of similar classes. Exercise 5.5 was inspired by an example of Harbison and Steele [HS91].

6 Conflict

> *Bring us together again.*
> — Richard Nixon

> *Everything is a name-space problem.*
> — Jerry Schwarz

Two pieces of software *conflict* if they cannot be used together easily in the same program. Reusable code should conflict with as little code as possible. Many conflicts between bodies of code involve uses of the same names in the same scope to mean different things. Names used in libraries can conflict with names in other libraries or in user code. Such conflicts can occur between global names, macro names, and environmental names. We discuss these kinds of conflict and describe the use of naming conventions and the `namespace` construct to avoid conflict. We also present the concepts of the *unclean library* and the *good-citizen library*.

6.1 Global Names

All the code in a C++ program — whether user code or library code — shares the same (single) global scope. Hence, libraries must be careful that the names they define in the global scope do not conflict with the global names defined in user code or other libraries. Consider two libraries, each of which provides a global `Widget` class. Because it is not legal for a C++ program to define two different classes in the same scope with the same name,[1] these two libraries conflict and cannot be used together in a program. Not all uses of names to mean different things create conflict,

---

1. The actual rules are slightly more complex, as we shall see in Section 6.1.2.

however. To understand when conflict exists, we must first consider in detail how C++ programs are organized and compiled.

6.1.1 Translation Units

Suppose that two files *a.h* and *a.c* contain the following:

a.h:

```
int i;
#define greeting "Hey, Guys and Gals!"
```

a.c:

```
#include <a.h>
int main() {
    char* s = greeting;
    // ...
}
```

The translation unit resulting from preprocessing *a.c* (assuming that the #include statement in *a.c* resolves to the *a.h* shown) is

```
int i;
int main() {
    char* s = "Hey, Guys and Gals!";
    // ...
}
```

Every C++ program consists of one or more translation units. *All the translation units in a program share the same global scope.* If the following two translation units are in the same program, then the definitions of i, j, and k are in the (one and only) global scope of that program:

unit1:

```
int i;
int j;
// ...
```

unit2:

```
int k;
// ...
```

6.1.2   Class Definitions

C++ has various rules specifying what declarations and definitions may legally appear in the global scope of a program. Let us consider class definitions. Any program containing a translation unit that contains more than one definition of a class with a given name — whether the definitions are the same or not — is illegal:

unit3:

```
class X { /* stuff */ };
// ...
class X { /* the same or different stuff */ };  // error
```

This error is detected by C++ compilers.

Now consider the following two translation units, each containing a single definition of a class named X:

unit4:

```
class X { /* ... */ };
// ...
```

unit5:

```
class X { /* ... */ };
// ...
```

A program containing these two translation units might or might not be legal. If these definitions are the same, then the program is legal, assuming that it has no errors elsewhere. If the Xs defined in the two translation units are different, then the legality of the containing program depends on the linkage of the class definitions. A class defined at global scope in a given translation unit has *external linkage* in that translation unit if, in that translation unit, it is involved in the declaration of something else with external linkage. (As of this printing, the ANSI/ISO committee is working toward a definition of what it means for an identifier to be involved in the declaration of something else.) If one or both definitions of X have internal linkage, then the program is legal, assuming that it has no errors elsewhere.

If both definitions of X have external linkage, however, the containing program is illegal. This error might or might not be detected by current compilation systems. If, for example, each of the classes contains a noninline member function named f, *unit4:*

```
class X {
    void f();
    // stuff
};
```

unit5:

```
class X {
    void f();
    // different stuff
};
```

then there might be two different definitions of `X::f()` given to the linker, and the linker might detect the error. (The conditions under which the linker detects multiple definitions of a function will be discussed in Section 6.1.3.) If the definitions of `X` are sufficiently different, however, this error will not be detected by any current compilation system. For example, if both `X`s contain only nonstatic data members (and no function members),

unit4:

```
class X {
public:
    int i;
    char c;
};
```

unit5:

```
class X {
public:
    int i;
    double d;
};
```

then current C++ compilation systems probably will not detect the error. If the containing program is built and executed, its behavior will be undefined.

6.1.3   Function and Data Definitions

Now consider function definitions. (Data definitions are similar except for the matter of argument types.) Any program containing a translation unit that has more than one definition of a function with a given name and signature (the number, order, and types of its arguments) is illegal. For example, the following is illegal:

unit6:

```
void f(int) { /* stuff */ }
// ...
void f(int) { /* the same or different stuff */ }  // error
```

This error is detected by C++ compilers.

If the function definitions are in separate translation units, the legality depends on the linkage of the definitions. If one or both has internal linkage (that is, if one or both is declared with the **static** keyword),

unit7:

```
void f(int) {
    // ...
}
```

unit8:

```
static void f(int) {
    // ...
}
```

then the program is legal, assuming that it has no errors elsewhere.

If both definitions have external linkage, however, the containing program is illegal. Whether this error is detected by the compilation system depends on how the translation units are presented to the linker. If both *unit7* and *unit8* are presented as object files, the linker will probably issue a "multiply defined" error.

If, however, one of these translation units — say *unit7* — is presented as a member of an object code archive, then, depending on how the rest of the code is organized, the linker might not pull *unit7* into the program. Although the resulting program will be legal, calls to f(int) that were intended to call the version defined in *unit7* will instead call the version defined in *unit8*. Hence, the program will have incorrect behavior.

6.1.4   Implications for Libraries

Now let us consider the implications of C++'s rules for declarations and definitions on the design of a C++ library. Suppose that a library defines a class `Widget` at global scope with external linkage.[2] This library conflicts with all other libraries and user code that also define a class `Widget` at global scope with external linkage. A programmer who tries to use two such libraries in the same program might get an error at compile or link time or might be unlucky enough to build a program with undefined behavior. It does not matter if one or both of the libraries defines and uses `Widget` only in the implementation of the library. If the following file

libimpl.c:

```
// used only in this file, has external linkage
class Widget {
    // ...
};
// ...
```

is part of the implementation of a library, then any program that pulls in the object code for *libimpl.c* will define the shown `Widget` at global scope.

Now suppose that a library defines a function `f(int)`. If the definition has internal linkage and is in a library implementation file, there is no possibility of conflict. Otherwise, the library conflicts with all other libraries and user code that also define an external `f(int)`. A programmer who tries to use two such libraries in the same program might get an error at link time or might build a program with incorrect behavior.

Not only do global name conflicts create the possibility of building programs with undefined or incorrect behavior, they are also difficult for library users to fix. To remove a conflict, the prospective user of the conflicting libraries must change the source code for one or both of the libraries. At best, this task is tedious and error prone; if the user does not have access to the source code, it is impossible. Hence, C++ library designers should make every reasonable effort to prevent global name conflict. To prevent global name conflict, C++ libraries should use the `namespace` construct (unless portability concerns preclude using `namespace`; see Section 9.2.2)

---

2. More precisely, suppose that at least one of the following is true: (1) A header file in the library contains code that causes one or more of the user's translation units to contain a definition of a class `Widget` at global scope with external linkage. (2) A translation unit in the implementation of the library contains a definition of a class `Widget` at global scope with external linkage. In the following discussion, we use less precise language.

and should follow a naming convention for names to which namespaces do not apply.

6.1.5   Naming Conventions

All the global names with external linkage defined by a C++ library should be names that are likely to be unique among all global names in all code that might ever be used in the same program as the library. To increase the likelihood of names being unique, every global name with external linkage should be prefixed. One-letter and two-letter prefixes are common in practice:

```
class XYwidget {
    // ...
};
void XYf(int);
```

To increase the odds that a library's names are unique, we might use a prefix containing the name of the library and the name of the company or organization that produced the library:

```
class Companyxyz_libabc_widget {
    // ...
};
void companyxyz_libabc_f(int);
```

The tradeoff is that such long names are unsightly and cumbersome.

Library providers can, if they like, give users a synonym mechanism by providing a synonym file, which users can edit to contain whatever names they prefer:

synonyms.h:

```
#define Widget Companyxyz_libabc_widget
#define f Companyxyz_libabc_f
// ...
```

Using the preprocessor to replace names is risky, however. Consider the following user code:

```
#include <synonyms.h>

class User_class {
    class Widget {  // whoops!
        // ...
    };
    // ...
};
```

Here, the user's identifier will be replaced — almost certainly unintentionally — with the library class name. If the user is lucky, such accidental
replacement will cause errors during compilation or linking. If not, a debugging session will ensue.

A library should apply its naming convention to all global names with
external linkage — even those names that appear only in the library implementation:

libimpl.c:

```
// has external linkage
class Companyxyz_libabc_used_only_in_this_file {
    // ...
};
// ...
```

If a library's implementation is large, two different implementors of that
library might both choose the same name accidentally. To reduce the odds
of conflict, global names in the implementation might also embed the name
of the containing subsystem:

libimpl.c:

```
class Companyxyz_libabc_subsystemq_used_only_in_this_file {
    // ...
};
// ...
```

Theoretically, not protecting a class's private member names can lead to
conflict. Suppose that a class X in some library declares a private member
function f and that some other library provides the following class Y:

```
class Y {
public:
    void f();
    //...
};
```

Further suppose that a user of both libraries derives from X and Y, as follows:

```
class XY : public X, public Y {
    // ...
};
```

If the user tries to call f on an XY object, a compile-time error will occur:

```
XY xy;
xy.f();  // error: ambiguous X::f and Y::f
```

Because ambiguities are detected in C++ before access protection is checked, the presence of the private member X::f renders the attempted call to Y::f ambiguous.

Thus, ideally, a library should apply a naming convention to all the private members of its classes. Doing so, however, would be a considerable burden for the library developers. Because in practice this conflict occurs rarely, most libraries do not apply a naming convention to private member names.

6.1.6   The namespace Construct

To reduce significantly the number of global names that need prefixing, libraries can use the namespace construct. For example,

```
namespace Companyxyz_libabc {
    class Widget {
        // ...
    };
    void f();
    // ...
};
```

Because they are nested within the namespace, Widget and f do not need prefixing. Because the namespace name is in the global scope, it follows a naming convention, as described in the previous section. The number of global namespaces in a typical library — even a large one — will be low, and thus the number of unwieldy names will be low.

Here is how programmers can use the names declared inside the
Companyxyz_libabc namespace:

```
Companyxyz_libabc::Widget widget;
Companyxyz_libabc::f();
```

Users can, if they like, access the names in a namespace without typing the
namespace name by taking advantage of the using construct:

```
using namespace Companyxyz_libabc;
Widget widget;
f();
```

The single disadvantage of using the namespace construct is that it is a relatively new addition to C++. Until all compilers implement it, portability
of code that uses it is limited.

6.2   Macro Names

In C++, preprocessor macros do not scope as other names do. Use of
macro names can cause conflicts with other macro names or other identifiers. Fortunately, almost all uses of macros can be eliminated from C++
libraries.

6.2.1   Macro Name Conflicts

Consider some library LIB-A, and suppose that LIB-A defines the following
macro in one of its public header files:

libA.h:

```
#define MACRO stuff
```

Suppose that LIB-B also defines a macro named MACRO in one of its public
header files:

libB.h:

```
#define MACRO different stuff
```

Then programs that use both libraries can get a redefinition error:

user.c:

```
#include <libA.h>
#include <libB.h>  // error: redefinition of MACRO
// ...
```

Even if no library other than LIB-A and no user code defines a macro named
`MACRO`, the presence of the macro definition in LIB-A can still cause conflict.
Suppose that LIB-B provides the following class:

libB.h:

```
class X {
    void MACRO();
    // ...
};
```

Then code that includes *libA.h* before it includes *libB.h* will change the
name of X's member function, probably with undesirable results.

Macros have other disadvantages that are perhaps even worse for users
than name conflicts. First, on most systems macro names are not available
during debugging. Second, macros are not type safe. Consider this macro:

```
#define ABS(X) ((X) > 0? (X) : -(X))
```

The author of this macro intended that it be called only on integer or
floating point values. Nevertheless, the following call will compile with
neither an error message nor a warning:

```
ABS('q'); // elicits no compiler diagnostic
```

To minimize the problems caused by macros, libraries should do the following two things:

1. Define as few public macros as possible (a *public macro* is a macro
   defined in a public header file).
2. Use a naming convention for all public macros that cannot be eliminated.

6.2.2   Eliminating Macros

C++ provides mechanisms that obviate the need for most macros. Virtually
all uses of the preprocessor in real C++ code, other than `#include`, fall into
at least one of the following categories [Str94a]:

- Commenting out code. For example,

  ```
  #if 0
  int not_needed_anymore;
  #endif
  ```

- Symbolic constant. For example,

```
#define TABLESIZE 1024
```

- Inline function. For example,

```
#define CLEAR(X) ((X) = 0)
```

- Generic function. For example, the macro

```
#define ABS(X) ((X) > 0? (X) : -(X))
```

might be called on both integers and floating point values:

```
ABS(-7);
ABS(-7.0);
```

- Generic type. For example,

```
#define Stack(T) Stack__ ## T
#define Stackdeclare(T) class Stack(T) { /* ... */ }

Stackdeclare(int);
Stackdeclare(char);
// ...
Stack(int) s1;
Stack(char) s2;
```

- Syntax extension. For example, suppose that `Set` is a class representing sets. Then a programmer might define a macro `FORALL` that enables writing the following:

```
Set<int> s;
int i;
FORALL(i, s)
        // ...
```

- Declaration macro. For example,

```
#define DECLARE_MEMBERS(X) X(); ~X(); X(const X&)
// ...
class Widget {
public:
        DECLARE_MEMBERS(Widget);
        // ...
};
```

- Code versioning. For example, the following function comes in debugging and nondebugging versions:

```
void f() {
#ifdef DEBUG
        // debugging version
#else
        // nondebugging version
#endif
}
```

All these uses of the preprocessor other than declaration macro and code versioning are rendered obsolete in C++. Use of the preprocessor to comment out code can be replaced by real comments:

```
// int not_needed_anymore;
/* int also_not_needed_anymore; */
```

(A slight disadvantage of using real comments is that it is easier to comment out a block of code by wrapping it in a `#if 0 ... #endif` pair than by placing a `//` at the beginning of each line in the block.)

Use of the preprocessor to define a symbolic constant can be replaced by either a `const` or `enum` value:

```
const int TABLESIZE = 1024;   // either this
enum { TABLESIZE = 1024 };   // or this
```

Use of the preprocessor to define a nongeneric inline function can be replaced by a real inline function. For example, if the macro `CLEAR` shown on page 148 is called on only `int` arguments, we can replace calls to `CLEAR` with calls to the following inline function:

```
inline void clear(int& x) { x = 0; }
```

Sometimes, replacing a use of the preprocessor with an inline function requires some additional program transformations. Consider this code:

```
#define CONTROL(c) ((c) - 64)
// ...
switch (c) {
case CONTROL('a'):  // ...
case CONTROL('b'):  // ...
// ...
}
```

Because it is illegal in C++ for a case label to be a function call, replacing the `CONTROL` macro with an inline function would result in illegal code. We can, however, transform the code as follows:

```
inline char decontrol(char c) {
        return c + 64;
}
// ...
switch (decontrol(c)) {
case 'a':  // ...
case 'b':  // ...
// ...
}
```

(Because it does the addition in `decontrol` at run time, this version is slightly slower than the version using the macro.)

Use of the preprocessor to implement a generic function or type can be replaced by a function or class `template`:

```
template<class T>
T abs(const T& t) { return t > 0 ? t : -t; }

template<class T>
class Stack { /* ... */ };
```

Finally, use of the preprocessor to extend the syntax of C++ can almost always be replaced by use of one or more C++ classes. For example, rather than define the `FORALL` macro, a C++ programmer can define a `Set_iter` class that makes it possible to write the following:

```
Set<int> s;
int i;
Set_iter<int> iter(s);
while (iter.next(i))
        // ...
```

This code is only slightly less terse than the code using the `FORALL` macro.

6.2.3 Naming Conventions for Macros

Public macros that cannot be eliminated should adhere to a naming convention, as described in Section 6.1.5. For example,

```
#define COMPANYXYZ_LIBABC_MACRO stuff
```

Remember to follow a naming convention for *all* public macros. In particular, macros used to guard public header files against multiple inclusion (and every public header file provided by a library should be guarded) should obey a naming convention:

libA.h:

```
#ifndef COMPANYXYZ_LIBABC_WIDGET_H
#define COMPANYXYZ_LIBABC_WIDGET_H
// ...
#endif
```

Macros defined within a library's implementation do not have to follow a naming convention:

libimpl.c:

```
#define MACRO ...
```

This macro cannot cause a conflict with other libraries or user code, and presumably the implementor of *libimpl.c* knows that this macro does not conflict with any of the code in the containing translation unit.

6.3 Environmental Names

The kinds of names discussed in Sections 6.1 and 6.2 all appear within the source code of a C++ library. Not all the names used by a C++ library are found within the source code. For example, a typical library provides several header files, each of which has a name. A library might also come with on-line manual pages, perhaps provide some executable programs, and maybe use some environment variables; each of these things has a name too. We call such names *environmental names*.

Environmental names in different libraries can conflict. Suppose, for example, that two libraries LIB-A and LIB-B each provide a public header file named *Widget.h*. If a user of LIB-A and LIB-B keeps the header files for all libraries in a single directory, then the installation procedure for whichever of LIB-A or LIB-B is installed second will try to overwrite (one hopes unsuccessfully) the header file for the first.

Suppose that, to avoid this conflict, a user keeps the header files for different libraries in separate directories and specifies these directories in an #include path to the compiler. Unfortunately, this scheme merely moves the conflict; it does not resolve it. If the user writes

```
#include <Widget.h>
```

the preprocessor will use the first *Widget.h* found on the #include path, which might not be the desired one. Reordering the #include path moves the problem to another header file.

To reduce the odds of environmental name conflict, all the files associated with a library should be under a directory whose name is likely to be unique. For example, all the files for company XYZ's ABC library might be located under a directory named *Companyxyz_libabc*. Further, all code that refers to any of the files associated with a library should always use path names relative to that library's unique directory. For example, if *Widget.h* is in the *incl* subdirectory of the directory *Companyxyz_libabc*, then programmers should #include *Widget.h* like this:

```
#include <Companyxyz_libabc/incl/Widget.h>  // right
```

rather than like this:

```
#include <Widget.h>  // ill-advised
```

Both the users and the implementors of a library should adhere to this convention. If the implementors do not adhere to it, then conflicts might arise when users of library source code try to compile it in their environments. Unfortunately, as we shall discuss in Section 9.9, this approach to reducing environmental name conflicts trades off with portability.

On some systems, file names are not case sensitive. Thus, for example, a library header file named *Widget.h* can collide with a system file named *widget.h*.

6.4 Unclean Libraries

A library is *name clean*, or *clean* for short, if every global name, public macro name, and environmental name obeys a naming convention as described in Sections 6.1 through 6.3. Sometimes, a library can be unclean without risk of conflict. Specifically, consider some unclean library UN-CLEAN, and suppose that at least one of the following statements is true for every piece of code C that will ever appear in the same program as UNCLEAN:

1. C is clean.
2. C was written with the knowledge that it will appear in the same program as UNCLEAN.

Then it is easy to see that UNCLEAN will not cause a name conflict.

What libraries might be unclean safely? The standard C++ library is one example: Every piece of C++ code that might ever appear in the same program as the standard C++ library should be written with knowledge of that possibility. Another example is a C++ library intended solely for its author's personal use. Such code will be used with other code written by the same author, which thus should satisfy property (2), or with code from some other library that satisfies — or should satisfy — property (1). Of course, if our personal libraries are unclean, then colleagues who discover that they would like to use our libraries cannot do so without risk of name conflict. Beware: Libraries that start out as personal libraries often do not remain solely personal libraries — especially if they are useful.

6.5   Good-Citizen Libraries

Suppose that a library, LIB-Q, wants to allocate all its free-store objects from a special pool of memory. It might, therefore, define the global operator **new**. The drawback of this scheme is that all calls to global **new** — not just calls from within LIB-Q — will invoke LIB-Q's operator **new**. If the user also tries to link with some other library, all its **new**s will call LIB-Q's **new**, which might conflict with what the other library is trying to do.

We say that LIB-Q is not a *good-citizen* library. It has assumed ownership of a global resource — operator **new**. By usurping a global resource, a library will conflict with any other library or user code that wants to use or own that resource. A good-citizen library refrains from assuming ownership of any global resources. Other global resources in C++ include the global operator **delete**, the new-handler, and the **terminate** and **unexpected** functions for exception handling. Further, a good-citizen library does not assume ownership of application-specific resources. A good-citizen library would not, for example, assume ownership of the root window in a windowing system.

Sometimes, we might knowingly design even a nonpersonal library in a way that renders it not a good citizen. For example, suppose that for some reason our library needs to allocate all free-store objects created by anyone anywhere in the user's program in a special pool of memory. If we must have this behavior, then we can define our own version of **new** and require our users to use that version. Although the resulting library is not a good citizen, we might nevertheless choose this design if alternative designs would present even larger problems for our users.

6.6   Summary

When two libraries conflict, use of both of them in a single program will be difficult, if not impossible. To maximize reusability, library designers should avoid conflicting with other code. Use of sound naming conventions and the **namespace** construct is essential for all global, public macro, and environmental names defined by a library unless the library can safely be unclean. Good-citizen libraries avoid another form of conflict: conflicting attempts to own global or application-specific resources.

Exercises

6.1 (**) State precisely the C++ rules specifying what declarations and definitions may appear legally in the global scope of a program without conflicting.

6.2 Explain why a C++ library should not define classes named `Root` or `Object` in the global scope.

6.3 Suppose that you are designing a library to be marketed to real estate agencies. Your first cut at one of your class declarations is as follows:

```
class Listing {
public:
    Listing();
    void reduce_asking_price(Price new_price);
    // ...
private:
    Price asking_price;
    bool has_attached_garage;
    int nbedrooms;
    // ...
};
```

  a. Revise this declaration using a suitable naming convention so that your customers will not encounter conflicts with your class's names.
  b. Write a synonym file for your customers' convenience in using your revised `Listing` class.
  c. Revise the declaration of `Listing` using the `namespace` construct.

6.4 Before C++ contained the `namespace` construct, some library designers used *scoping classes* to help reduce name conflicts. A scoping class is a class used not for the sake of creating objects but for the sake of the scope it provides. For example, instead of declaring

```
int abc_val;
void abc_func();
class ABC_Widget { /* ... */ };
```

we could write

```
class ABC_lib {
public:
    static int val;
    static void func();
    class Widget { /* ... */ };
private:
    ABC_lib();
};
```

The identifiers `val`, `func`, and `Widget` would be in the scope of `ABC_lib`. Users would reference the identifiers with the class scoping operator, as follows:

```
int i = ABC_lib::val;
ABC_lib::func();
ABC_lib::Widget w;
```

a. Why did we give `ABC_lib` a private constructor?

b. What will be the scope of a macro declared within a scoping class? For example, what is the scope of `some_macro` in the following?

```
class ABC_lib {
#    define some_macro X
     // ...
};
```

c. What will happen if we attempt to nest a template within a scoping class, as follows?

```
class ABC_lib {
    template<class T>
    class ABC_Another_widget { /* ... */ };
    // ...
};
```

d. Can a library use a scoping class or scoping classes to avoid introducing *any* names into the global scope? Explain your answer.

6.5   Suppose that a header file in library LIB-A uses the same macro name for its header file guard as a header file in library LIB-B. Show how a conflict can arise in a program that tries to use both libraries. Will a C++ compilation system detect all such conflicts? Explain.

6.6   The definition of a macro is *guarded* if it is embedded within a similarly named `#ifndef` construct, like this:

```
#ifndef MACRO
#define MACRO ...
#endif
```

Show that even if all libraries and user code guard all their macro definitions, the conflicts described in Section 6.2 are not eliminated.

References and Further Reading

The C++ rules specifying what declarations and definitions may legally appear in the global scope of a program are still under active discussion by the C++ ANSI/ISO committee. (In particular, the One Definition Rule must be clarified. Under what conditions is it legal for the definition of a class to appear in different translation units? What does it mean for two class definitions to be the same?) The rules as of this printing can be found in the ANSI/ISO working paper [ANS94].

Kendall and Allin [KA94] explain further the notion of class linkage.

Conflict among C++ libraries is discussed by Berlin [Ber90].

7 Compatibility

> *Ours is not to reason why;*
> *ours is but to code and cry.*
> — Rob Murray

Most providers of reusable code will need to be concerned with compatibility between releases of that code. Releases of code can provide different forms of compatibility: source compatibility, link compatibility, run compatibility, and process compatibility.

In this chapter, we define these forms of compatibility and discuss how to provide them. We also advise documenting incompatibilities and warn library providers about the possibility of users relying on undocumented properties of reusable code.

7.1 Backward and Forward Compatibility

The users of a changing library often need to upgrade to the latest release of the library. For example, users might want to exploit new functionality, optimizations, or bug fixes introduced in the latest release, or they might need to stay synchronized with other code that uses the latest release of the library. If upgrading from release m of a library to release n is easy (in any of the senses defined in the next section), then release m is *forward compatible* to release n, and release n is *backward compatible* to release m.[1]

Backward compatibility and forward compatibility are two sides of the same coin: If you have done a good job of providing forward compatibility, you will have an easier time providing backward compatibility. In

---

1. Not everyone uses the terms *backward* and *forward* compatibility as we have defined them. Our definitions correspond to the most widely accepted usage.

the remainder of this chapter, we shall talk about compatibility from the perspective of providing backward compatibility to library users.

7.2   Forms of Compatibility

Consider the typical sequence of steps a C++ programmer follows to build a program, shown in Figure 7.1. First, the programmer writes source code that is intended to implement some desired behavior. Next, the source is compiled into object code. One or more translation units of object code are then linked, creating executable code. Finally, the executable code is executed, creating a process on the underlying machine. If every step in the sequence was implemented correctly, the process exhibits the desired behavior.

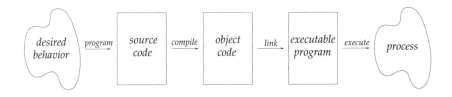

Figure 7.1   The build sequence.

Suppose that a program written, built, and executed with release m of a library needs to be upgraded to use release n of the library. How easy the upgrade will be depends on which steps in the build sequence need redoing.

- If no users have to change their source code in any way, then release n of the library is *source compatible* with release m.
- If no users have to recompile anything, then release n is *link compatible* with m.
- If no users have to relink anything, then n is *run compatible* with m.
- If even currently executing programs can be upgraded while they are executing, then n is *process compatible* with m.

Let us consider more closely the definition of source compatibility. What exactly do we mean by "no users have to change their source code"? Sometimes, changes to a library can force users to change their source code for reasons not foreseen by the library developers. Suppose, for example, that we change the implementation of a noninline function f without changing f's semantics but that unbeknownst to us one of our users has stringent resource limits. If our change causes this user's program to exceed its code size limit, the source code for the program will have to be changed somehow to bring it back under the limit. Even so, we would not usually consider this change to be source incompatible.

We shall therefore refine our definition of source compatibility such that a change is considered to be source incompatible only if it requires users to change their code because of changed semantics:

> Release *n* of a library is *source compatible* to release *m* if every legal program that uses release *m* is legal and has the same semantics using release *n*.

Our change to f is source compatible according to this definition.

Although this definition is more precise than the earlier one, it raises a question: What do we mean by "every" in "every program"? Do we mean every possible program, or do we mean every existing user program? We shall refer to the former as *compatibility in theory* and the latter as *compatibility in practice*. Henceforth, when we say "source compatible," for example, with no qualifier, we shall mean "source compatible in practice." Similar distinctions can be made between theory and practice for the other forms of compatibility. In Sections 7.4 through 7.7, we discuss the forms of compatibility in greater detail.

7.3   Source Compatibility in Theory

Almost every change to a C++ library is source incompatible in theory. We believe that for almost any nontrivial change to a library, it is possible to construct a hypothetical user program that would have to be rewritten to accommodate the change. Consider, for example, a seemingly innocuous change to a library: adding a member function to a class. Here is the class X with the added function:

```
class X {
public:
    void added();
    // ...
};
```

Now consider the following hypothetical user code:

```
class User_x : public X {
public:
    void f();
    // ...
};
```

Suppose that the user's program contains a definition of a function at global scope whose name just happens to be added. Suppose further that the implementation of User_x::f is as follows:

```
extern void added();

void User_x::f() {
    added();
    // ...
}
```

Using the version of X without added, User_x::f calls the global added; using the version of X with added, User_x::f calls X::added. The user's code must be changed because of changes in semantics. Hence, adding a public member to a class is source incompatible in theory.

"Okay," you might say, "but that was a change to the *interface* of the library. I'll bet any change to the *implementation* of a library is source compatible in theory, right?" Sorry. Suppose that the member function we wish to add is a private member of X:

```
class X {
private:
    void added();
    // ...
};
```

Because access protection is checked *after* name lookup in C++, the same hypothetical user program becomes illegal when this change is made. Hence, even this change is source incompatible in theory.

7.4   Source Compatibility in Practice

Most library writers cannot examine each of their users' programs, so it can be difficult to determine whether a given change to a library is source compatible in practice. A bit of reasoning, however, frequently will give us the answer. For example, suppose that class X was not designed for derivation. Although it is *possible* that a determined user will have derived from X, *probably* none will have (see Section 3.4 for a discussion of the difficulty of deriving from classes not designed for derivation). If we assume that no user has derived from X, then our changes to X are source compatible in practice.

Usually, changes that neither remove nor change existing functionality are source compatible in practice. The following changes, for example, are source compatible:

- Adding a member function.
- Granting a friendship.
- Loosening the protection of a member or base class (that is, changing from private to protected or public, or from protected to public).
- Making a previously out-of-line function inline.
- Making an inline function out-of-line.

Changes that remove functionality, on the other hand, are almost always source incompatible. Suppose, for example, that later we wish to remove X::added from our library. Then every program that calls X::added will have to be changed. Of course, if we *know* that no one uses X::added, we can remove it without breaking compatibility.

Dealing with source incompatibilities can be made easier for users by a migration technique called *deprecation* (or *denigration*). Rather than remove a function from a library, we would warn in the documentation that it should not be used. Code that used to work will continue to work, while new code will be written without using it (we hope). Users will be able to change their source to accommodate the change in the library at their convenience. By the time the deprecated functionality is removed (if ever), some programs that relied on it will no longer be in use and will never have to be changed.

Even if a function is deprecated, a description of it should remain in the documentation because there will be programmers who must maintain old code that uses the function. When we deprecate a function, we might document it in a special section of the manual and remove all references to it from the rest of the documentation. If we expect to remove the function from the library eventually, we should warn users to that effect.

Deprecation can be applied not only to individual functions; it can be applied at any level of granularity. One can deprecate a group of functions, a class or group of classes, or even an entire library.

7.5 Link Compatibility

Programmers with a large base of existing software do not want to have to recompile all their code to upgrade to a new release of a library that they use. Recompiling all the code for some projects takes days. Rarely, a project does not have access to all the source code from which its object code was built, or something in the build procedure depends on software that is no longer available. Thus, many users prefer that a new release of a library be link compatible with the previous release and sometimes with older releases. To upgrade a program from a release m of a library to a link-compatible release n, all a programmer must do is relink.

Unfortunately, providing link compatibility (sometimes also called "binary compatibility") is often easier said than done. Many of the kinds of changes one typically makes to a library as it evolves render it link incompatible with older releases. In this section, we discuss which kinds of changes are link compatible and which are not. In Section 8.2, we show how to design classes and inheritance hierarchies to increase the odds that a desired change to a library will be link compatible.

Probably the most frequently seen link-compatible change is changing the implementation of an out-of-line function without changing its interface. Any change that does not affect any of a library's public header files must be link compatible. Such changes are restricted to changes to types that users cannot construct, objects that users cannot access, and functions whose implementations cannot appear in users' object code (through inlining). In the remainder of this section, we shall consider changes that affect one or more of a library's public header files.

All source-incompatible changes are also link incompatible. For example, the following changes are both source and link incompatible:

- Removing a function (from the interface of the library).
- Changing a function's return type or argument types.
- Tightening the protection of a member (changing it from public to private or protected or from protected to private).

Here are some additional link-incompatible changes:

- Any change in the layout or size of a class — adding, removing, or changing the size or offsets of data members.
- Changing a function from out-of-line to inline. Code compiled with the older release requires an out-of-line definition, which will not be present in the newer release.
- Almost any change to an inline function.
- Adding a virtual function to a class that previously had none. A class that has one or more virtual functions will have a virtual function table; in most C++ implementations, any object of that type will contain a pointer to the virtual function table.

Some nontrivial changes to a library's public header files are actually link compatible. Here are some link-compatible changes:

- Adding a new nonvirtual function — inline or out-of-line — provided that the new function does not overload or hide any existing function.
- Loosening the protection of a base class (changing it from private to protected or public or from protected to public).
- Granting a friendship.

Changing a function from inline to out-of-line might or might not be link compatible. If users have object files created with the old (inline) version of the function and they link with the new version of the library, they will not invoke the new version of the function. Thus, if the semantics of the function changes in the new version, the change is link incompatible. On the other hand, if the function has the same semantics and has merely been made more efficient, for example, and the old implementation will still work correctly with the new release of the library, then the change is link compatible.

The link compatibility *in practice* of many changes depends on the compilation system our users have. For example, consider the following changes:

- Loosening the protection of a data member. An implementation may order data members with different access specifiers any way it chooses. With a C++ implementation that lays down data members in the order they are declared, for example, loosening the protection of a data member will be link compatible. With a C++ implementation that groups data members by access protection, loosening the protection of a member could cause the layout of objects of the class type to change, which would be a link incompatibility.
- Rearranging virtual function declarations in a class definition. Some C++ implementations lay down function entries in a class's virtual function table in the order the virtual functions were declared; with such an implementation, rearranging virtual function declarations will be link incompatible. Other implementations will order virtual function tables independently of the order of declaration — alphabetically by function name, for example; with such an implementation, rearranging virtual function declarations will be link compatible.
- Adding a new virtual function to a class that already had one or more virtual functions. Such a change will change the size and layout of the virtual function table. If, however, the C++ implementations to be used lay down virtual function entries in the order the functions

are declared, and if the new function is declared after all other virtual functions, then the addition of the new function will not affect existing code that uses the virtual function table.

- Adding an exception specification to a function, changing a function's exception specification, or deleting a function's exception specification. With most implementations of exception handling, these will be link compatible.

Of course, we do not advocate relying on the implementation dependencies of users' compilation systems. If you must rely on such implementation dependencies, be sure that you know what compilation systems are used to compile your code, and be absolutely certain you know how those systems implement whatever it is you are depending on.

7.6   Run Compatibility

If release n of a library is run compatible with an earlier release m, programs that use release m can be upgraded merely by being executed. The most commonly used mechanism for providing run compatibility is *dynamic linking*.

Suppose that we create a program by nondynamically linking two object files, t1.obj and t2.obj, and an archive file my.lib:

```
% link t1.obj t2.obj my.lib
```

If the link succeeds, the resulting executable file will contain a copy of all the code in t1.obj and t2.obj plus the object files in my.lib containing the definitions of any functions or data used in the program.

Now suppose that we dynamically link. Although the mechanism for dynamic linking varies across systems, typically the programmer must first create (or have available) a *dynamic link library* (DLL) — that is, an archive suitable for dynamic linking. (DLLs are called *shared libraries* on some systems.) Suppose that we have created a DLL my.dynlib containing the code in my.lib. If we link with my.dynlib,

```
% link t1.obj t2.obj my.dynlib
```

then the resulting executable will contain copies of the code in t1.obj and t2.obj but *no copy* of any of the code in my.dynlib. Run-time support for dynamically linked programs will cause calls to functions defined in my.dynlib to execute the appropriate code.

Many implementations of dynamic linking also provide a DLL versioning mechanism. With such an implementation, a DLL is assigned a version number when it is created; this version number might be assigned for us automatically, or we might have to assign it explicitly. We also specify (using some system-dependent mechanism) with which other versions of the DLL this version is link compatible. Suppose that we link our program with version m of `my.dynlib`. At run time, a call to a function `f` defined in `my.dynlib` will execute the code for `f` that is found in the highest available version of `my.dynlib` that is designated as link compatible with version m.

Using dynamic linking to make a release n of a library run compatible with release m thus involves the following steps:

1. Ensuring that release n is link compatible with release m
2. Building DLLs for releases m and n
3. Designating n as link compatible with m

Step 2 can be difficult. Certain C++ implementations do not work correctly when used in conjunction with some implementations of dynamic linking. Consider the following code:

```
class X {
public:
    X();
    // ...
};

X x1;

void f() {
    static X x2;
    // ...
}
```

With some combinations of C++ implementations and dynamic linking, if this code is in a DLL, the objects `x1`, `x2`, or both will never be initialized.

Note that if a library adheres to the recommendations we shall discuss in Section 12.1, then `x1` would not be declared as shown. If the implementation of dynamic linking correctly initializes local static objects such as `x2`, then in practice the odds are high that the given C++ implementation and dynamic linking mechanism work correctly together.

7.7 Process Compatibility

If release n of a library is process compatible with an earlier release m, then programs that were written and built with release m can be upgraded *while they are executing*. For example, we might want to upgrade an air traffic

control system without bringing it down. Process compatibility is difficult
to provide and thus is rarely seen. The mechanisms used are highly system
dependent and are beyond the scope of this book. Here, we shall merely
sketch a few of the requirements of such a system.

Suppose that a library contains a single class X and that release n of
this library is link compatible with release m. To upgrade an executing
program from m to n, the following (at least) must happen:

- All calls to member functions of X must be upgraded during program
  execution to call the release n versions.
- All extant instances of X objects must become instances of release n
  X objects.

One way to upgrade extant instances of X is to have each member function
of X test, before doing anything else, whether the X object for which it has
been called has been upgraded; if not, we upgrade the object:

```
// release n of library
void X::f() {
    if (!is_version_n(this)) {
        // upgrade *this to version n
        // ...
    }
    // ...
}
```

Programmers interested in the details of how to provide process compatibility should see Coplien's book [Cop92].

7.8   Documenting Incompatibilities

Every release of a library should document all source and link incompatibilities with the previous release. Further, library designers who want to
assist users should explain, for each source incompatibility, how users must
change their code to upgrade. The documentation might say, for example,

> The function `Widget::operator++` has been removed; use `Widget::`
> `next` instead.

All compatibility notes should be in one place in the documentation.

Not all users of a library upgrade their programs with every new release.
For example, some users elect not to upgrade to "point 0" releases (1.0, 2.0,
3.0, and so on) because such releases have the reputation for being faulty.
Such a user might want to upgrade from the most recent release preceding

3.0 to release 3.1 (skipping 3.0). Let us assume that the release preceding 3.0 was 2.9. To upgrade from 2.9 to 3.1, this user might first follow the directions for upgrading from 2.9 to 3.0, then follow the directions for upgrading from 3.0 to 3.1. Besides being a nuisance, this process might be expensive — such users will have to purchase the 3.0 documentation even though they do not intend to use release 3.0. For the convenience of these users, library providers sometimes document the incompatibilities with several previous releases. (Documentation and compatibility are discussed further in Section 10.2.4.)

7.9   Undocumented Properties

Suppose that our library provides a `Gizmo` class with an `operator<<`

```
ostream& operator<<(ostream& o, const Gizmo& g);
```

and suppose that we have documented this operation as follows:

> Prints on `o` a human-readable representation of `g`, then returns `o`.

This documentation neither describes the format of the resulting output nor guarantees that the format will remain unchanged in future releases of the library. Thus, we might think that changing the format of the output of `operator<<` would not break source compatibility. Unfortunately, if `Gizmo` is widely used, some users somewhere will have written code that depends on that format. If we change that format, those users will have to change their source code to deal with the new format. Hence, just because something is undocumented does not imply that changing it will not break compatibility.

There are two reasons that a user might rely on an undocumented property of a library. First, the user might have to. For example, the user of `Gizmo` might need to write a program P_1 that analyzes the output of another program P_2. If P_2 ever calls the `Gizmo` stream-insertion operator, P_1 will have to rely on the format of the output of that operator. Unfortunately, there is little a library designer can do to prevent this sort of reliance on undocumented properties.

The second reason a user might rely on an undocumented property is that the user might enjoy reading header files. For example, suppose that the implementation of `Gizmo` contains a member function `useful_function` that we need to call from many other classes in our library. We might make `useful_function` private and every other class a friend of `Gizmo`:

```
class Gizmo {
    friend class A;
    friend class B;
    friend class C;
    friend class D;
    friend class E;
    friend class F;
    friend class G;
    // and so on, and so on, and so on ...
    // ...
private:
    void useful_function();
    // ...
};
```

Making a class a friend of Gizmo, however, gives it access not only to useful_function but to the entire implementation of Gizmo. Giving so many classes access to the entire implementation of Gizmo is error prone. A better approach is to make useful_function a public, but undocumented, function:

```
class Gizmo {
public:
    void useful_function();   // undocumented
    // ...
};
```

Unfortunately, users who enjoy reading header files looking for interesting functions might call useful_function in their code. To prevent such use, the library header file should contain a warning such as the following:

```
class Gizmo {
public:
    // WARNING: useful_function is public to make this
    // library easier to implement. It is undocumented
    // and should not be called by library users.  It
    // is not guaranteed to exist in future releases
    // of this library.
    void useful_function();
    // ...
};
```

Users who call useful_function, in spite of the comment, deserve whatever they get.

7.10   Summary

Library developers should be concerned with providing backward compatibility for their current users and with anticipating forward compatibility so that they can provide backward compatibility in future releases. A library should try to provide source compatibility, link compatibility, and run compatibility whenever possible. Some libraries will also try to provide process compatibility. Providing compatibility requires careful thought about changes to a library. Deprecating, rather than removing, functionality provides source compatibility and allows users to change their code at their convenience.

Incompatibilities between releases of libraries should always be documented clearly, along with instructions on how to upgrade user programs. Library providers should also be aware of the possibility that users are relying on undocumented properties of a library.

Exercises

7.1   Suppose that you are developing a library containing the `Path` class discussed in Exercise 1.2. In your first release, `Path`s are not automatically canonicalized; instead, you provide a public `canonicalize` function:

```
class Path {
public:
    Path(const char*);
    void canonicalize();
    // ...
};
```

Suppose that you discover, after this first release of `Path` has been in use for a while, that `Path`s are always canonicalized immediately after their construction. To simplify use of `Path`, you decide in release 2 to canonicalize automatically:

```
class Path {  // release 2, automatically canonicalized
public:
    Path(const char* p) { /* ... */ canonicalize(); }
private:
    void canonicalize();
    // ...
};
```

You also move `canonicalize` to the private interface because users no longer need to call it.

    a.   Is this change source compatible in theory? Is it source compatible in practice? If so, is it link compatible?

    b.   Suppose that in release 2 you instead left `canonicalize` public. Assume that calls to `canonicalize` on a `Path` that has already been canonicalized are harmless. Is this change source compatible in theory? Is it source compatible in practice? If so, is it link compatible?

    c.   What would you do in release 2 if you would like in some future release to make `canonicalize` private?

7.2   For each of the following possible changes to a library, give an example of user code for which that change is source incompatible. Which changes would you consider source compatible in practice?

    a.   Rearranging the data members in a class.

    b.   Changing the number of array elements in a data member of a class.

    c.   Changing the order of appearance of the base classes in a class declaration.

7.3   Show that each of the following proposed changes to a class is source incompatible.

    a.   Changing the return type of a member function.

    b.   Adding a conversion function.

    c.   Changing the derivation of a base class from public to private.

7.4   Which of the following changes to a library are source compatible? Which are link compatible?

    a.   Changing the type of a private data member such that it does not change the size of the class.

    b.   Changing a default value for a function parameter.

    c.   Changing a derivation from nonvirtual to virtual.

    d.   Changing a derivation from virtual to nonvirtual.

    e.   Adding a `friend` declaration.

    f.   Adding a nested class to the private section of a class.

    g.   Adding a definition for a pure member function.

    h.   Changing a class from abstract to nonabstract without adding, deleting, or changing the implementations of any member functions. Assume that all pure virtual functions in the class already had noninline definitions and that the change to the class definition is to delete the pure specifier (= 0) from each formerly pure virtual function.

i.   Making a formerly nonabstract class abstract without adding, deleting, or changing the implementations of any member functions. That is, a pure specifier (= 0) is added to one or more virtual functions that were already defined for the class.

7.5   On page 163, we said that a new nonvirtual function can be added without breaking link compatibility, but only if the new function does not overload or hide any existing function. Why must the new function not hide any existing function? Why must it not overload any existing function?

7.6   Certain functions will be generated automatically for a class if they are not defined explicitly.
   a.   For which of the following member functions can explicit definitions be added to a class without breaking source compatibility?

- Default constructor
- Destructor
- Copy constructor
- Assignment operator
- Operator **new** (without additional arguments)
- Operator **delete**

   b.   Which of the member functions listed in part a could be deleted from a class within a library that must maintain source compatibility?
   c.   Can a library add an explicit definition for any of these functions and maintain link compatibility? What would happen if a user's compilation system had inlined the default version of the function when users compiled with the previous release of the library?
   d.   Can a library delete any of these functions and maintain link compatibility?

7.7   (∗) Suppose that a C++ library contains the function `might_throw`, which might throw or propagate an exception. In release 1 of the library, `might_throw` was declared as follows:

```
void might_throw() throw(User_blunder, System_oops);
```

Keep in mind that

1. Some users do not catch exceptions.
2. Some users want to handle every possible exception thrown and have handlers as follows:

```
try {
    // ...
}
catch (User_blunder) {
    // ...
}
catch (System_oops) {
    // ...
}
```

3. Some users catch all exceptions with this handler:

```
try {
    // ...
}
catch (...) {
    // ...
}
```

a. Suppose that `User_blunder` and `System_oops` were the only two exceptions to be thrown from or propagated out of `might_throw` in release 1. How might users be affected if the library is changed such that in release 2 `Library_glitch` propagates to `might_throw` but `might_throw`'s exception specification is not changed?

b. Again suppose that `User_blunder` and `System_oops` were the only two exceptions to be thrown from or propagated out of `might_throw` in release 1. How might users be affected if in release 2 `might_throw` throws `Library_glitch` and its exception specification lists `Library_glitch`?

c. Suppose that in release 1 `Library_glitch` was sometimes propagated to `might_throw`. How might users be affected if in release 2 `might_throw`'s exception specification is changed to list `Library_glitch`?

d. Suppose that in release 2, `System_oops` is deleted from `might_throw`'s exception specification. How might users be affected if `System_oops` propagates to `might_throw`?

e. Again suppose that in release 2, `System_oops` is deleted from `might_throw`'s exception specification. How might users be affected if `might_throw` never throws `System_oops` and `System_oops` never propagates to `might_throw`?

f. Which (if any) of the scenarios discusssed in parts a through e would you consider source-compatible changes?

7.8   (∗) Suppose that you plan to provide a collection of container classes:
Set, List, Ordered_list, Queue, and so on. All your container classes have
add, remove, and next functions. You believe your users can afford the
run-time overhead of virtual function calls and so you factor the common
functions into a base class, Container:

```
template<class T>
class Container_int {
public:
    virtual void add(const T&) = 0;
    virtual void remove(const T&) = 0;
    virtual void next(const T&) = 0;
};
```

The container classes inherit from Container_int:

```
template<class T>
class Set : public Container_int<T> {
    // ...
};
// other container classes similarly ...
```

You distribute your first release and soon you begin to hear from customers who are deriving their own container classes from your base class
Container_int. Sometimes, they say, they are designing classes for which
no remove function can be provided. They complain that they are forced
to do something like this:

```
template<class T>
class User_class_with_no_remove : public Container_int<T> {
public:
    void remove(const T&) { /* print an error message */ }
    // ...
};
```

Undoubtedly, they would rather get a diagnostic at compile time than at
run time.

To your chagrin, you realize that your customers are right — there
are many container classes for which providing a remove operation is not
appropriate. Now you realize that you should have designed your class with
a more fine-grained hierarchy (see Section 3.4.7), like this perhaps:

```
template<class T>
class Container_int {
public:
    virtual void add(const T&) = 0;
    virtual void next(const T&) = 0;
};

template<class T>
class Container_with_remove_int : public Container_int<T> {
public:
    virtual void remove(const T&) = 0;
};

template<class T>
class Set  : public Container_with_remove_int<T> {
    // ...
};
// other container classes similarly ...
```

a.   What compatibility problem will your customers have if you change your class hierarchy to this one? What kinds of uses of your library would be affected?

b.   You could change your design to this:

```
template<class T>
class Container_with_no_remove_int {
public:
    virtual void add(const T&) = 0;
    virtual void next(const T&) = 0;
};

template<class T>
class Container_int :
  public Container_with_no_remove_int<T> {
public:
    virtual void remove(const T&) = 0;
};

template<class T>
class Set  : public Container_int<T> {
    // ...
};
// other container classes similarly ...
```

For what kinds of uses of your library would there be a compatibility problem if you make this change to your class hierarchy?

    c.   If you have to satisfy the customers who are complaining, which of
the changes discussed in parts a and b would be the lesser evil? Why?

    d.   Setting aside compatibility considerations, why would this design
be ill advised?

7.9   (∗) Declaring a class's public data members first, protected data
members next, and private data members last has been proposed as a way
to facilitate link compatibility [ES90]. The intention is that protected and
private data members can be added or changed without requiring code that
uses only the public data to be recompiled and that private data members
can be added or changed without requiring code that uses only public and
protected data to be recompiled.

    a.   Explain how inlined member functions could interfere with provid-
ing link compatibility even when data members are always declared in the
order recommended. Is the problem limited to public and protected inline
member functions?

    b.   Changes to data members of a class often change the size of objects
of that type. Where might dependencies on the size of an object appear
within object code?

References and Further Reading

Dorward, Sethi, and Shopiro [DSS90] and Section 9.4 of Coplien [Cop92]
provide more information about upgrading a program while it is running.

8 Inheritance Hierarchies

> *Enjoy what thou hast inherited from thy sires*
> *if thou wouldst really possess it.*
>
> — Goethe

In this chapter, we define the rootedness, depth, and fanout of an inheritance hierarchy. Contrary to the recommendations of some writers, the appropriate number of roots, depth, and fanout of a hierarchy depends on the domain the hierarchy is intended to model and the properties the hierarchy is intended to have. Next, we discuss the various styles of inheritance hierarchies. The simplest inheritance hierarchy is usually the most efficient and is often the best choice. More complex hierarchy styles use interface classes, object factories, and handle classes to increase extensibility and link compatibility. Finally, we discuss template-based versus inheritance-based designs. Although inheritance-based designs have their uses, they are used too often where a template-based design would be more appropriate.

8.1 Rootedness, Depth, and Fanout

Consider the directed graph whose nodes are the classes that a library provides to its users and whose edges represent derivations (that is, the graph has an edge from node x to y if the class X represented by node x inherits from the class Y represented by node y). We shall call the hierarchy this graph represents the *inheritance hierarchy* of the library.

A class is a *root* if it does not derive from any class. A class's *depth* is the number of classes from a root to that class along a longest possible sequence of derivations. The *fanout* of a class in a given inheritance hierarchy is the number of classes in that hierarchy that derive directly from that class. The *rootedness* of a hierarchy is the number of roots in the hierarchy. The *depth*

177

of a hierarchy is the maximum depth of any class in the hierarchy. The *fanout* of a hierarchy is the maximum fanout of any class in the hierarchy.

Various well-meaning authors have advocated the design rules for inheritance hierarchies shown in Table 8.1. Obviously, because the first two rules contradict each other, not all of these rules can be well founded. In fact, *none* of these proposed rules is good advice universally. On the contrary, the best rootedness, depth, and fanout of a given library's inheritance hierarchy depend on the domain the library seeks to model and the properties (such as extensibility or efficiency) the library is intended to have. For some libraries, a singly rooted hierarchy is best; for other libraries, a multiply rooted hierarchy is best. For some libraries, large depth or large fanout would be best.

Table 8.1   Unfounded inheritance hierarchy design rules.

Singly rooted hierarchies are best.
Multiply rooted hierarchies are best.
The depth of a hierarchy should be no more than 7 ± 2.
The fanout of a hierarchy should be no more than 7 ± 2.

Suppose, for example, that we are designing a library of type fonts. (Sixteen-point Times Italic is an example of a font.) Perhaps the best design for this library will provide a common base class `Font` from which all font classes derive, directly or indirectly. The fanout of `Font` will almost certainly be at least as large as the number of font families we wish to provide. (Times is an example of a font family.) Attempting to make our library conform to an arbitrary limit on fanout would restrict senselessly the number of font families we could provide.

For a more complex example, suppose that we are designing a library whose classes model the various C++ language constructs — `if` statements, `for` loops, function definitions, constructor initializers, and so on. (In this class definition,

```
class X {
public:
    X() : i(0) {}
private:
    int i;
};
```

the i(0) is a constructor initializer.) Figure 8.1 shows part of a reasonable hierarchy for this library. Construct represents any C++ programming construct. One kind of construct is a statement (Statement). A statement is either a declaration (Decl) or an expression (Expr). Three kinds of expressions are if statements (If), for loops (For), and constructor initializers (Ctor_init). A declaration might declare a type (Type_decl) — a typedef (Typedef) or a class (Class). Otherwise, a declaration declares something other than a type (Nontype_decl). Nontype_decls are definitions (Defn) and functions declarations (Function_decl). A definition defines either data (Data_defn) or a function (Function_defn). Notice that a function definition is also a function declaration. Two kinds of function definitions are constructor (Ctor_defn) and destructor definitions (Dtor_defn). Even this simplified hierarchy is singly rooted and has a depth of 7; a real library for this domain would have an even deeper hierarchy. For this domain, a singly rooted, moderately deep hierarchy is a good design.

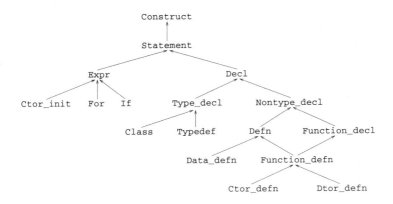

Figure 8.1   A C++ language construct hierarchy.

In a misguided effort to adhere to a limit on hierarchy depth, we might decide to collapse our hierarchy by eliminating some of the derivations. Two classes that might seem to be candidates for elimination are Ctor_defn and Dtor_defn. Suppose that we eliminate these classes and instead model all function definitions only by the class Function_defn. Suppose further that our original, deep design provides the following function, which returns the list of constructor initializers for a given constructor definition (using a class List that represents lists):

```
class Ctor_defn {
public:
    List<Ctor_init*> initializers() const;
    // ...
};
```

When we eliminate `Ctor_defn`, we must also move `initializers` up into `Function_defn`:

```
class Function_defn {
public:
    List<Ctor_init*> initializers() const;   // moved here
    // ...
};
```

Now we must decide what `Function_defn::initializers` will do when it is called on a `Function_defn` that is not a constructor definition. We might have `initializers` return an empty `List`, or we might give `initializers` the precondition that it not be called on any definition other than a constructor definition. Whichever design we choose, it will be legal for users to invoke `initializers` on a function definition that is not a constructor definition. With our original, deeper hierarchy, such an attempt was a compile-time error. Thus, attempting to reduce the depth of our hierarchy has caused us to create a less type-safe design. A deeper hierarchy was better.

Now suppose that we also wish to provide in our library a class `Parser`, representing a C++ parser:

```
class Parser {
public:
    Construct* parse(const char* code);
    // ...
};
```

The function `parse` builds a tree representing the C++ code in the null-terminated string `code`. Each node in the tree is an instance of one of the classes in our `Construct` hierarchy. The function `parse` returns a pointer to the root of the newly built tree.

Our library now has two roots — `Construct` and `Parser`. Suppose that we attempt to change our classes so that our library will be singly rooted, to conform to the first rule in Table 8.1. To do so, we shall have to derive both `Construct` and `Parser` from a common base class; let us call that class `Construct_or_Parser`. Because C++ language constructs and C++ parsers are such different kinds of things, `Construct_or_Parser` will almost certainly have no data members and probably will have no non-nice member functions. Because users of our library probably will never need to write a function that can take either a `Construct` or a `Parser` polymorphically, `Construct_or_Parser` would be useless — merely adding to the complexity of our library. For this version of our library, a multiply rooted hierarchy is better than a singly rooted one.

8.2 Hierarchy Styles

The design of a reusable library can be based on one of several inheritance hierarchy styles or on a combination of styles. The simplest and most efficient is the direct hierarchy. Interfaced hierarchies, interfaced hierarchies with object factories, and handle hierarchies confer several advantages over direct hierarchies — notably, they increase extensibility and link compatibility — but they have certain drawbacks.

8.2.1 Direct Hierarchies

Suppose that we are designing a consumer electronics library. Our library is to provide classes representing televisions (TVs), compact disc players, (CDs), personal computers (PCs), and so on. Suppose that all the electronic devices in our library have certain functions in common — they all have serial numbers and they can all be turned on, to name two. The simplest, most straightforward design for our library inherits all the electronic device classes from a common base class `CED` (short for *consumer electronic device*):

```
class CED {
public:
    String serial_number() const { return _serial_number; }
    virtual void turnon() = 0;
    // ...
private:
    String _serial_number;
    // ...
};
```

The implementation of `serial_number` is the same for all our electronic devices.

Here is TV:

```
class TV: public CED {
public:
    void turnon();
    void set_channel(int channel);
    int current_channel() const;
    // ...
};
```

TV implements the function turnon, declared pure virtual in CED, and provides functions specific to televisions (set_channel, current_channel, and so on). Classes for CD and PC are similar.

Part of the consumer electronic devices inheritance hierarchy is shown in Figure 8.2. This design is simple and easy to understand. It is also

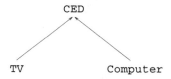

Figure 8.2   Inheritance hierarchy of consumer electronics library.

more efficient than the designs we shall present in the following sections. It has two disadvantages, however. First, it is not as extensible as a design that uses interface classes (see Section 3.2.1). Second, as we showed in Section 7.5, the odds are high that a change to the implementation of any of our classes will be link incompatible.

In the next three sections, we shall present alternative designs that increase extensibility and link compatibility at the cost of increased complexity and decreased efficiency. As always, the best design for a particular library will depend on the needs of the library's users.

8.2.2   Interface Hierarchies

We saw in Section 3.2.1 that interface classes can increase a library's extensibility. Figure 8.3 shows an interfaced version of part of our library's hierarchy.

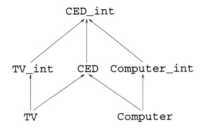

Figure 8.3   Interfaced version of consumer electronics library.

Here is the interface class `CED_int`:

```
class CED_int {
public:
    virtual String serial_number() const = 0;
    virtual void turnon() = 0;
    // ...
};
```

and here is the interface class `TV_int`:

```
class TV_int : public virtual CED_int {
public:
    virtual void set_channel(int channel) = 0;
    virtual int current_channel() const = 0;
    // ...
};
```

The common implementation of `serial_number` is defined in the noninterface class `CED`:

```
class CED : public virtual CED_int {
public:
    String serial_number() const { return _serial_number; }
    // ...
private:
    String _serial_number;
    // ...
};
```

Users who want, for example, to create a new kind of television with a completely different implementation from that of our TV class can now inherit from TV_int.

In addition to increasing extensibility, interface classes increase link compatibility. Notice that we can change the implementation of TV without breaking link compatibility for code that uses only TV_int and never uses TV directly. Fortunately, it is possible to write almost exclusively in terms of TV_int. Here, for example, is a function for channel surfing that is implemented using only TV_int:

```
void surf(TV_int& tv) {
    int i = tv.current_channel();
    while (!showing_program_viewer_likes(tv))
        tv.set_channel(++i);
}
```

Only when programmers need to create a TV object must they use the TV class:

```
TV_int* new_TV() {
    return new TV;   // TV, not TV_int
}
```

To make upgrading to new releases of our library as easy as possible, programmers can isolate all their code that uses our noninterface classes in as few files as possible and recompile only those files when they upgrade.

A hierarchy is *interfaced* if each of its classes is interfaced. If a library's hierarchy is interfaced, users can write almost all their code in terms of the library interface classes. Only when they need to create instances of library classes must programmers use the noninterface classes.

Interfaced hierarchies have several disadvantages compared to noninterfaced hierarchies. First, interfaced hierarchies are more complex than noninterfaced hierarchies. Programmers who do not care about extensibility or link compatibility will not like this added complexity. Further, interfaced hierarchies are typically somewhat harder to implement. Finally, they usually have many virtual derivations and virtual functions. For example, all the derivations in Figure 8.3 from the class CED_int and the function serial_number must be virtual. In the direct hierarchy of Section 8.2.1, there were no virtual derivations and serial_number was not virtual. Virtual derivations and virtual functions are less efficient than nonvirtual derivations and functions.

8.2.3   Object Factories

We saw in the previous section that an interfaced hierarchy provides link compatibility only for code that does not need to create instances of the classes in the hierarchy. To enable library users to write programs that will need no recompiling whatsoever to upgrade to a new release of the library, we can provide an *object factory* (also called a *kit*) along with our interfaced hierarchy. Here is an object factory for our consumer electronics library:

```
class CED_factory {
public:
    static TV_int* new_TV();
    static PC_int* new_PC();
    // ...
};
```

The parameter list of each factory function is usually the same as the parameter list of a constructor of the corresponding class. The definitions of the factory functions must be out of line:

```
TV_int* CED_factory::new_TV() {
    return new TV;
}

PC_int* CED_factory::new_PC() {
    return new PC;
}
```

Any changes to the implementations of a library's classes will be totally link compatible for programs that use only the library's object factory and interface classes.

Factories have two additional advantages besides increasing link compatibility. First, they can simplify the inheritance hierarchy that a library presents to its users. Suppose that part of our library's inheritance hierarchy looks like this:

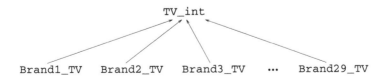

We can move all the Brand X_TV classes to the implementation of our library if we provide factory functions to create all the kinds of televisions:

```
class CED_factory {
public:
    enum TV_brand { Brand1, Brand2, /* ... */, Brand29 };
    static TV_int* new_TV(TV_brand brand);
    // ...
};
```

Many users will consider the library interface with a single enumerated type to be simpler than the library interface with a collection of classes.

Factories can also be used to hide some implementation decisions. Suppose that we wish to provide two kinds of television: high density and low density. Suppose further that we consider two alternative designs for our library. In the first design, instances of a single class represent both high-density and low-density televisions:

```
class TV : public virtual TV_int {
public:
    TV(bool high_density = false);
    // ...
};
```

In the second design, we represent high-density and low-density televisions with different classes:

```
class HDTV : public virtual TV_int {
public:
    // ...
};

class LDTV : public virtual TV_int {
public:
    // ...
};
```

Whichever design we choose, we can hide our decision from the library user by moving all noninterface classes to the implementation of our library and providing a factory:

```
class CED_factory {
public:
    static TV_int* new_TV(bool high_density = false);
    // ...
};
```

A person looking only at the interface classes and the factory cannot tell whether high-density and low-density televisions are represented by a single class or by two classes. Thus, we shall have given ourselves the flexibility to change the way we implement high-density and low-density televisions in a future release, should the need arise.

Providing library users only interface classes and a factory (and not providing noninterface classes) has several disadvantages. Because library objects then would always have to be created via the factory, all library objects would have to be in the free store. Allocating objects in the free store is less efficient than allocating objects in static storage or on the stack. Using objects in the free store is also more error prone. (Section 8.3.1 elaborates on the disadvantages of moving objects into the free store.) Another disadvantage of providing only interface classes and a factory is that programmers who could have used some of our noninterface classes to implement their own classes will be out of luck. In practice, a library should provide any noninterface classes whose omission would make user code too inefficient, error prone, or difficult to implement.

8.2.4   Handle Hierarchies

We saw in Sections 8.2.2 and 8.2.3 that interface classes and object factories can be used to provide link compatibility (among other things). An alternative way to provide link compatibility is to use handle classes. A *handle class* is a class whose instances contain only one data member, which is a pointer to some other object. Suppose, for example, that we implement TV as a handle and that we do not inherit TV from an interface class:

```
class TV_rep {
    // ...
};
class TV {
private:
    TV_rep* rep;  // the only data member
    // ...
};
```

Any change to the implementation of TV_rep will be link compatible for users of TV. The library documentation should state clearly which classes are handles and should remind the reader that link compatibility is guaranteed only for code that uses no library classes other than handle or interface classes.

Typically, every member function of a handle class simply forwards to the corresponding member function of the representation class:

```
class TV_rep {
public:
    int current_channel() const;
    // ...
};
```

```
class TV {
private:
    TV_rep* rep;
    // ...
public:
    int current_channel() const {
        return rep->current_channel();
    }
    // ...
};
```

Note that either one, but not both, of `TV_rep::current_channel` or `TV::current_channel` can be inline. Inlining both would defeat our purpose because compiled code for the implementation of the function would appear in users' object files, and changes to the implementation of `TV_rep` would require users to recompile.

Handle classes are less efficient than nonhandle classes even if all the member functions of the handle class are inline. Every call of a member function of `TV` is really an indirect call of the corresponding function in `TV_rep`.

To satisfy users who want link compatibility as well as users who want maximum efficiency, we can provide both the handle and the representation class. Providing both classes, however, renders the library interface more complex and the library itself harder to maintain. Hence, library writers usually hide representation classes in the library implementation.

Handle classes get more interesting when we try to implement all the classes in a hierarchy as handles. Suppose that we provide the hierarchy shown in Figure 8.4, and that we want all the classes in that hierarchy to be handles. Then the first thing we will do is create a representation hierarchy, as shown in Figure 8.5.

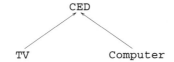

Figure 8.4   A hierarchy of handle classes.

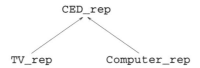

Figure 8.5   A hierarchy of representation classes.

Here is `CED_rep`:

```
class CED_rep {
public:
    String serial_number() const {
        return _serial_number;
    }
    virtual void turnon() = 0;
    // ...
private:
    String _serial_number;
};
```

Here is `TV_rep`:

```
class TV_rep :public CED_rep {
public:
    void turnon();
    void set_channel(int channel);
    int current_channel() const;
    // ...
};
```

Now we can implement our handle hierarchy. The class `CED` forwards to `CED_rep`:

```
class CED {
public:
    String serial_number() const {
        return rep->serial_number();
    }
    void turnon() {
        rep->turnon();
    }
    // ...
protected:
    CED(CED_rep* r) : rep(r) {}
    CED_rep* rep;
};
```

(Remember that at least one of `CED::serial_number` or `CED_rep::serial_number` must be out of line.) Although **turnon** is virtual in the representation hierarchy, it need not be virtual in the handle hierarchy, because the implementation shown for `CED::turnon` is correct for all the handle classes. Further, because `CED_rep` is an abstract class, `CED` provides no public constructors; the protected constructor shown will assist in constructing derived class objects.

Here is the implementation of **TV**:

```
class TV: public CED {
public:
    TV() : CED(new TV_rep) {}
    void set_channel(int channel) {
        ((TV_rep*)rep)->set_channel(channel);
    }
    // ...
};
```

We must downcast `rep` before forwarding `set_channel`. The downcast is legal because `CED_rep` is a nonvirtual base class of `TV_rep`; it is safe because the **TV** constructor initializes `rep` to a `TV_rep`. (Any derived class of **TV** should set `rep` to a `TV_rep` or to a class derived from `TV_rep`.) If `CED_rep` had been a virtual base class of `TV_rep`, then we would have had to use one of the downcasting mechanisms discussed in Exercise 8.9.

Handle hierarchies are not as extensible as direct or interface hierarchies (see Exercise 8.10). To provide some extensibility in a hierarchy of handle classes, we can add interface classes, as shown in Figure 8.6. This hierarchy is the same as that of Figure 8.3, with one important difference: In Figure 8.3, the noninterface classes were not handles; in Figure 8.6, they are. To provide complete link compatibility for users of the hierarchy of Figure 8.3, we had to provide an object factory; users who wanted link compatibility were able to create instances of our classes only in the free store, via the factory. The hierarchy of Figure 8.6, on the other hand, provides link compatibility without an object factory. Users can therefore create instances of our classes wherever they wish — in static storage, on the stack, or in the free store. (The underlying representation objects will be in the free store, but that is an implementation detail and is not visible to the user.) Thus, for users who want link compatibility, interfaced handle hierarchies are preferable to interfaced (nonhandle) hierarchies with factories.

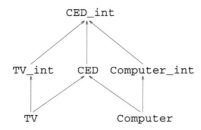

Figure 8.6   Interfaced version of the handle hierarchy of Figure 8.4.

An interfaced handle hierarchy has two disadvantages over an interfaced (nonhandle) hierarchy with a factory. First, the interfaced handle hierarchy is more difficult to implement. Designing and implementing the dual handle and representation hierarchies for a real library is tedious and time consuming. The handle design is also more difficult to maintain because changes often must be applied to both hierarchies.

Second, an interfaced handle hierarchy, although more extensible than a noninterfaced handle hierarchy, is still less extensible than an interfaced (nonhandle) hierarchy with a factory. Suppose, for example, that our users wish to model a new kind of computer, a personal computer with a math coprocessor, called Math_PC, and that Math_PC can reuse most of the implementation of PC. In an interfaced (nonhandle) hierarchy with a factory, we can simply provide the class PC and design it inheritably; the user will derive Math_PC from PC. With an interfaced handle hierarchy, we must design both PC and PC_rep inheritably (PC, which is a simple handle, probably does not require much effort to be inheritable). Further, we must provide users with both the handle and the representation hierarchies. The user must then derive Math_PC from PC and Math_PC_rep from PC_rep, making sure to implement all the forwarding functions correctly.

8.3   Templates or Inheritance?

Templates and inheritance are both powerful features of C++. Unfortunately, there is some confusion among C++ programmers about whether to base a design for a class hierarchy on templates or on inheritance. Library designers sometimes use inheritance when use of templates would produce a better design.

Consider the design of container classes. Throughout this book, we have been designing container classes using a template argument to specify the type of contained value. Recall our Stack template of Sections 2.6 and 5.1:

```
template<class T>
class Stack {
public:
    void push(const T& t);
    T pop();
    // ...
};
```

Another way that some people have designed containers (especially before templates were part of the C++ language) is to provide an abstract base class and require that the element type inherit from that class. For example, here is a stack class that requires that its element type inherit from an abstract class named Stackable:

```
class IBStack : public Stackable {
public:
    void push(Stackable* s);
    Stackable* pop();
    // ...
};
```

We name our class `IBStack` (for *inheritance-based stack*) to avoid confusion in this discussion with the template-based `Stack`. The function `push` inserts the value `s` onto the top of the `IBStack`; `pop` removes the top value from the stack and returns it. We derive `IBStack` from `Stackable` because users might want to construct an `IBStack` of `IBStacks` (actually, an `IBStack` of pointers to `IBStack`). A user who wants to create an `IBStack` of some type `Widget` (actually, pointers to `Widget`) must derive `Widget` from `Stackable`:

```
class Widget : public Stackable {
    // ...
};
```

This inheritance-based stack has several serious drawbacks that the template-based stack does not. We leave it to the reader (see Exercise 8.11) to show that `Stack` does not have any of the drawbacks of `IBStack` discussed in the following sections.

8.3.1   Pointer Manipulation

The first serious drawback of inheritance-based containers is that they require users to manipulate pointers. (The `IBStack` `push` and `pop` operations take and return pointers.) Unfortunately, pointer manipulation is error prone. Consider the following code:

```
IBStack create_stack() {
    IBStack s;
    Widget w;
    s.push(&w);
    return s;  // oops
}
```

The `IBStack` returned by `create_stack` will contain an invalid pointer to what used to be `w`. The lifetime of an `IBStack` should be no longer than the shortest lifetime of any of the objects pointed to by its elements. It is difficult for a library to prevent users from making lifetime errors.

To reduce the risk of creating an invalid `IBStack`, many users will insert into an `IBStack` only objects allocated in the free store. This practice typically will force the user to move into the free store objects that would otherwise have been in static or stack storage. For example, such users would rewrite `create_stack` as follows:

```
IBStack create_stack() {
    IBStack s;
    Widget* w = new Widget;
    s.push(w);
    return s;   // ok
}
```

Moving objects into the free store increases the risk of a memory leak. The caller of this version of `create_stack`, for example, must remember to delete (eventually) all objects pointed to by the returned stack. The implementor of a program that manipulates many inheritance-based containers might have trouble preventing leaks.

8.3.2 The Derivation Requirement

Suppose that a user would like to create an `IBStack` of integers. Such a user might like to do something like this:

```
int* i;
IBStack int_stack;
int_stack.push(i);   // error
```

Unfortunately, this code is illegal because `int` does not inherit from `Stackable`. To manipulate a stack of integers, the user must write a new class:

```
class Int : public Stackable {
    int val;
    // ...
};
```

Now the user can create an `IBStack` of `Int`s:

```
Int* i = new Int;
IBStack int_stack;
int_stack.push(i);
```

This solution is easier said than done, however. Writing an `Int` class that models the `int` built-in type is surprisingly difficult (see Exercise 2.8). Furthermore, writing `Int` probably would be just the beginning: The user might also need `Bool`, `Char`, `Short`, `Long`, `Float`, and `Double`.

Having to derive from `Stackable` presents a problem not only with built-in types but also with user-defined types. Not all classes in the universe will derive from `Stackable`. Many classes will be designed by people who have never heard of `Stackable`, and many people who know of `Stackable` will nevertheless decide not to inherit their classes from `Stackable`. For example, the designers of other C++ libraries might not want to compile their libraries with ours.

Consider a class `Fidget` that does not derive from `Stackable`. There are two things that the user of `IBStack` could do to make it possible to stack `Fidget`s. The first alternative is to change the declaration of `Fidget`, as follows:

```
class Fidget : public Stackable {  // added derivation
    // ...
};
```

Of course, it is rarely possible to add a new base class to a given class without also having to change the interface or implementation of the derived class in other ways.

Even if the programmer knows how to change `Fidget`, adding a new base class is not a possibility for programmers who do not have access to the source code for `Fidget`. Such programmers will have to implement the second alternative — deriving a `Stackable` version of `Fidget`:

```
class Stackable_fidget : public Fidget, public Stackable {
    // ...
};
```

Although this approach works in theory, consider the programmer who uses five libraries, each of which contains its own analogue of `Stackable`, and each of which contains at least 10 classes that the user wants to be insertable into other libraries' containers. The task before such a user is daunting, and the resulting heavy use of multiple inheritance will, on most systems, yield inefficient code.

8.3.3   Implementing Unneeded Functions

Consider a library that provides several inheritance-based container classes — `IBStack`, `IBSet`, and `IBSorted_list`, for example. To keep the number of derivations required of users manageable (see Exercise 8.12), the library designer probably will use the same abstract base class, here named `Containable`, for all containers:

```
class IBStack : public Containable {
public:
    void push(Containable*);
    // ...
};

class IBSet : public Containable {
public:
    void insert(Containable*);
    // ...
};
```

Suppose that `IBSet` requires inserted objects to have a `hash` function, `IBSorted_list` requires inserted objects to have a `compare` function, and so on. Then these functions must be declared in `Containable`:

```
class Containable {
public:
    virtual long hash() const = 0;
    virtual int compare(const Containable*) const = 0;
    // ...
};
```

But now a user who wishes to insert `Widgets` into an `IBStack` must define `Widget::hash`, `Widget::compare`, and perhaps others — even though `IBStack` does not need these functions. Most users, when forced to implement functions their programs do not need, will take the easy way out:

```
class Widget : public Containable {
public:
    long hash() const {
        assert(0);
        return 0;
    }
    int compare(const Containable*) const {
        assert(0);
        return 0;
    }
    // ...
};
```

Unfortunately, if these functions are called accidentally, a run-time error results rather than a compile-time error.

Libraries should not require users to implement unneeded functions.

8.4   Summary

The appropriate rootedness, depth, and fanout for an inheritance hierarchy depend on the domain the hierarchy is intended to model and on the desired properties of the hierarchy.

Although a direct inheritance hierarchy is easiest style to implement and understand as well as the most efficient, interfaced hierarchies, object factories, and handle hierarchies facilitate link compatibility between releases of a library. Further, interfaced hierarchies increase a library's extensibility. Table 8.2 summarizes the most important differences among the hierarchy styles discussed in Section 8.2. As always, no single design is best for all libraries. Library designers must decide which is the best choice for their library and their users.

Table 8.2   Tradeoffs of hierarchy styles.

Hierarchy Style	Complexity	Efficiency	Extensibility	Link Compatibility
Direct	simple	maximal	mediocre	minimal
Interfaced	complex	reduced	good	partial
Interfaced + Factory	complex	reduced	good	total
Handle	simple	reduced	poor	total
Interfaced Handle	complex	reduced	good	total

Library designers should be careful not to use inheritance when use of templates would produce a better design.

Exercises

8.1   Suppose that you are designing a library intended for multimedia applications — that is, applications that manipulate various kinds of media, such as text, audio, video, and synced media. (A *synced* medium is a synchronized combination of two or more media — a motion picture with a soundtrack, for example.) Show a direct inheritance hierarchy for a multimedia library with the classes Medium, Text, Audio, Video, and Synced.

8.2   Now suppose that your multimedia library (described in Exercise 8.1) will provide digital (as opposed to analog) implementations of audio, video, and synced media. Show an interfaced hierarchy for your multimedia library with concrete classes representing the required digital implementations.

8.3   A reasonable implementation of the direct hierarchy of Exercise 8.1 will have factored common parts of the implementation of `Audio` and `Video` into `Medium`. Consider a new medium, `Olfactory`, for representing aromas.

   a.   Assuming that the implementation of `Olfactory` will have little in common with the implementations of `Audio` and `Video`, show how you would add a digital implementation of `Olfactory` to the direct multimedia hierarchy you designed for Exercise 8.1.

   b.   Show how you would add classes for digital and analog implementations of `Olfactory` to your interfaced multimedia hierarchy of Exercise 8.2.

8.4   Write an object factory for your interfaced multimedia library of Exercise 8.2.

8.5   Recall that handle hierarchies can be interfaced or noninterfaced.

   a.   Show a noninterfaced handle hierarchy for the multimedia library of Exercise 8.1.

   b.   Suppose that an audio medium has a virtual function `volume` that returns the current volume of the audio object, stored in a private data member `_volume`. Show the bodies of the `volume` functions in your handle and representation classes for an audio medium. Remember to show whether the functions are `const` and whether they are inline.

   c.   What are the advantages and disadvantages of noninterfaced handle hierarchies over direct hierarchies?

   d.   Interface the handle hierarchy you designed for part a.

   e.   What are the advantages and disadvantages of interfaced handle hierarchies over interfaced hierarchies without handles?

8.6   Suppose that you are designing an on-line reservations system for travel agents. Your inheritance hierarchy will include the following classes derived from `Reservation`:

`Car_rental_reservation`	`Limo_reservation`
`Lodging_reservation`	`Airline_reservation`
`Train_reservation`	`Cruise_ship_reservation`

Show how you can use an object factory to simplify your library's interface.

8.7   Suppose that in some library you wish to model two kinds of audio media — tape and compact disc (CD) — and that you are considering two design possibilities. Objects representing tapes and CDs could be instances of a single class:

```
class Audio_medium : public Medium {
public:
    Audio_medium(bool tape = false);
    // ...
};
```

Alternatively, audio tapes and CDs could be represented by different classes:

```
class Tape : public Medium { /* ... */ };

class CD : public Medium { /* ... */ };
```

Show how you can use an object factory to hide your design decision from your users.

8.8   Show how to use an object factory to solve the "complicated constructor" problem discussed in Exercise 3.8 in a way that does not require the derivation of any new class such as `Childrens_toothpaste`.

8.9   The downcast in the class `TV` on page 190 would not be legal if `CED_rep` were a virtual base class of `TV_rep`. In this exercise, we consider alternative designs for which virtual inheritance will not present a problem.

    a.   Show how to replace the cast on page 190 with a use of the `dynamic_cast` construct. What is the principal disadvantage of this approach?

    b.   Let $\{X_1, X_2, \ldots, X_n\}$ be the set of classes that directly or indirectly inherit from `CED_rep`. Consider the following functions:

```
class CED_rep {
public:
    virtual X1* cast_to_X1();
    virtual X2* cast_to_X2();
    // ...
    virtual Xn* cast_to_Xn();
    // ...
};
```

If the function `cast_to_Xi` is called on an object of type Xi or a class derived from Xi, then `cast_to_Xi` returns a pointer to that object; otherwise it returns 0. Show how to implement these functions without using the `dynamic_cast` operator. Explain why your implementation will work even when used with virtual inheritance.

c. Is the design in part b extensible? Why or why not?

d. Show how to collapse the `CED` representation hierarchy into a single class so that the cast on page 190 can simply be removed. What are two disadvantages of this approach?

e. Suppose that we replace the `CED::rep` data member on page 190 with a pair of data members:

```
class CED {
private:
    void* rep;
    int reptype;
    // ...
};
```

Show how, using these data members, the handle and representation hierarchies can be redesigned such that no downcasting is required.

f. In what way is the design in part e inefficient and nonextensible?

g. If you were implementing the `CED` library and if `TV_rep` were to derive virtually from `CED_rep`, which of the designs described in parts a, b, d, and e would you use?

8.10 On page 190 we said that handle hierarchies are not as extensible as interfaced hierarchies. Explain why they are not.

8.11 Recall the `Stack` template of Sections 2.6 and 5.1.

a. Show that `Stack` does not have any of the drawbacks of `IBStack` discussed in Section 8.3.

b. What is one drawback of `Stack` that `IBStack` does not have?

c. Is the single drawback of `Stack` worse than the sum of the drawbacks of `IBStack`? Justify your answer.

8.12 Show that using a different abstract base class for each of the inheritance-based containers mentioned in Section 8.3.3 might cause many derivations to be necessary in user code.

References and Further Reading

Martin [Mar91], Nackman and Barton [NB94], and Linton and Pan [LP94] discuss the use of interface classes in a C++ library as well as the associated inefficiencies. Linton [Lin92] presents an example of an object factory.

Gorlen, Orlow, and Plexico [GOP90] document an example of a C++ library that provides inheritance-based container classes. Carroll [Car95] discusses the disadvantages of inheritance-based containers in more detail.

Exercise 8.9 was inspired by a discussion with Rich Kempinski, Deborah McGuinness, and Elia Weixelbaum.

9 Portability

> *Jewels are handed down from age to age;*
> *less portable valuables disappear.*
>> — Lord Stanley

The more portable code is, the more reusable it is. In this chapter, we discuss the major issues that affect the portability of C++ code: the changing state of the C++ language definition, undefined behaviors, implementation-defined and unspecified behaviors, implementation dependencies, template instantiation, run-time libraries, and other system-dependencies.

9.1 Should You Write Portable Code?

For many programming projects, portability is not a concern; for others, it is a primary goal. No nontrivial code works on every platform. Code is *portable* to a platform if the code can easily be made to work properly on that platform. Changing code to make it work on a given platform is called *porting* it to that platform.

When we design code, we have (or we should have) some idea of the range of platforms on which we want the code to run. We might care only that the code work on the nearly identical platforms sitting on the desks of the three programmers on our development team, we might want our code to work on all platforms running the Windows operating system, or we might want it to work on several different kinds of hardware running several different operating systems.

9.1.1   Tradeoffs of Portability

Portability often trades off with efficiency and ease of implementation. Specifically, portable code that is easy to implement is often not efficient enough on one or more platforms. Suppose, for example, that we wish to clear the n bytes starting at location p in memory. We might write

```
memset(p, n, 0);
```

This code is portable to every platform that provides the ANSI/ISO C++ library, in which memset will be defined. Now suppose that the section of code in which we need to clear this memory is time critical. We might want to call the function bzero, which is provided on some platforms and clears memory faster than memset:

```
bzero(p, n);   // faster than memset(p, n, 0)
```

The function bzero, however, probably will not be in the ANSI/ISO C++ library, so calling bzero would make our code less portable.

To maintain portability and get efficiency on systems where bzero is available, we might write

```
#ifdef HASBZERO
    bzero(p, n);
#else
    memset(p, n, 0);
#endif
```

We then ensure somehow that HASBZERO gets defined on platforms that provide bzero. Alternatively, if we call bzero in several places, we might write a version of bzero for use on platforms that do not provide it:

bzero.h:

```
#include <stdlib.h>
#include <memory.h>

#ifndef HASBZERO
inline void* bzero(char* p, size_t n) {
    return memset(p, n, 0);
}
#endif
```

If all platforms that provide bzero declare it in *stdlib.h*, then anywhere we need to clear memory we can write

```
#include <bzero.h>    // bzero.h #includes stdlib.h
// ...
bzero(p, n);
```

This code is both portable and efficient. It was, however, not as easy to write as a simple call to `memset`. Real code that is ported to many platforms can easily become complex and inelegant.

9.1.2   Object Code and Build Procedure Portability

When we think of portability, we usually think of source code, but portability also applies to object code. Specifically, a piece of object code is portable to a platform if it can be copied to that platform and used without change. As the `memset` example showed, programmers can take measures to increase source code portability; programmers can do nothing to increase object code portability. Whether object code is portable depends on the platforms in question, not on the source code from which the object code was produced.

Object code portability is rare in practice. Hence, if we wish to produce object code for our library for a new platform P, usually we must port our source code to P and then build it on P. This procedure requires that the build procedure for our library be portable. If our code is simple enough, the build procedure will involve only a few commands, but if our code is large and complex, the build procedure will be correspondingly large and complex. To build code that uses our `bzero` function, for example, the build procedure will have to know whether `bzero` is available on P and will have to set `HASBZERO` appropriately. Complex code might have many more such dependencies. We would like not only our source code but also our build procedures to be portable. Unfortunately, writing portable build procedures for complex bodies of code can be difficult or impossible because of the wide variation in build tools available on different platforms.

In the following sections, we shall discuss issues that complicate writing portable C++ source code and build procedures.

9.2   The Evolving Language Definition

As of this writing, C++ has not yet been standardized. The ANSI/ISO standard is scheduled for completion in 1996. Until then, there is a de facto standard: *The Annotated C++ Reference Manual* [ES90], often called the ARM. The ARM contains the base document for the ANSI/ISO standard as well as extensive annotations and commentary explaining the rationale for many of the language design decisions.

The first C++ translator, *cfront*, was originally written at AT&T Bell Laboratories and was later developed and marketed by Novell's UNIX System Group under the official name C++ Language System. The translator *cfront* was also considered a de facto standard for some time.

9.2.1 Controversy

The ARM and *cfront* do not always agree. Other existing implementations of C++ differ in their interpretations of some language constructs. Some differences among implementations and the ARM are controversial. Consider this code:

```
class A {
private:
    class B { /* ... */ };
    B* f();
};

A::B* A::f() { /* ... */ }    // legal?
```

A strict reading of the ARM implies that the commented line is not legal, because the private type B is referenced outside its containing class A. The construct is allowed by *cfront* — to enable users to define f out of line — but some other implementations disallow the construct. This conflict will be resolved by ANSI/ISO.

Note, incidentally, that even after the ANSI/ISO standard is published officially, ANSI/ISO-conformant code will not be guaranteed to be portable. It will take a while — possibly several years — for C++ implementations to catch up to the standard.

9.2.2 Completeness of Implementations

Many current C++ implementations do not implement the entire language. Not all C++ compilers implement templates and exception handling, both of which were described in 1990. Until all (or most) C++ implementations become ANSI/ISO conformant, C++ programmers will need to write code that conforms to the subset of C++ that is supported by all implementations to which the programmers want their code to be portable. As of this printing, not all C++ implementations support the newer language features, including exception handling, run-time type information,

covariance of member function return type, namespaces, the type `bool`, the
`mutable` keyword, the new cast syntax (`static_cast`, `reinterpret_cast`,
and `const_cast`), default arguments to templates, and template arguments to templates. Further, some C++ implementations do not implement
nested classes fully:

```
class A {
public:
    class B;        // implemented?
    class C {
        void f();
    };
};

void A::C::f() { }    // implemented?
```

The incomplete declaration of the nested class `B` and the definition of the
member function `f` of the nested class `C` are not implemented by all C++
compilation systems. Some implementations that do support these constructs do not support the template version (that is, the code that would
result from changing `A` to a class template). Finally, a few C++ implementations still do not support templates at all (and those that do present an
entire category of portability problems, as we shall discuss in Section 9.7).

Most implementations of C++ are incomplete as of this writing; nevertheless, some implementations provide extensions to C++. Most versions
of C++ running on personal computers, for example, define `near` and `far`
as keywords that allow programmers to work around the unfortunate designs of certain processors used in those systems. Programmers who use
extensions should be careful that they are not preventing their code from
being portable to platforms on which they will someday want it to run.

9.3 Undefined Behavior

For certain usages, the ANSI/ISO C++ standard will impose no requirements on the behavior of a C++ implementation. For example, the result
of a left-shift or right-shift operation (`<<` or `>>`) will be undefined if the
right operand is negative or if the right operand is greater than or equal to
the number of bits in the left operand. The effect of calling a pure virtual
function from a constructor for the object being constructed will also be
undefined, unless explicit qualification is used.

There are about a dozen constructs with undefined behavior in the
C++ language definition. The response of a C++ compilation system to
a program containing such a construct may, according to the standard, be

anything. Given such a program as input, a compiler may do any of the following:

- Produce a diagnostic.
- Abort.
- Remove all the files in the file system (although any compilation system that did that would not survive for long).
- Produce neither an error message nor a warning and generate executable code.

Further, if the compilation system produces executable code, that code may do anything. It may

- Yield the results the programmer expected.
- Yield incorrect results.
- Abort.
- Remove all the files in the file system.

Unfortunately, few C++ implementations notify a programmer when a program has undefined behavior. To produce portable C++ code, you must be careful to avoid writing undefined constructs.

An area of particular concern for code that must be portable is memory layout — sizes and alignments of objects and pointer and address manipulation. Many C++ programmers think of the address space of an executing program as a contiguous sequence of bytes, each of which is addressable by a char* or void* variable set to the appropriate value. There are many platforms, however, that do not conform to this simple model. Code that depends on this model will not be portable to such platforms.

9.3.1 Alignment and Padding

In C++, many types have alignment restrictions. Consider the following:

```
char x[sizeof(int)];
int* p = (int*)x;
*p = 0;
```

If the array x does not reside in memory on a boundary allowed for type int, the third statement will have undefined behavior (it probably will abort.)

For maximum portability, code must not rely on assumptions about the internal layout of objects that are not guaranteed by the language definition. This code, for example,

```
int i;
char* p = (char*)&i;
```

is not guaranteed to make p point to the least significant byte (or any other particular byte) of i.

Now consider this code:

```
static union {
    int i;
    int bits: 32;
};

bits ^= 1;
```

Even if we know that this code will be run on a machine on which there are 32 bits in an int, there is no guarantee that the assignment statement sets the least significant bit (or any other particular bit) of i.

Further, code that must be portable should not assume anything about the internal padding of class objects. Here, for example,

```
struct X {
    char c1;
    char c2;
};
int main() {
    X x;
    char* p = &x.c1;
    ++p;
    // ...
}
```

there is no guarantee that after the increment p points to x.c2.

Attempts to overlay different **structs** are fraught with portability problems. Consider this code, which attempts to overlay **structs** X and Y:

```
struct X {
    char c1;
    char c2;
};
```

```
struct Y {
    int bits: 8;
    char c2;
};

int main() {
    X x;
    Y* y = (Y*)&x;
    y->c2 = 0;
    // ...
}
```

Even if we know that this code will be run on a machine on which there are eight bits in a char, there is no guarantee that the assignment to y->c2 clears the c2 field of x.

9.3.2   Address Manipulation

Contrary to popular belief, the C++ language definition does not guarantee that a variable of type void* can point to an arbitrary location in a program's address space. In particular, pointers to functions cannot be converted to void* portably:

```
void g();

int main() {
    void* q = (void*)g;  // nonportable
    // ...
}
```

An attempt to convert a function pointer to the type void* will work only on platforms on which sizeof(void*) is large enough to hold a function pointer. A library that contains such a conversion will compile and execute properly on some platforms, will compile and have bizarre behavior on other platforms, and will fail to compile on still other platforms.

Some programmers try to use long variables to store and manipulate memory addresses, but such use is nonportable — a long might not be big enough to hold a pointer. After this code executes

```
char x[10];
long addr = (long)x;
char* p = (char*)addr;
```

p is not guaranteed to point to x[0]. On many platforms, it will not.

9.4   Legal, Nonportable Code

C++ inherits from the programming language C many implementation-defined and unspecified behaviors and adds a few new ones. Although C++ programs may rely legally on implementation-defined or unspecified behaviors, code that does so will not be maximally portable. Unfortunately, it is easy to write code with such dependencies unintentionally.

9.4.1   Implementation-Defined Behavior

The C++ language has more than 40 implementation-defined constructs. For example, the result of a right-shift operation (>>) is implementation defined when it is not undefined (see Section 9.3) and when the first operand is a signed type with a negative value. The operation may be either a logical right shift (the most significant bits will be zero filled) or a signed right shift. A C++ implementation is required to specify the behavior it implements for the appearance of each implementation-defined construct in a program. The behavior of programs containing such constructs may vary when compiled with different C++ implementations.

Whether char is signed or unsigned is also implementation-defined. This code

```
char c;
// ...
c >>= 1;
```

will clear the sign bit of c if char is unsigned or if operator>> is defined as logical right shift, but the sign bit will be propagated if char is signed and operator>> is defined as arithmetic right shift.

The complete set of implementation-defined behaviors is given in the ARM and will also be given in the ANSI/ISO standard. Unfortunately, few C++ implementations notify a programmer when the program being built relies on an implementation-defined construct. Thus, the burden falls on C++ programmers who wish to write portable code to be careful to avoid writing such constructs.

9.4.2   Unspecified Behavior

C++ leaves the behavior for at least six program constructs unspecified. Whereas a C++ implementation presented with a construct for which behavior is undefined may do anything, the ANSI/ISO C++ standard will list the possible behaviors for constructs for which behavior is unspecified. A

C++ implementation is *not* required to document which behavior it implements for the appearance of such a construct in a program.

For example, the order of evaluation of arguments to functions is unspecified. Thus, given the function `print_args` defined as follows

```
void print_args(int arg1, int arg2) {
    cout << arg1 << arg2 <<endl;
    return;
}
```

and this call to `print_args`

```
int i = 0;
print_args(++i, i);
```

the output might be either

        1 0

or

        1 1

A C++ implementation need not say which output it will produce. A single implementation may behave differently on different function calls.

The order of initialization of global objects defined in different translation units is also unspecified. The failure of the language to specify this ordering can cause difficulties for library writers. Section 12.1 will discuss this problem at greater length as well as what library writers can do about initialization.

A program that relies on unspecified behavior might work as intended fortuitously when built and executed on a particular platform. Suppose, for example, that our program consists of two translation units, f and g, and that it contains an initialization dependency such that the program works correctly only if the global variables defined in f are initialized before the global variables defined in g. Suppose that we link the program as follows:

```
% link f.obj g.obj
```

If our compilation system has the property that global variables in translation units are initialized in the order that those units are specified to the link command, then our program will work when built with this compilation system. When we try to port our program to another platform that has a different compilation system, chaos might ensue when we run the program.

C++ programmers who want their code to be portable should be careful to avoid relying on unspecified behavior.

9.5   Implementation Dependencies

The C++ language definition does not, of course, say anything about how
the language must be implemented. (The ARM describes many commonly
used implementation techniques, but none of these techniques is mandated.)
C++ programmers who wish to write portable code should avoid relying
on details of their particular C++ implementation.

To understand why a programmer might be tempted to rely on an implementation detail, consider the following code:

f.c:

```
void f(int i) {
    // ...
}

void f(char c) {
    // ...
}
```

main.c:

```
void f(int);
void f(char);

int main() {
    f(0);
    f('0');
    // ...
}
```

When this program is linked, each reference to f in *main.c* must call the
appropriate instance of f defined in *f.c*. To ensure that that happens, all
current implementations of C++ encode the types of the parameters of a
function in the function's name in the object code. For example, a C++
implementation might use the encoded names f__Fi and f__Fc for f(int)
and f(char), respectively. Encoded function names vary from compilation
system to compilation system, or even from one release of a system to
the next. Thus, a programmer who relied on a particular name-encoding
scheme would be writing nonportable code.

Suppose, however, that our compiler is generating egregiously inefficient
code for the two definitions of f, and suppose that we know how to write
better code in some language other than C++, say C. Then we might be
tempted to replace the definitions of f in *f.c* with the following C code:

```
/* C code */
void f__Fi(int i) {
    /* efficient C code */
}

void f__Fc(char c) {
    /* efficient C code */
}
```

Rewriting the code this way would be quick and easy; unfortunately, it would not be portable. To implement the more efficient code portably, we must first change the names of the C functions (see Exercise 9.5) to names such as the following:

```
/* C code */
void f_int(int i) { /* ... */ }
void f_char(char c) { /* ... */ }
```

Next, we rewrite the C++ definitions of f as follows:

```
extern "C" {
    void f_int(int i);
    void f_char(char c);
}
void f(int i) { f_int(i); }
void f(char c) { f_char(c); }
```

Notice, as usual, that the portable code took more effort to write.

9.6   Portable Data Files

Often, we need data files to be portable across platforms. For portability, a data file should be read in the same way it was written. Consider, for example, this struct:

```
struct X {
    char c1;
    char c2;
};
```

Suppose that we write a value of type X to a file as follows:

```
X x;
ofstream f("datafile");
f.write((const char*)&x, sizeof(x));
```

Then we should read that value using the same type and the corresponding read function:

```
X x;
ifstream f("datafile");
f.read((char*)&x, sizeof(x));
```

This approach guarantees that if the following conditions are met then the read operation will read the value that was written:

- The programs containing the write and read operations were compiled with the same C++ compilation system or with compilers that generate object code with the same alignments and padding.
- The write and read are executed on the same platform.
- Both the write and the read operations succeed.

This approach does *not* guarantee, however, that a file written on one platform will be read properly on another. If the external representation of X is different on the two platforms, the read will not recover the correct value.

One way to make data files portable across platforms is to write and read data one byte at a time, in a predetermined order. For example, if we write X as follows

```
X x;
ofstream f("datafile");
f.write(&x.c1, 1);
f.write(&x.c2, 1);
```

and we read X as follows

```
X x;
ifstream f("datafile");
f.read(&x.c1, 1);
f.read(&x.c2, 1);
```

then a data file written on platform P will be portable to any platform that has the same external representation for char values as P. Of course, if X contained any nonchar data members, we would have to write and read recursively each of those one byte at a time in a predetermined order (see Exercises 9.2 through 9.4).

The principal tradeoff of this one-byte-at-a-time technique for making data files portable is run time. This code

```
f.write((const char*)&x, sizeof(x));
```

probably executes faster than this code

```
f.write((const char*)&x.c1, 1);
f.write((const char*)&x.c2, 1);
```

In practice, the additional overhead for writing and reading one byte at a time is usually not large enough to prohibit use of the technique.

9.7 Template Instantiation

The template instantiation mechanism on users' platforms will affect the design and implementation of a C++ library. Some instantiation mechanisms require that a library's source code be organized in a certain way if the library contains templates in either its interface or its implementation. If we are preinstantiating any templates (see Section 4.2.2), the library's build procedure must know how to use the instantiator. Unfortunately, instantiators vary widely. Thus, writing code that is portable to more than one instantiator can be difficult, if not impossible. Designers of C++ code intended for reuse must understand the various template instantiation mechanisms their potential users will invoke to build and use the libraries. In the following sections, we discuss various kinds of template instantiation mechanisms.

9.7.1 Automatic Instantiators

The ANSI/ISO definition of C++ probably will require that a C++ programming environment be able to instantiate automatically all the template specializations (recall the definition of *specialization* from page ix) used by a program being built. Suppose that our library provides the following two templates:

List.h:

```
template<class T>
class List {
public:
    void insert(const T& t);
    //...
};
```

Hashtable.h:

```
template<class T>
class Hashtable {
public:
    Hashtable();
    void insert(const T& t);
private:
    List<T> the_table[1024];
    //...
};
```

A `List<T>` is a list of values of type `T`. A `Hashtable<T>` is a fixed-size hash table of values of type `T`; the hash table uses open chaining (that is, when more than one value hashes to the same location, the values are kept on a list). The implementation of `Hashtable` uses a fixed-size array of `Lists`, `the_table`.

Suppose that a user of our library creates a `Hashtable<Widget>`, where `Widget` is one of the user's classes. An automatic instantiator must detect that the containing program uses both `Hashtable<Widget>` and `List<Widget>` and must instantiate everything that is needed from both classes.

There are many ways to design an automatic instantiator. The following two sections discuss two frequently used designs. (Another design is discussed in Exercise 9.9.)

Compile-Time Instantiators

In each translation unit, a compile-time instantiator instantiates all the template specializations that that translation unit uses, directly or indirectly. Compile-time instantiators typically require that the user explicitly `#include` any files needed to perform the instantiation (unlike link-time instantiators, which we shall discuss in the next subsection).

Suppose that `Hashtable::insert` calls `List::insert`:

```
template<class T>
void Hashtable<T>::insert(const T& t) {
    int i;
    //...
    the_table[i].insert(t);   // calls List::insert
    //...
}
```

If some user's translation unit calls `Hashtable<Widget>::insert`, a compile-time template instantiator will generate in the object code for that translation unit the definitions of `Hashtable<Widget>::insert`, `List<Widget>::insert`, and any other specializations those functions use, directly or indirectly.

Of course, an effect of generating in each translation unit all the specializations directly or indirectly used by that translation unit is that the object files for several translation units linked into a program might have duplicate definitions. When the program is linked, only one copy from each duplicated definition should be incorporated into the executable program. Thus, compile-time instantiators typically come with special linkers that strip out duplicate specializations.

A big drawback of compile-time instantiators is efficiency. If a certain specialization is generated in n translation units, it is compiled n times and n copies are made of it. For developers of large programs that use templates heavily, this duplicated time and space can be frustrating and wasteful.

Link-Time Instantiators

Link-time instantiators generate at link time all the template specializations needed by a program. When a program is linked, the instantiator generates the object code for missing specializations repeatedly until none are missing. Generating missing specializations requires executing the compiler. Thus, a link-time instantiator *compiles* code at link time. The resulting object code is placed in a location reserved for storing template specializations, usually called a *repository*.

The algorithm as we have described it is conceptually simple. Implementing it, however, such that it is correct, efficient when a program is first built, and efficient when a program is rebuilt after a change is difficult. Fortunately, writing a correct, efficient template instantiator is the concern of compiler vendors, not the concern of designers and implementors of reusable code.

Some link-time instantiators, to simplify instantiation, require that the source code for templates be organized according to certain conventions. Suppose that the definition of `Hashtable` is in a file *Hashtable.h*:

Hashtable.h:

```
template<class T>
class Hashtable {
    // ...
};
```

Then some instantiators require that the definitions of all the noninline member functions and static data members of `Hashtable` be in a file named *Hashtable.c* located in the same directory as *Hashtable.h*:

Hashtable.c:

```
template<class T>
void Hashtable<T>::insert(const T& t) {
    // ...
}
// ...
```

The source code organization requirements for link-time instantiators typically are not onerous, but they can cause portability problems. Different instantiators impose different, sometimes conflicting, requirements. Thus, trying to write code that can be compiled on platforms with different instantiators can require extra effort in the build procedures for that code.

Comparison of Efficiency of Automatic Instantiators

Typical link-time instantiators generate the code for a given template specialization in only one place — the repository. Recall that compile-time instantiators generate the code for a given template specialization in each translation unit that uses that specialization, directly or indirectly. Hence, the output of link-time instantiators requires less space than that of compile-time instantiators.

A naive analysis might conclude that link-time instantiators are faster than compile-time instantiators. In fact, instantiating at link time can be faster than instantiating at compile time, can be equally fast, or can even be slower. Consider the following program:

main.c:

```
#include <Hashtable.h>
#include <Hashtable.c>  // for compile-time instantiator

int main() {
    Hashtable<int> table;
    table.insert(7);
    return 0;
}
```

Let us assume that the functions `Hashtable<int>::Hashtable()` and `Hashtable<int>::insert(const int&)` do not use any other template

specializations. If we build this program using a compile-time instantiator, the definitions of these two functions will be generated in the object
code for *main.c*. When that object code is linked, all the needed specializations will be present, and there will be no duplicates that have to be
identified and removed.

Now suppose that we build the same program using a link-time instantiator. When *main.c* is compiled, no specializations will be generated. When the object code for *main.c* is linked, the instantiator
will have to generate definitions for `Hashtable<int>::Hashtable()` and
`Hashtable<int>::insert(const int&)`. To do that, the instantiator
might create a file that looks like this:

Hashtable_int.c:

```
#include <Hashtable.h>
#include <Hashtable.c>

#pragma instantiate Hashtable<int>::Hashtable()
#pragma instantiate Hashtable<int>::insert(const int&)
```

After writing this file, the link-time instantiator invokes the compiler on it.
When the compiler returns, the instantiator adds the resulting object file
to the program being linked.

When we built the program using a compile-time instantiator, the contents of *Hashtable.h* and *Hashtable.c* were compiled only once — when
main.c was compiled. When we built the program using a link-time instantiator, the contents of *Hashtable.h* and *Hashtable.c* were compiled twice
— once when *main.c* was compiled and again when *Hashtable_int.c* was
compiled. Thus, a link-time instantiator probably will be slower than a
compile-time instantiator on this program. For a large program, a link-
time instantiator might spend much time compiling header files repeatedly.

The efficiency of template instantiation — whether by compile-time or
link-time instantiators — is currently a concern for C++ users. In Sections 4.2.2 and 4.3.3, we showed techniques for improving the efficiency of
template instantiation for users of a library.

9.7.2 Manual Instantiation

Because implementing a correct, efficient, automatic instantiator is difficult,
some (incomplete) C++ programming environments do not provide one.
Such implementations force users to specify what should be instantiated
and where, through various manual instantiation schemes.

ANSI/ISO C++ probably will provide a manual instantiation directive:

```
template class Hashtable<Widget>;
```

This statement means "Generate definitions for all the noninline member functions and static data members of Hashtable<Widget> here." The syntax for function templates is analogous. For example, given the function template

```
template<class T> void f(const T&);
```

the statement

```
template void f(const Widget&);
```

means "Generate the definition of f<Widget> here."

Some current C++ environments recognize manual instantiation constructs different from that just described. A common alternative construct uses #pragma. The syntax for specifying what to instantiate might let the programmer say things like "Generate the definition of all noninline member functions of Hashtable<Widget> whose names begin with 'put' here." Of course, relying on such mechanisms is not portable.

Some C++ implementations offer both automatic and manual instantiation. Judicious use of manual instantiation can often reduce program build time significantly from what it would be if only automatic instantiation were used. Often, the programmer and not the instantiator can best judge what to instantiate and where. As discussed in Section 9.7.1, automatic instantiators tend to consume much time and space on large, complex programs. Manual instantiation can reduce resource consumption at the cost of increasing the time the programmer must spend determining what to instantiate and where.

Using Manual Instantiation

Because of transitive dependencies, determining what to instantiate and where can be surprisingly difficult. Suppose that our program uses a Hashtable<Widget>, and suppose that we have decided to instantiate manually all specializations used by our program:

```
template class Hashtable<Widget>;
```

We must also remember to instantiate manually any specializations needed by Hashtable<Widget>:

```
template class List<Widget>;
```

If List<Widget> used another template, we would have to instantiate that one too.

If we were the implementors of `Hashtable`, then having to instantiate `List<Widget>` might not be onerous. If, however, we were not familiar with the implementation details of `Hashtable`, then we probably would write only the first manual instantiation; when we try to link the program, we would get errors indicating that certain functions and data involving `List<Widget>` are undefined:

```
error: undefined function:
List<Widget>::insert(const Widget&)
```

If the program is large, we might have no idea where the program needed `List<Widget>::insert`, and we probably would not want to spend time figuring out where we needed it. Instead, we would simply add the second manual instantiation to our program. We would then repeat the process of linking our program and adding manual instantiations until no symbols are undefined.

When we add a manual instantiation, we must also `#include` the appropriate files:

```
#include <List.h>
#include <Widget.h>
//...
template class List<Widget>;
```

Note, however, that the error message did not tell us the name of the file in which `List` is declared. To enable users to determine the name of the file, the library containing `Hashtable` and `List` must either use a uniform file-naming scheme or document the name of the containing file for each template the user might need to instantiate manually. Even if the presence of `List` is an implementation detail of the library and it is not intended for public use, the location of the `List` template must be publicized.

Linking a large program is often a slow process; repeatedly linking a program to identify all needed manual instantiations might take a very long time. To reduce the number of needed links, the library documentation can specify the instantiation dependencies:

> A program that instantiates `Hashtable<T>` must also instantiate `List<T>`.

A programmer who reads this documentation will write both manual instantiations at once and thereby save a link step.

Manual Instantiation and Code Changes

If programs were written only once and never changed, manual instantiation might not be too unwieldy, but difficulties arise when we modify programs. Suppose that we reimplement `Hashtable` to use closed instead of open chaining (that is, when a collision occurs, we find, by some algorithm, another location in the table at which to store the given value). We change `Hashtable` to the following:

```
template<class T>
class Hashtable {
private:
    T* table[1024];   // was "List<T> the_table[1024];"
    //...
};
```

Each entry in the fixed-size table points to the value stored at that position or is 0 if there is no such value. Because there are no open chains, we no longer need to use `List` to implement `Hashtable`.

After this change, a program that used a `Hashtable<Widget>` might or might not still need to instantiate `List<Widget>` (because `List<Widget>` might be used somewhere else in the program). If a program no longer needs `List<Widget>`, then the manual instantiation directive

```
template class List<Widget>;
```

contained in it would cause unneeded code to be generated, bloating the executable.

Even a small change to a program can change radically the set of instantiations that program needs. How does a programmer determine the minimal set of instantiations needed after a change to a program? With a manual instantiator, the only realistic approach that is guaranteed to find all unneeded instantiations is to remove *all* the manual instantiations and repeat the entire manual instantiation process from scratch.

9.8   Run-Time Libraries

Most platforms provide a set of libraries that C++ programmers can use. For example, platforms that have file systems will provide functions to create and modify files. A platform without a file system — a platform used for executing programs embedded inside an automobile engine, for example — will not have such functions. Because there is considerable variation among the libraries available on different platforms, C++ code should use only the library functionality known to be present on all platforms to which the code is to be portable.

Although not described in the ARM, a standard library will be defined in the ANSI/ISO C++ standard. As of this writing, the draft standard C++ library addresses the following areas of functionality:

- Language support
- Diagnostics
- General utilities
- Localization
- Containers
- Iterators
- Algorithms
- Numerics
- Input and output (the `iostream` library)

To date, most C++ implementations do not provide the entire draft library. Many implementations provide only the following:

- Some variant of an `iostream` library. The implementations available differ from the draft standard `iostream` library.
- Most of the ANSI/ISO C (not C++) library, with modifications.

A de facto standard `iostream` library was originally created at AT&T around 1988. This library was an improvement in several ways over an earlier `stream` library. First the `stream` library, and later the `iostream` library, were provided with the then de facto standard compiler, *cfront*. The ANSI/ISO C++ committee has taken the opportunity to improve the design of the `iostream` library. As of this writing, interfaces of `iostream` libraries vary, and few C++ implementations support the draft standard `iostream` library. Until most C++ implementation provide the ANSI/ISO standard `iostream` library, programmers who wish to write portable code that does input or output must be careful to use only functionality that is common to all the `iostream` libraries that will be used with that code.

The ANSI/ISO C library, with some modifications, will be a proper subset of the ANSI/ISO C++ library. Changes will be made to the standard C library because of small differences between the C and C++ type systems. Consider the function `strchr`, declared in the C library as follows:

```
char* strchr(const char* p, int c);   /* ANSI/ISO C */
```

The function `strchr` returns a pointer to the leftmost occurrence of the character `c` in the null-terminated string pointed to by `p`, or 0 if `c` is not in the string. The second argument has type `int`. In C, a literal character such as `'x'` has type `int`, not `char`. In C++ literal characters have type `char`. Notice also that the C `strchr` has a type hole:

```
/* C code */
void modify_string(const char* p) {
    char* q = strchr(p, p[0]);
    q[0] = 'x';
}
```

Here, we use the value returned by `strchr` to modify the string pointed to by `p`. To fix these problems, in ANSI/ISO C++ `strchr` probably will be overloaded and declared as follows:

```
// C++ code
char* strchr(char* p, char c);
const char* strchr(const char* p, char c);
```

As of this writing, the ANSI/ISO C++ committee is discussing the changes to be applied to the C library for C++.

Even after the ANSI/ISO C++ standard library is defined officially, not all platforms will provide the entire library. Consider again a program that executes in an automobile engine. What should that program do if it were to execute the following statement?

```
cout << "Hello, Officer!\n";
```

Embedded programs often have no appropriate output device on which to print a message. Hence, a platform designed for programmers writing embedded code might not provide the entire `iostream` library or might provide the `iostream` library only in test mode (see Section 5.3.1).

Most platforms provide libraries in addition to the standard C++ library. For example, many platforms provide the libraries defined in the System V Interface Definition (SVID) [AT&89]. The SVID defines a C interface to a range of functionality, which is also available to C++ programmers. The Portable Operating System Environment for Computer Environments Standard (POSIX) [IEE90] defines a library of functions for interacting with the underlying operating system. Some platforms provide libraries that are not described in any standards document but are nevertheless de facto standards. We refrain from discussing these libraries here; C++ programmers should become acquainted with the libraries provided on the platforms to which they wish their code to be portable.

9.9   Other Portability Concerns

Many other differences among platforms complicate the portability of C++
source code and build procedures. One problematic area is system commands — for example, commands for displaying the contents of a file or
commands (typically called `make` or `build`) for building programs. Most
platforms provide one or more command-line interpreters, or shells, in which
system commands can be executed; almost every shell also provides its own
programming language. Unfortunately, shells and system commands vary
widely across platforms. Even commands with the same names on different platforms might do different things or might have different interfaces.
The differences among system commands render it impossible to use the
standard C++ library function `system` portably (`system` passes a string
argument to the operating system, and that string is interpreted as a command and executed). Trying to write a portable build procedure amid these
inconsistencies is challenging.

Another source of portability problems is file systems. Many platforms
provide a hierarchical file system. Unfortunately, the syntaxes for naming
files differ. For example, to refer to a file *file1.c* in a directory *dir* in the
directory containing the current directory on a UNIX system, we would say

```
../dir/file1.c
```

On a VMS system, we would say

```
[-.dir]file1.c
```

On a Windows system, we would say

```
..\dir\file1.c
```

This difference affects both C++ source code and C++ build procedures,
which typically manipulate many path names. For example, the code

```
#include "../dir/file1.h"
// ...
ifstream f("../dir/file2.c");
```

is portable only to platforms that recognize the UNIX path syntax. To
increase the portability of code, some platforms recognize more than one
path syntax. For example, most (perhaps all) C++ compilers running on
Windows platforms recognize both Windows and UNIX path syntaxes.

We shall merely mention one other source of portability problems: windowing systems. Different platforms provide different window systems, with
different application programmer interfaces (APIs). Trying to write code

that is portable to several window systems can be monumentally difficult. Some libraries try to solve this problem by layering a single interface over several window system APIs.

9.10   Summary

Currently, writing highly portable C++ code is challenging. Part of the challenge comes from the continuing evolution of the C++ language. There is controversy over how an implementation should interpret certain constructs. Further, many implementations of the language are not complete.

Even after the ANSI/ISO C++ standard is finalized, the language will allow legal programs that will not be portable. C++ inherits from C many undefined, unspecified, and implementation-defined behaviors and adds a few new ones. Memory and object layout, in particular, need careful attention in code that must be portable.

Template instantiation mechanisms vary considerably among C++ implementations. Some automatic instantiation schemes require template code to be organized in specific ways, but the requirements vary from implementation to implementation. Manual instantiation schemes use a variety of directives to give users control over template instantiation. Thus, porting code that uses templates can involve some effort.

Finally, portability can be complicated for programs that depend on standard as well as nonstandard run-time libraries, system commands, file systems, and window systems.

Exercises

9.1   Discuss in detail the portability of the following pieces of code:

Exercise9.1a.c:

```
namespace {
    class Secret {
        char _c;
        // ...
    };
};
```

Exercise9.1b.c:

```
ofstream o("dir1/file");
o << "Engage!\n";
```

Exercise9.1c.c:

```
class Oops { /* ... */ };
void shifty() throw(Oops) {
    char c = -1;
    try {
        c <<= 4;
        // ...
    }
    catch (Oops) {
        // ...
        throw;
    }
}
```

Exercise9.1d.c:

```
#include <iostream.h>
static union {
    char c1, c2;
    // ...
};
main() {
    c1 = 'a';
    if (c2 == 'a')
        cout << "as I expected\n";
}
```

9.2 Section 9.6 showed how to write and read a sequence of `chars` portably.

   a. Write a pair of functions `portablewrite(ostream& o, long l)` and `portableread(istream& i, long& l)` that write and read, respectively, a `long` one byte at a time in a predetermined order.

   b. Specify the conditions under which a `long` written by `portablewrite` on platform P will be read correctly by `portableread` on platform Q.

c. (∗) Write a pair of functions `portablewrite(ostream& o, double d)` and `portableread(istream& i, double& d)` that write and read a double one byte at a time in a predetermined order.

d. (∗) Specify the conditions under which a `double` written by `portablewrite` on platform P will be read correctly by `portableread` on platform Q.

9.3 (∗) Suppose that we write a value `val1` of type T to an `ostream o` positioned at the beginning of some file, as follows:

```
T val1;
o << val1;
```

We then copy the resulting file to a different platform. Next, we run some other program in which we read in a value `val2` of the same type T from an `istream i` positioned at the beginning of that file:

```
T val2;
i >> val2;
```

a. Under precisely what conditions is `val2` equal to `val1` if T is the type `char`?

b. Under what conditions is `val2` equal to `val1` if T is `int`?

c. Under what conditions is `val2` equal to `val1` if T is `float`?

9.4 (∗) Again suppose that we write a value `val1` to an `ostream o` positioned at the beginning of some file, this time using `write`:

```
T val1;
o.write((char*)&val1, sizeof(val1));
```

We copy the resulting file to a different platform, and we run some other program in which we read in a value `val2`, using `read`:

```
T val2;
i.read((char*)&val2, sizeof(val2));
```

a. Under precisely what conditions is `val2` equal to `val1` if T is the type `char`?

b. Under what conditions is `val2` equal to `val1` if T is `int`?

c. Under what conditions is `val2` equal to `val1` if T is `float`?

9.5 Why did we say (in Section 9.5) that to write a portable program we would have to change the names of the C functions `f__Fi` and `f__Fc`?

9.6 Suppose that template instantiator $T1$ requires that the definition of a function template be contained in a file that has the same name, except for a different suffix, as the file containing the declaration of the function template. Suppose further that template instantiator $T2$ requires the definition of a function template to be present in all translation units that call any specialization of that function.

    a. Show how a library's source code could be organized such that it would be portable to platforms running instantiator $T1$ and to platforms running instantiator $T2$.

    b. Does your solution to part a minimize users' compile time on both platforms?

9.7 (∗) Discuss the problems involved in writing code that is portable both to platforms with automatic instantiators and to platforms that support only manual instantiation.

9.8 (∗∗) Recall from Section 4.2.2 that a library must preinstantiate certain template specializations.

    a. Write a program that will add to a library's archive the object code for a given set of specializations. Your solution may use the template instantiator and platform of your choice.

    b. How portable is your program?

9.9 (∗∗) In Section 9.7.1, we discussed two popular designs for automatic template instantiators. Another design works as follows: When compiling a translation unit t, instantiate into a repository all the specializations used directly or indirectly by t that are not already in the repository. Discuss the advantages and disadvantages of this design.

References and Further Reading

Lapin [Lap87] discusses writing portable C source code and build procedures; C++ programmers will also find it useful. Stevens' work [Ste92] is essential reading for C++ programmers who wish to write portable code for UNIX platforms.

    The perils of undefined and unspecified behaviors have long been known in the programming language community. In some modern programming languages (for example, ML [Wik87]), executable programs cannot have undefined or unspecified behavior.

Memory and object layout are discussed in Harbison and Steele's Chapter 6 [HS91].

Writing and reading floating point values portably is difficult. Interested readers should see papers by Clinger [Cli90] and Steele and White [SW90].

McCluskey and Murray [MM92] discuss the difficulties of C++ template instantiation. The implementation of an automatic link-time instantiator is described in Chapter 8 of Novell's *C++ Language System Release 3.1 Manual, Selected Readings* [Nov92].

The C++ standard library is discussed by Vilot [Vil95]. A draft version of the library (as of February, 1994) is discussed in detail by Plauger [Pla95]. Teale [Tea93] discusses variations among implementations of `iostreams`. The C standard library is defined in the ANSI/ISO C standard [ANS89]. The Standard Template Library is a recent, large addition to the ANSI/ISO C++ draft standard — too recent and too large to be discussed in this book; Vilot [Vil94], Stroustrup [Str94b], and Plauger [Pla95] provide more information.

Exercise 9.1 was inspired by Becker's discussion of portability [Bec94].

10 Using Other Libraries

> *If a better system is thine, import it;*
> *if not, make use of mine.*
>
> — Horace

In this chapter, we discuss whether a C++ library should reuse part of another library. We discuss drawbacks of using other libraries in code intended for reuse: requiring users to obtain the reused code, concerns about efficiency, the potential for name-space conflicts introduced by reusing other libraries, and the problem of synchronizing releases of libraries. We also discuss writing *self-contained libraries* — an alternative to reusing other libraries.

10.1 Why Reuse Other Libraries?

Sometimes, when we are writing a library, we discover that we would like to reuse part of some other library. For example, suppose that we are writing MEDLIB, a library for use in medical applications. We want our library to provide the domain-specific functionality that is common to many medical application programs — programs for hospitals, medical laboratories, and other health-care establishments. Because many medical applications need to manipulate diagnostic tests — blood tests, X-rays, CAT scans, and so on – we provide in our library a class `Diagnostic` representing a diagnostic test. We also provide a function that, given a collection of diagnostic tests, sends invoices to the parties responsible for payment for those tests:

```
void send_invoices(const Some_type<Diagnostic>& diags) {
      // send an invoice for each Diagnostic in diags ...
}
```

What collection type should we use for the parameter of this function? If we do not have any collection classes in our library, we have two reasonable alternatives for *Some_type*: We can design and implement our own collection class, or we can reuse a collection class that exists in some other library.

There are strong reasons to prefer reusing another library's collection class. First, why should we write yet another collection class if a suitable one already exists? Second, if we are the aspiring authors of a *medical* library, not a container class library, we might not have experience writing high-quality container classes. Third, because we are providers of a library intended for reuse, we would like to set a good example by practicing reuse ourselves.

Suppose that we choose reuse. In a library called CONTAINER, we find a Set class we can reuse:

Set.h, from CONTAINER:

```
template<class T>
class Set {
    // ...
};
```

We complete the interface of our invoicing function as follows:

Medical.h:

```
#include <Set.h>
void send_invoices(const Set<Diagnostic>& diags);
// ...
```

Our users will write code like this:

```
#include <Medical.h>

int main() {
    Set<Diagnostic> diags;
    // ...
    send_invoices(diags);
    // ...
}
```

Reusing another library has produced an elegant interface that is easy to implement.

10.2   Drawbacks of Using Other Libraries

Unfortunately, using another library within reusable code can have drawbacks. Using another library will impose on users the requirement to acquire the reused library; it might impair efficiency; it can introduce potential name-space conflicts; and it might require synchronization with releases of the reused library.

10.2.1   Acquisition

The first drawback of reusing another library is that we impose on our users the requirement to acquire that other library. In our example, programmers who wish to use MEDLIB must acquire a copy of CONTAINER. It is not guaranteed that programmers who need MEDLIB already have a copy of CONTAINER— these two libraries address different problem domains.

Acquiring, installing, and maintaining a copy of CONTAINER (or any library) will cost our users some amount of money, time, and effort. If these costs are too high, then potential customers will elect not to use our library, even if the costs of acquiring, installing, and maintaining *our* library are low. Indeed, even if the costs of acquiring CONTAINER are insignificant, the mere necessity of acquiring it will discourage some fraction of our intended users from using MEDLIB.

10.2.2   Efficiency

Reusing another library might cause our library to be too inefficient. In this section, we illustrate the sort of analysis a library designer should do to determine whether reusing another library is efficient enough.

First, consider compile time. If we reuse `Set`, users of MEDLIB who `#include` *Medical.h* will have their compilations slowed by the time it takes to compile *Set.h*. Even users who do not use `send_invoices` must compile *Set.h*. If compiling *Set.h* is too time consuming, we can forward declare `Set` instead of including *Set.h* (see Section 4.2.1):

Medical.h:

```
template<class T> class Set;
void send_invoices(const Set<Diagnostic>& diags);
// ...
```

Now compile time should be acceptable.

If we reuse `Set`, then `Set<Diagnostic>` will have to be instantiated in user programs. Instantiation can be slow (see Section 4.2.2). If, however, we preinstantiate (see Section 4.2.2) `Set<Diagnostic>` in MEDLIB, users will incur no overhead for instantiation.

Now consider run time. Although the use of a general-purpose class such as `Set` can result in code that is not as fast as code designed for a particular use, we expect that most of our users will generate invoices only once or twice per month. Further, generating invoices will probably involve read and write operations and database accesses. These are slow operations, and their run time will swamp any differences in execution speed attributable to using `Set`. Therefore, the effect on run time of using `Set` in `send_invoices` should not be a problem.

Similarly, because most of our users will generate invoices infrequently, we expect that any increase in memory use caused by our use of `Set<Diagnostic>` will be acceptable to our users.

Thus, we conclude that reusing `Set` will be efficient enough. An analysis, like the one we have done here, of some other proposed reuse of code from another library might reveal that reuse as too inefficient.

10.2.3   Conflict

Another drawback of reusing another library is that the other library might conflict (see Chapter 6) with code in which users would like to use our library. Suppose, for example, that CONTAINER defines a class `List` somewhere in its global scope. Suppose further that it is irrelevant to MEDLIB that `List` is defined globally in CONTAINER because MEDLIB never refers to anything named `List`. If user code, however, defines a `List` at global scope, then CONTAINER conflicts with the user code. Such code will have to be changed before it can use MEDLIB. Forcing users to change their code does not promote the popularity of a library.

Once the namespace feature (see Section 6.1.6) is widely implemented by C++ compilers, however, name conflicts between libraries should rarely be a problem. If CONTAINER defines `List` in a namespace, then there will be no conflict with anything called `List` in user code.

10.2.4   Release Synchronization

Libraries change over time; new releases add new functionality, modify the functionality of the previous release, and occasionally remove outdated functionality. Suppose that library X reuses part of library Y. Each release of X will have been designed to work with and tested against some particular release or releases of Y; usually, not all releases of Y will work with every release of X. Therefore, programmers who wish to use a particular release of X must have a release of Y that works with that release of X.

To simplify our discussion, let us assume that there is only one release of MEDLIB and that MEDLIB was tested against a single release C_m of CONTAINER, as shown in Figure 10.1.

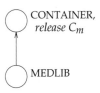

Figure 10.1   Dependency of MEDLIB on a particular release of CONTAINER. MEDLIB was designed to work with and tested against release C_m of CONTAINER.

Unfortunately, some potential users of MEDLIB might not have release C_m of CONTAINER, and they might not be able to acquire it. Some users might have acquired CONTAINER before we did and might therefore have an earlier release. Users with an earlier release of CONTAINER might not be willing or able to upgrade to C_m; some of their code might depend on features in the earlier release that are removed or changed in C_m, or they might be unwilling to pay for an upgrade.

On the other hand, if a new version of CONTAINER was released *after* MEDLIB, our potential users might have a release of CONTAINER that is later than C_m. Users with a later release of CONTAINER almost certainly do not want to downgrade to an earlier release. Let us call the release of CONTAINER that our potential users have release C_u, as shown in Figure 10.2.

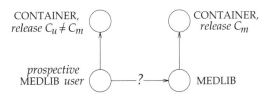

Figure 10.2   Release synchronization problem. Prospective users of MEDLIB have a release of CONTAINER other than C_m.

What are users who have a release of CONTAINER other than C_m to do? The good news is that some of those other releases of CONTAINER might work with MEDLIB. The bad news is that users might not be able to determine whether the release of CONTAINER they have is one of the releases that work.

If we are planning to distribute only the source code for MEDLIB, then our users will be concerned about source compatibility (see Section 7.4) between releases of CONTAINER. If release C_u of CONTAINER is source compatible with release C_m, then C_u will work with MEDLIB. This conclusion follows directly from the definition of source compatibility. If we shall be distributing object code for MEDLIB, then our users will be concerned about link compatibility (see Section 7.5) between releases of CONTAINER. If release C_u of CONTAINER is link compatible with release C_m, then C_u will work with MEDLIB. This conclusion follows from the definition of link compatibility.

How does a programmer determine whether a given release C_u of a library is source or link compatible with some other release C_m? There are three cases (see Figure 10.3):

1. If C_u is an earlier release than C_m, then the user probably is out of luck. The documentation for C_u will not say whether C_u is compatible with C_m because C_m did not exist when the documentation for C_u was written. Further, library users in practice rarely need to know whether an earlier release of a library is compatible with a later release, so the documentation for C_m will usually not address the issue.

2. If C_u is C_{m+1} — the next release after C_m — then the documentation for C_u should say whether C_u is compatible with C_m.

3. If C_u is later than the next release after C_m, then the documentation for C_u might or might not say whether C_u is compatible with C_m. The more releases that C_u is beyond C_m, the lower are the odds that the implementor of C_u went to the trouble of determining whether C_u is compatible with C_m. If C_u is later than the second release after C_m, rarely will the documentation for C_u answer the question (despite our recommendation in Section 7.8).

The user unable to determine whether C_u is compatible with C_m must err on the side of safety and assume that C_u is *not* compatible with C_m and hence that C_u *cannot* be used safely with MEDLIB. Applying this conclusion to Figure 10.3 yields Figure 10.4.

Figure 10.4 might appear discouraging. It implies not only that library developers must make sure that they know which releases of the libraries they use can be used with which releases of the libraries they develop, but

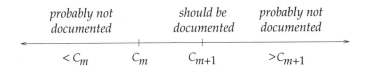

Figure 10.3   Release timeline showing documentation of compatibility
with release C_m.

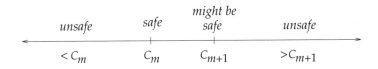

Figure 10.4   Release timeline showing which releases of CONTAINER
can be used safely with MEDLIB.

also that users must take pains to ensure that they keep the releases of the
libraries they use synchronized.

The situation is not as bleak as it first seems, however. A typical library
vendor will have only a few releases in use in the field at any one time —
usually not more than three. Thus, the MEDLIB developers might be able to
test MEDLIB with all the releases of CONTAINER that are in the field when
MEDLIB is released. Furthermore, unless MEDLIB uses obscure features of
CONTAINER (which would be ill advised), MEDLIB is likely to work with
C_{m+1} — libraries typically add functionality and seldom change or delete
functionality.

Some C++ implementations assist users in dealing with the synchronization problem by providing a library versioning mechanism (see Section 7.6).
The library provider uses the versioning mechanism to specify with which
other releases of the library a given release is link compatible.

10.3   Self-Contained Libraries

One way to avoid the problems caused by reusing other libraries is to make
our library self-contained. A *self-contained library* defines and implements
all the functionality it needs and uses no other libraries, except perhaps

those libraries whose interfaces are well established — such as the standard
C and C++ libraries (see Section 9.8).

We can make MEDLIB self-contained in either of two ways. We can
buy the right to use CONTAINER within MEDLIB and the right to distribute
CONTAINER as part of MEDLIB, or we can write our own collection class.
Let us consider the second approach. Suppose that we call our collection
class **Medset** to avoid confusion with the CONTAINER class **set**:

Medlib.h:

```
template<class T>
class Medset {
    // ...
};

void send_invoices(const Medset<Diagnostic>& diags);
// ...
```

Once we make MEDLIB self-contained, our users no longer have to worry
about acquiring a release of CONTAINER (or any other library) that works
with it. Further, users will not encounter conflicts with names used in
some other library but not needed in MEDLIB. Of course, making a
library self-contained has drawbacks, which we discuss in Sections 10.3.1
through 10.3.4.

10.3.1 Difficulty of Implementation

A self-contained library usually is more difficult to implement than a library
that reuses other libraries. If we elect to make our library self-contained, we
must provide all the functionality ourselves. (Recall that ease of implementation was one of our primary motivations for choosing to reuse an existing
library in the first place.)

We might be able to simplify the job of implementing a self-contained
library by scavenging (see Section 1.1.1) — that is, by *copying* the code of
some already existing set class (for example, the **Set** class in CONTAINER)
into our library. Of course, we can copy code into our library only if we
have a flexible enough licensing agreement with the owner of that code.
As we mentioned in Section 1.1.1, however, scavenging can be difficult and
should not be undertaken lightly.

10.3.2 Difficulty of Use

A self-contained library can be less convenient to use than a library that
reuses other libraries. Users of a self-contained MEDLIB who also use CON-

TAINER must understand two set classes (`Set` and `Medset`) rather than the one (`Set`) they would have to understand with the non–self-contained version of MEDLIB.

A further complication of self-contained libraries involves conversion functions. Consider a self-contained version of MEDLIB that defines its own `Medset` class, and consider a user of MEDLIB who also uses CONTAINER. Suppose that such a user tries to pass a `Set` of `Diagnostics` to our `send_invoices` function:

```
Set<Diagnostic> diags;
// ...
send_invoices(diags);  // error
```

This call might seem perfectly reasonable to the user — `diags` is a collection of diagnostic tests, and `send_invoices` is supposed to generate invoices for a given collection of diagnostic tests. Unfortunately, this call to `send_invoices` will fail to compile because `send_invoices` takes a `Medset<Diagnostic>`, not a `Set<Diagnostic>`, and there is no conversion defined from `Set<T>` to `Medset<T>`.

There are two places where you might think that a conversion from `Set` to `Medset` could be defined. First, perhaps `Medset` could provide the conversion via a single-argument constructor:

```
template<class T>
class Medset {
public:
    Medset(const Set<T>&);
    // ...
};
```

Alternatively, perhaps `Set` could provide the conversion via a conversion function:

```
template<class T>
class Set {
public:
    operator Medset<T>() const;
    // ...
};
```

The conversion function in `Set` is unlikely to exist, however. The designers of CONTAINER, which is a general-purpose container class library, probably do not know of the existence of MEDLIB, which is a domain-specific library. Even if they do know of MEDLIB, and even if they wanted to provide the conversion, they could not do so without making *their* library non–self-contained.

Suppose, therefore, that we were to provide the first conversion, in MEDLIB. To make MEDLIB consistent and complete, should we not also provide similar conversions from the set classes in all other well-known container class libraries? If we were to provide all such conversions, however, Medset might have too many constructors. Should we choose to provide only certain conversions?

For once, we are saved from having to make a difficult decision because even if we *did* want to provide the shown conversion in Medset, we could not. Consider what the implementation of the conversion would look like:

```
#include <Set.h>  // from CONTAINER library

template<class T>
Medset<T>::Medset(const Set<T>& s) {
    // ...
    // access some of s's members
    // ...
}
```

To construct a Medset from a Set, we would have to access some of Set's members. To access Set's members, we would have to #include the header file from CONTAINER that contains the definition of Set, but that inclusion would render MEDLIB no longer self-contained.

Because neither of the conversion functions will exist, users of MEDLIB and CONTAINER who want to manipulate Sets of Diagnostics and call send_invoice on such Sets will themselves have to implement a conversion from Set to Medset:

usercode.c:

```
template<class T>
Medset<T> set2medset(const Set<T>& s) {
    // ...
}
```

With this explicit conversion function, users can write the following:

```
Set<Diagnostic> diags;
// ...
send_invoices(set2medset(diags));
```

Of course, it is inconvenient for the user to implement the conversion from Set to Medset.

10.3.3   Efficiency

Self-contained libraries can be too inefficient. For example, calling the conversion function set2medset will consume run time. In contrast, code that uses the non–self-contained version of MEDLIB requires neither the implementation nor the execution of a conversion function. Self-contained libraries can also increase the user's code size. If MEDLIB defines its own set class and the user's program uses another set class, then the user's executable will be bloated with the code for both set classes.

If *every* library were self-contained, the code size for complex programs using several libraries probably would become unacceptably large. As reliance on libraries grows, both within applications and among libraries themselves, this problem will be exacerbated.

10.3.4   Isolation

In isolating themselves from dependence on other libraries, self-contained libraries also isolate themselves from beneficial changes to libraries they otherwise would have used. Suppose that the provider of CONTAINER issues a new release containing a faster version of Set. If MEDLIB is self-contained, its users will not reap the benefits of the improvement.

This drawback is offset, however, by the control designers have over the classes in their own libraries. For example, if MEDLIB is self-contained, we might be able to release a faster version of Medset before the developers of CONTAINER release a faster version of Set. In fact, if MEDLIB is self-contained, we can custom optimize Medset for the specific uses to which it is put in MEDLIB. The designer of CONTAINER is unlikely to optimize Set for the uses to which it is put in some other library.

10.4   Summary

Using other libraries eases implementation but brings the problems of acquisition, conflict, release synchronization, and possibly efficiency.

Self-contained libraries avoid these problems, but they trade off ease of implementation, ease of use, and efficiency. Some programmers also use the library that otherwise would have been reused. Self-contained libraries can reduce ease of use for those programmers by requiring them to learn multiple interfaces and to write and invoke conversion functions explicitly. Self-contained libraries can also cause such users' executables to be bloated. Finally, self-contained libraries isolate themselves from other libraries — with both desirable and undesirable effects.

Exercises

10.1   Suppose that you are developing the `Path` class discussed in Exercises 1.2 and 7.1. Consider the following member function, which uses a `List` class to represent a list of `Paths`:

```
class Path {
public:
    List<Path> expand_wildcards() const;
    // ...
};
```

The function `expand_wildcards` looks at the file system on the machine on which the program is executing and returns the list of files that match (according to some defined set of rules) the given `Path`.

Perform an analysis (like the analysis in Section 10.2.2) of the efficiency of reusing a commercially available general-purpose list class versus using a specialized list class that you implement and optimize for lists of `Paths`.

10.2   Suppose that the only thing our library reuses from library CONTAINER is `Set` and that the only way we reuse `Set` is as the argument type of `send_invoices` (see Section 10.1). Explain why even if we preinstantiate `Set<Diagnostic>` in our library's archive, users of our library must still acquire CONTAINER.

10.3   Suppose that the only place we use `Set<Diagnostic>` is in the implementation of our library (that is, not in a public header file).

   a.   Now does preinstantiating `Set<Diagnostic>` free users of our library from having to acquire CONTAINER?

   b.   Is preinstantiating `Set<Diagnostic>` guaranteed to prevent the sort of conflicts described in Section 10.2.3? Why or why not?

11 Documentation

I have made this letter longer than usual,
because I lack the time to make it short.
                                    — Blaise Pascal

Good documentation is crucial to the success of any library. In this chapter, we define and describe each of the documents that should accompany every library — a design paper, tutorials, and a reference manual. We include suggestions for writing tutorials and a specification for what reference manuals should document.

11.1 Documentation and Reusability

Code that is not documented properly is not reusable. Poor documentation can lead to the failure of well-designed and otherwise well-presented libraries. Good documentation is essential for quickly learning how to use a library. Good documentation should not be overlooked for small libraries, even libraries that provide only a few, easily understood features. Few people will use a library if it is possible to design and implement the equivalent functionality in less time than it takes to learn the library.

Documentation should be clear and complete. Even if the design or intended use of some feature of your library seems obvious to you, many of your users will not find it obvious. Your perspective, if you have just spent months or years living with the design and implementation of a library, is not the same as that of users approaching the library for the first time.

Producing high-quality documentation often takes a significant fraction of the time required to design, implement, and test a library. The need for good documentation is one of the reasons developing reusable code is more expensive than producing single-use code.

A library should be documented *while* it is being designed and implemented. Documenting usually reveals ways to improve the code being documented. Postponing the effort of documenting, even for apparently simple library facilities, is a mistake. Donald Knuth's observations on designing the typesetting language TeX [Knu89] are germane:

> The designer of a new system must not only be the implementor and the first large-scale user; the designer should also write the first user manual. . . . If I had not participated fully in all these activities, literally hundreds of improvements would never have been made, because I would never have thought of them or perceived why they were important.

Every reusable C++ library should be accompanied by at least a design paper, a set of tutorials, and a reference manual. We discuss these in Sections 11.2 through 11.4.

11.2   The Design Paper

Throughout this book, we have shown that the designer of reusable code faces an almost dizzying array of design choices. Many of these design decisions will render the resulting library more usable for some potential users and less usable for others. In the design paper, the library designer should explain the choices made, why each was made the way it was, for whom the library is intended, and what the library provides those users. In particular, the design paper for a C++ library should answer at least the following questions:

- What classes does the library provide?
- What is the inheritance hierarchy?
- Are all the classes in the library nice (see Section 2.3)?
- How efficient is the library?
- In what ways is the library extensible?
- Does the library use any other libraries? If so, with what versions of those other libraries has the library been tested?
- Are future or past releases of the library guaranteed to be source, link, run, or process compatible?
- How are errors handled?
- How portable is the library?
- Does the library conflict with any other libraries?

The design document should also address issues particular to the problem domain addressed by the library.

11.3   Tutorials

Tutorials show how a library is typically used. Because their purpose is to assist users in getting started using a library, tutorials omit many details that are needed only in special or advanced uses of the library. Most libraries should have a single tutorial for the entire library and individual tutorials for each class or related set of classes in the library.

There is an art to writing a tutorial. The best way to learn that art is to read well-written tutorials by others and try to write some yourself. We shall not replicate an entire well-written tutorial here. Instead, we offer, in the following sections, several suggestions for tutorial writing style. Our tutorial examples are taken from a hypothetical tutorial for the following class:

```
class Regex {
public:
    Regex(const char* s);
    // ...
    bool match(const char* s);
    bool match(const char* s, String& t);
};
```

A `Regex` is a regular expression. The constructor shown here creates a `Regex` representing the regular expression given by the null-terminated string pointed to by `s`. For example, the following regular expression matches any string of zero or more digits:

```
Regex r("[0-9]*");
```

11.3.1   Know How Much Your Readers Know

Before writing a tutorial, determine how knowledgeable your typical readers will be. Consider this description of part of the `Regex` class:

> The following declares an instance of `Regex`, initialized to the empty regular expression:
>
> ```
> Regex r;  // default value is ""
> ```

This description is suitable for newcomers to C++. The reader who already knows C++ does not need to be told that the declaration "declares an instance of `Regex`." More advanced readers will prefer a terser explanation:

> The default value of a `Regex` object is the empty regular expression:
>
> ```
> Regex r;  // ""
> ```

Whatever level you choose, use it consistently both within and across tutorials for the same library.

You might also have to consider your users' knowledge of topics other than the C++ language. This description of `Regex` assumes that readers know what `egrep` and regular expressions are:

> A `Regex` is an `egrep`-style regular expression.

Many users might not know that `egrep` is the name of a pattern-matching program on some systems. The term *regular expression* might not be familiar to readers with no formal mathematical or computer science training.

If your users might be lacking in background knowledge necessary for understanding your documentation or for using your library, you will have to supply the needed information or provide references for that information.

11.3.2   Write in Terms of the Abstractions

Document the behavior of functions in terms of their effect on the abstract values of objects, not in terms of their underlying implementations. This presentation reveals an implementation detail:

> The function `match`
>
> ```
> if (r.match("Earl Grey"))  // ..
> ```
>
> efficiently matches the given string against an internal compiled form of the `Regex`.

In contrast, the following presentation is explained in terms of the abstract values of the objects involved:

> The function `match`
>
> ```
> if (r.match("Earl Grey"))  // ..
> ```
>
> returns `true` if the given string matches the regular expression.

Occasionally, some discussion of the underlying implementation will be of interest to the tutorial reader. Anytime the implementation is being discussed, that fact should be clear:

> `Regex` is implemented by compiling the given regular expression into an internal form that is efficient for matching.

The writer might consider placing all references to the implementation in a separate "Implementation Notes" section near the end of the tutorial.

11.3.3   Explain Common Uses First

Not everything about a facility must be explained fully or even mentioned
in a tutorial. The tutorial should cover enough to get users started, doing
the things they will typically want to do first and most often.

Some functions will have both commonly and infrequently needed uses.
For such a function, the less common use should not be mentioned the first
time the function is discussed in the tutorial. For example, only later in
the tutorial would we mention the following more advanced use of `match`:

> Earlier, we showed that the function `match` can be used to determine
> whether a `Regex` matches some string. This function will, when called
> with a second `String` argument, return the matching substring in
> that argument:
>
> ```
> String matching_substring;
> if (r.match("Earl Grey", matching_substring))  // ...
> ```

If two uses of a library are equally common, explain them in the order they
will occur in typical user code. For example, because users will construct
`Regex`s before matching them, construction should be described first:

> First, construct a `Regex` with the desired pattern, as follows:
>
> ```
> Regex r("[1-9]*");
> ```
>
> Then match the `Regex` against a target string:
>
> ```
> if (r.match("Earl Grey"))  // ...
> ```

11.3.4   Explain One Thing at a Time

The temptation to explain more than one idea at a time can be great.
Consider this ill-advised presentation:

> A `Regex` can be matched against a target string by calling `match`:
>
> ```
> String matching_substring;
> // optional second argument
> if (r.match("Earl Grey", matching_substring))  // ...
> ```
>
> This call returns `true` if the match was successful, in which case
> the `String` argument `matching_substring` is set to the matching
> substring in the target string.

This last sentence, if it were to appear in a tutorial, would be unclear to a
significant fraction of readers.

11.3.5   Explain Use, Not Design

A tutorial for reusable code teaches how to use the code, not why it was designed the way it was. Instead of writing

> Users often need the index and length of the matching substring. To minimize the number of overloaded instances of the function `match`, the following interface is provided:

simply say this:

> Users who need the index and length of the matching substring can get them as follows:

Information about the design of the library should be mentioned in the tutorial only if that information would help users understand and remember how to use the library. For example, if our users are familiar with the UNIX system, it would be helpful to include the following information about the design of `Regex`:

> The behavior of the functions provided by `Regex` corresponds, whenever possible, to the behavior of the UNIX `egrep` command.

11.3.6   Write Clearly and Simply

Originality of style is valued in literature, but in technical writing adherence to a uniform style is preferable. The purpose of a tutorial is to show how to use a library. Any writing style that interferes with that goal should be avoided. In particular,

- *Avoid subtlety.* Even the slightest subtlety will confuse readers, not because tutorial readers lack intelligence but because while they are reading a library tutorial they have other things on their minds — notably, learning how to use the library.
- *Fight the temptation to be witty.* Humor, except in small doses, does not belong in a tutorial. It is frustrating to have to wade through someone's idea of humor to find the technical information one wants to learn.
- *Keep it simple.* A tutorial that reads as if it were written by the great Italian author Dante might be great literature, but it would not be a great tutorial.

11.3.7   Use Language Precisely

Library documenters should write precisely in whatever language (English, Japanese, Russian, ...) they are using. Here is a counterexample, taken from a real program, that illustrates the point. When processing a statement like this

```
x = (f(y) ? w++ : throw 19, 1);
```

an alpha version of a C++ compiler issued this warning:

```
warning:  throw is not last operand of comma
expression, entire expression will not be evaluated
```

The compiler implementors meant to say that *not all* of the expression will be evaluated; what the warning says, however, is that *none* of the expression will be evaluated. Users who understand C++ will realize that this is a poorly worded diagnostic, but less sophisticated users might be misled. This example shows that it is important to have good writers review your writing. This message no doubt looked perfectly fine to the person who wrote it. It is difficult to see mistakes in your own writing.

11.3.8   Use Commonly Accepted Terminology

If commonly accepted terms are in use, use them rather than inventing your own. For example, stick to the established

    `T::T(const T& t)` is the *copy constructor* for `T`.

rather than

    `T::T(const T& t)` is the *clone function* for `T`.

Even if you think your term is better, you will serve your readers better if you use the established terminology. If no established terminology exists and you must coin a term, then define it precisely at its first use. For example,

    In the following, we shall call `T::T(int i)` the *int constructor* for `T`.

When writing about C++, use C++ terminology. In particular, do not substitute or intersperse the terminology of other object-oriented languages. There is nothing wrong with the terminology of other languages, but readers of a tutorial for a C++ library have no wish to juggle two vocabularies. What some languages call a *method* is a *member function* in C++; what some languages call *sending a message* is in C++ *calling a member function*.

11.3.9   Beware of Overloaded Terms

Be careful with words that have more than one meaning. Consider the following five uses of the word *instance*:

1. An *instance* of class T
2. The *instance* T<int> of the class template T
3. The f(int) *instance* of function template f
4. The g(int) *instance* of the overloaded function g
5. An *instance* of the general rule

A discussion that used *instance* for all these uses would be difficult to comprehend. Better wordings for the first three of these phrases would be as follows:

1. An object of class T
2. The specialization T<int> of the class template T
3. The f(int) specialization of function template f

(The meaning of the term *specialization* is discussed on page ix.)

11.3.10   Show Legal, Error-Free Code

Code in a tutorial should contain no unintentional errors. Syntax or logic errors reveal that the examples were not tested; they make the writer appear careless and lazy, and they cause the reader to lose confidence in the tutorial or the library or both.

Code in examples should also be free of intentional errors. Generally, it is more effective to teach by showing what to do rather than what not to do. Thus, say

```
f(1);  // call f with a nonzero argument
```

rather than

```
f(0);  // it is an error to pass zero to f
```

Sometimes, however, showing an error helps the reader understand and avoid it. For example,

> If the user specifies an invalid regular expression, an exception is thrown:
>
> ```
> Regex r("[0-9"); // erroneous regular expression,
>                  // throws Regex::Invalid
> ```

Always label coding errors in examples. If this example appeared in a tutorial without the comment on the faulty line, readers scanning the tutorial might not notice that the code is faulty, and they might be misled into duplicating the error in their own code.

11.3.11   Keep Code Fragments Short

Try to keep code fragments in tutorials short (usually under 20 lines; certainly under one page). The longer a code example is, the greater the risk that readers will skip it or be confused by it. If the point you are illustrating requires many lines of code, break up the code with interspersed text. For example, instead of writing

> Users must do the following:
>
> ```
> // long
> // code
> // fragment
> // ...
> ```

write something like this:

> Users must first do the following:
>
> ```
> // short code fragment
> ```
>
> Then they must do this:
>
> ```
> // another short code fragment
> ```

11.3.12   Avoid Huge Functions

Huge functions are poor style, both in example code in tutorials and in real code. A tutorial writer should be careful not to present several code blocks, each of reasonable length, that collectively constitute a huge function. Consider this example:

> The users must provide a function f as follows:
>
> ```
> void f() {
>     while (some_condition)
>         // ...
> }
> ```
>
> The body of the while loop looks like this:

```
if (another_condition) {
    // ...
}
else {
    // ...
}
```

When `another_condition` is `true`, `f` should do this:

```
switch (expression) {  // ...
}
```

If this style of exposition continues for a page or so, `f` is a huge function, even though it might not appear to be on the tutorial page. The right way to present `f` (and to implement it) would be to break it into several functions:

The users must provide a function `f` as follows:

```
void f() {
    while (some_condition)
        g();
}
```

The function `g` looks like this:

```
void g() {
    if (another_condition)
        h(expression);
    else
        // ...
}
```

The function `h` is as follows:

```
void h(int expr) {
    switch (expr)
        // ...
}
```

Smaller, more modular functions are easier for readers of both code and documentation to digest.

11.3.13   Provide Examples On-line

Most of the code in tutorials should be provided on-line as part of the library distribution. Users will be frustrated if they have to type the examples to try them, when they know that the examples are already on-line on the library writer's machine.

11.4   Reference Manual

The reference manual for a library should document the library in complete, precise detail. Most C++ libraries are made up primarily of a collection of classes. Thus, a library documenter needs to know how to document a class completely and precisely. Documentation for a class X should do the following:

1. Tell the user what files to #include to get a definition of X. Unless there is a good reason to do otherwise, every public header file in a library should #include or declare (see Section 4.2.1) everything it needs. When this recommendation is followed, the user will never have to #include more than one file to get a definition of any given class.
2. Define X's abstraction.
3. Show X's syntactic interface.
4. Describe the semantics of each function in X's interface.
5. State any restrictions on template arguments.

The first of these points should be self-explanatory; we elaborate on the latter four in the following sections.

11.4.1   The Abstraction

It is difficult to overstate the importance of defining clearly every class's abstraction. To use a class intelligently, a user must know what abstraction that class models. Unfortunately, much existing documentation does not document class abstractions properly. Rather than define Regex's abstraction, for example, typical existing library documentation might say something like any of the following:

- The class Regex is useful for manipulating regular expressions.
- Regex should be used to perform regular expression matching.
- Regex provides a way for programmers to manipulate regular expressions conveniently.

Although each of these statements is true, none of them defines Regex's abstraction.

The appropriate level of precision at which to define a class's abstraction will depend on the class being documented and on the backgrounds of the intended users. If, for example, the class is Regex and the users are technically astute, then merely saying "A Regex is a regular expression" will suffice.

11.4.2   The Syntactic Interface

What parts of the definition of a class X should be shown in the reference manual? Certainly not the entire definition. Many parts of a typical class definition are implementation details that should not concern users of X. Consider the following:

```
class X {
    friend ostream& operator<<(ostream& o, const X&);
    // ...
};
```

That the output operator is a friend of X should not affect users of X; hence, we need not show this friend declaration (or any friend declaration) in the reference manual. (We should, of course, show the output operator somewhere.)

Obviously, we should show all public and protected base classes and members:

```
class X : public Document_this_base {
public:
    void document_this_function();
protected:
    void and_this_one_too();
    // ...
};
```

For a function member, the syntactic interface is its prototype: the return type, the types of the arguments, and whether the function is virtual, const, or static.

Automatically Generated Member Functions

Recall that the definition of C++ provides that if a class X does not declare any constructors, a public default constructor will be generated by the compiler. Similarly, the compiler will generate a copy constructor, an assignment operator, and a destructor when these functions are not declared.

There are two ways that the reference manual for a library can handle automatically generated functions:

- It can make no mention of them and let the user infer their existence. For example, if a class X is documented as having the following public interface

```
class X {
public:
    X();
    X(const X&);
    void f();
};
```

then the user can infer that an assignment operator and a destructor are automatically generated for X.

• Alternatively, the reference manual can show automatically generated functions explicitly, even though they do not appear in the class declaration in the code:

```
class X {
public:
    X();
    X(const X&);
    const X& operator=(const X&);
    void f();
    ~X();
};
```

That an assignment operator and a destructor are generated automatically is an implementation detail, and it should not affect users.

Either approach can be used. The reference manual should say how automatically generated members are documented. Whichever approach is chosen, it should be used consistently.

Private Members

The documenter's first impulse might be that private members need not be shown in the reference manual. The following private members, however, should always be shown:

• A private member function that would be generated automatically if the private declaration were not present
• A private declaration of operator&

For example, we should document the private members of the following class to show that copying and taking the address of X objects is prohibited:

```
class X {
private:
    X(const X& x);
    X* operator&();
public:
    X();
    // ...
};
```

What about other private members? If, for example, X declares a private member function f, should the reference manual show f? As pointed out in Section 6.1.5, C++'s checking of ambiguities before access protection can lead to private names in libraries causing ambiguities in user code. Documenting all private names would clutter user documentation. Thus, most libraries do not document private names other than the ones mentioned previously. For similar reasons, most library reference manuals do not show private base classes.

11.4.3   Function Semantics

The reference manual should state the semantics of each function (except regular functions, as will be discussed) in the syntactic interface of a class being documented. Documenters should adhere to these conventions:

- As discussed in Section 11.3.2, semantics should always be explained in terms of the abstract values of the objects involved, not in terms of the underlying implementations.
- When a virtual function is documented, its inheritance semantics (see Section 3.3) should be specified.
- When a function returning a pointer or reference is documented, the lifetime of the returned value (see Section 4.4.3) should be specified.
- If a function throws any exceptions (see Section 5.3.4), the type of each exception and under what conditions it will be thrown should be specified.

The semantics of the regular functions (see Section 2.2) need not be documented. It would not be necessary, for example, to document that X's destructor frees all the memory internally allocated by X. If X's destructor does *not* free the memory X allocated, then X is implemented incorrectly and should be fixed.

If a class is designed properly, but a documenter nevertheless perceives a need to document the semantics of one of the class's regular functions, it might be that the class's abstraction has not been defined properly. Suppose, for example, that a library provides the following class and associated function:

```
class File {
public:
    File(const char* path);
    // ...
};

bool operator==(const File& file1, const File& file2);
```

Suppose that the documentation reads as follows:

> A File represents a file name. The constructor creates the given file name. The equality operator returns true if f and g are the same file name or refer to the same file.

As stated, the semantics of the equality operator is not regular. We can make it regular by correcting the definition of the abstraction:

> A File represents a file in the underlying operating system. The constructor creates a File representing the file to which the given path refers. Different paths might refer to the same file.

If the equality operator has regular semantics, it will return true if f and g have the same abstract value — that is, if f and g refer to the same file. With a well-written definition of the File abstraction, this behavior of the equality operator goes without saying.

11.4.4   Template Argument Restrictions

Any restrictions on the arguments to a class template or function template should be documented in the reference manual. Suppose that a library provides a sort template:

```
template<class T>
void qsort(T* t, int n);
```

This function sorts the array of n Ts beginning at t. Suppose that qsort uses < to compare array elements:

```
template<class T>
void qsort(T* t, int n) {
    T* t1;
    T* t2;
    // ...
    if (*t1 < *t2)
        // ...
    // ...
}
```

For code that calls qsort to compile, the use of < in qsort must be legal for the type T. The documentation should state this restriction, perhaps as follows:

> T must be a type such that if x and y are objects of type T, the expression x < y is legal and returns true if x is to be considered less than y.

Documenting template argument restrictions properly is tricky. The documenter of qsort might be tempted to write this:

> The type T must provide a < operation.

This statement, however, demands more than the code requires. Consider this class:

```
class X {
public:
    operator int() const;
    // ...
};
```

Even if X provides no < operation, calling qsort on an array of Xs will be legal because the expression *t1 < *t2 will convert *t1 and *t2 to ints, then apply the built-in int operator <.

11.5 Summary

Good documentation is crucial for reusable code. Documentation for a C++ library should include at least a design paper, tutorials, and a reference manual.

The design paper for a library should discuss significant decisions made in the design of the library, why each was decided the way it was, for whom the library is intended, and what the library provides those users.

Tutorials should be written clearly and simply, and should be written appropriately for the background of the library's intended users. They should discuss the library functionality in terms of abstract values, not implementation. Examples in tutorials should show legal, correct code.

A library reference manual should define the abstraction of each library class, show the syntactic interface for each class, give the semantics of each function in the interface of each class, and present any restrictions on template arguments.

Exercises

11.1   Consider the following version of the `Path` class discussed in Exercises 1.2, 12.14, and 7.1:

```
class Path {
public:
    enum Style { UNIX, Windows, VMS };

    Path();
    Path(const Path& p);
    Path(const String& str, Style style = UNIX);
    const Path& operator=(const Path& p);
private:
    void canonicalize();
    Style the_style;
};

ostream& operator<<(ostream& o, const Path& p);
```

Which of these functions should be documented in the reference manual?

11.2   (∗) In Section 11.4.2, we discussed whether private member functions should be documented in a library reference manual.

    a.   Give an example of reasonable user code that will fail because of a private base class in a library.

    b.   (∗) Under what conditions would a library need to document its private base classes, and why?

References and Further Reading

Writing good English (or Japanese, or whatever language) is more difficult than most people realize. Writing good documentation is particularly difficult. Works by Strunk and White [SW79], Dupré [Dup95], and Hodges and Whitten [HW67] are excellent sources of valuable advice for writing in English.

12 Miscellaneous Topics

> *The beginnings and endings of all human undertakings are untidy, the building of a house, the writing of a novel, the demolition of a bridge, and, eminently, the finish of a voyage.*
>
> — John Galsworthy

In this chapter, we discuss several miscellaneous but important library design issues. First, we describe the problem of static initialization and present several techniques for implementing a library in the face of this problem. After defining the principle of *localized cost*, we caution that a library can violate that principle if it is not designed carefully. Containers are widely used reusable classes; therefore, we address two important issues related to containers: differentiating endogenous and exogenous containers and designing iterators. Next, we discuss the advantages and disadvantages of class coupling — the use in one class of another class in the same library. Finally, we show how a C++ library designer can avoid making a difficult design decision by deferring the decision to users.

12.1 The Static Initialization Problem

C++ inherits from C the notion of initialization of static objects. (*Static object* means an object in static storage; such an object might or might not be declared with the `static` keyword.) For example, the following definition, if it appears at global scope, initializes the static object i with the value 0:

```
int i = 0;
```

Unlike C, which restricts initializers for static objects to constant expressions (that is, expressions that can be evaluated during either compile time or link time), C++ allows arbitrary expressions to appear in initializers. This feature of C++ has created the static initialization problem. In the following sections, we shall elaborate on what the language definition has to say about the order of initialization of static objects, why there is a problem for writers of C++ libraries, and what library writers can do about initialization of statics.

12.1.1 Construction and Destruction Times

The C++ language makes certain guarantees about the construction and destruction times of the objects in a program. Consider a class with both a constructor and a destructor — the special-purpose memory allocator class `Pool` of Section 2.4.1, for example. A stack object p of type `Pool` is guaranteed to be constructed when the flow of control passes through p's definition and destroyed when the flow of control leaves p's immediately containing block:

```
{
    // ...
    Pool p(20);  // p constructed now
    // ...
}  // p destroyed now
```

Further, all the objects in a given block are guaranteed to be destroyed in the reverse order of their construction. An object allocated from the free store is guaranteed to be constructed when it is allocated and destroyed when it is deleted:

```
Pool* p = new Pool(20);   // *p constructed now
// ...
delete p;                 // *p destroyed now
```

If an object is neither on the stack nor in the free store, then it is in static storage. What the language will guarantee about construction and destruction times for static objects is, as of this writing, still being debated by the ANSI/ISO C++ committee. We are confident, however, that ANSI/ISO C++ will make certain guarantees. First, the language undoubtedly will guarantee that a local static will be constructed when the flow of control first passes through the object's definition:

```
{  // open a block
   // ...
   static Pool p(20);   // p constructed when control first
                        // passes here
   // ...
}
```

The C++ standard probably will also guarantee (with one exception, which we shall discuss) that all the nonlocal static objects (a *nonlocal* object is one not defined within a function) defined in a given translation unit will be constructed in their order of appearance in that translation unit and destroyed in reverse order of appearance. For example, if this code appears at global scope in a translation unit

```
Pool p1(20);
// ...
Pool p2(20);
// ...
Pool p3(20);
```

then p1, p2, and p3 will be constructed in that order and destroyed in the reverse order.

The exception to this order of construction and destruction of nonlocal statics is for what we shall call simple objects. An object x is *simple* if both of the following are true:

- x is not a class object or x's class has no explicit constructor.
- x's definition initializes x to a compile-time or link-time constant.

The language probably will guarantee that all simple, nonlocal, static objects defined in a translation unit T will be constructed when the object code for T is loaded (which might be after the program has started executing, if T is linked dynamically). In the following translation unit, for example,

```
Pool p1(20);
// ...
int i = 7;  // definition of a simple object
// ...
Pool p2(20);
```

i will be constructed when the object code for this translation unit is loaded, which will be before p1 and p2 are constructed and before any functions in the translation unit are executed.

ANSI/ISO C++ probably will make additional guarantees about the construction and destruction times of static objects. The language almost certainly will *not*, however, guarantee that a nonlocal static object is constructed before `main` is called. Such a guarantee would preclude dynamic linking of object files.

One guarantee that C++ programmers would like to have is that, in any program that builds successfully, objects are always constructed before they are used and never used after they are destroyed. Unfortunately, the language cannot make such a guarantee. It is not always possible to determine, when a program is built, whether there is an ordering in which to construct nonlocal static objects such that all objects are used only between construction and destruction (see Exercise 12.5).

12.1.2 Implications for Libraries

If a C++ library defines and uses *any* nonsimple, nonlocal, static objects, it will be possible for a user of the library to build successfully a program that uses an object before it is constructed (unless the library implementors have taken precautions to prevent such uses; see Section 12.1.6). Such a program will have undefined behavior. Suppose, for example, that our library provides the following `Widget` class:

Widget.h:

```
class Widget {
public:
    void* operator new(size_t) {
        return pool.alloc();
    }
    void operator delete(void* p) {
        pool.free(p);
    }
    //...
private:
    static Pool pool;
};
```

Widget.c:

```
Pool Widget::pool(sizeof(Widget));
```

We have used a `Pool` to implement the class-specific operators **new** and **delete**. Notice that `Widget::pool` is a nonsimple, nonlocal, static object.

Now suppose that the following user code appears at global scope:

```
Widget* w = new Widget;
```

Notice that `w` is also a nonsimple, nonlocal, static object and that the definitions of `w` and `Widget::pool` will be contained in different translation units. When the program containing this user code is built, `Widget::pool` might or might not be constructed before `w` is initialized. If it is not, then `Widget::pool` will be used (in `Widget::operator new`) before it is constructed. Hence, the containing program has undefined behavior.

It would be possible for a compilation system to insert checks into the generated code such that any use of an uninitialized object would cause a run-time error. The resulting program, however, typically would be too slow. Some programmers would like a compilation system that generates such checking optionally, so that the checks can be turned on during program development and turned off when efficiency matters. We know of no such compilation systems.

If a library contains code that allows users to use an uninitialized library object, it can be difficult for users to identify the problem. Further, even if they do identify the problem, they might have no remedy.

Libraries should always avoid the possibility of user programs using uninitialized library objects. In general, C++ libraries should not define and use nonsimple, nonlocal, static objects. Whenever we think we have a need for such an object, we should move the object to the free store. Moving `Widget::pool` to the free store yields this code:

Widget.h:

```
class Widget {
public:
    void* operator new(size_t) {
        assert(pool != 0);
        return pool->alloc();
    }
    void operator delete(void* p) {
        assert(pool != 0);
        pool->free(p);
    }
    //...
private:
    static Pool* pool;
};
```

Widget.c:

```
Pool* Widget::pool = 0;
```

Now `Widget::pool` is a *simple*, nonlocal, static object, and therefore it is guaranteed to be initialized when the object code for *Widget.c* is loaded, which will be before `Widget::operator new` ever executes.

Now that we have moved our object to the free store, we must allocate and deallocate it somewhere in our code. Several approaches, which we shall discuss in the following sections, are used commonly in C++ libraries. In discussing the various approaches, we shall use the following `Widget` member functions:

```
class Widget {
private:
    static void new_pool() {
        if (pool == 0)
            pool = new Pool(sizeof(Widget));
    }
    static void delete_pool() {
        delete pool;
    }
    // ...
};
```

None of the approaches we shall discuss is without disadvantages. C++ library designers must choose the approach that is least objectionable for each particular library.

12.1.3   Init Functions

One way that some C++ libraries try to deal with static initialization is to provide a library initialization function. For example, the library containing the class `Widget` might provide a global function `initwidgetlib` that a program would be required to call before using any of the functionality in the library:

```
void initwidgetlib() {
    Widget::new_pool();
    // ...
}
```

(This function would have to be a friend of `Widget`.) Using any functionality in a library before that library's init function has been called should be documented to have undefined behavior.

A library that provides an init function usually must also provide a finalization function that must be called when the program is finished using the library:

```
void finalizewidgetlib() {
    Widget::delete_pool();
    // ...
}
```

(This function would also have to be a friend of `Widget`.)

There are several drawbacks to library init functions. First, it is not always easy for the library user to determine when to call a given init function. The naive strategy would be to call all init functions at the beginning of `main`:

```
int main() {
    initwidgetlib();
    initsomeotherlib();
    // ...
}
```

For this approach to work, the user must own the implementation of `main`; this requirement sometimes will preclude relying on init functions. Further, if any functionality from one of these libraries were used during the initialization of any static objects that are initialized before the call of `main`, then the program would have undefined behavior. Thus, an init function does not, in fact, solve the static initialization problem.

Further, even if a program uses no libraries during the initialization of static objects and can therefore safely wait until `main` is executed to call library init functions, it can be difficult to identify which library init functions to call. Suppose that a large program is being written by a team of many developers. The developer of `main` might have a difficult time identifying all the libraries called, directly or indirectly, in the program. If the developer of `main` does manage to determine which library init functions should be called, there will still be the problem of determining a safe order in which to call them. Suppose, for example, that some part of library `X` uses some part of library `Y`. Then library `Y`'s init function must be called before library `X`'s init function. Keeping track of such dependencies in a large project could be a nightmare.

A further problem with init functions is that they sometimes initialize more than a program needs. Suppose that a program uses only certain parts of the `Widget` library and that those uses do not involve the `Widget` class.

Nevertheless, when the user calls `initwidgetlib`, the program will allocate `Widget::pool`. Instead of providing a single init function, a library might provide several init functions, each of which initializes some documented subset of the library. This attempted solution, however, could quickly become unmanageable.

Finally, library init functions do not work well with templates. Suppose that `Widget` were a class template:

```
template<class T>
class Widget {
    // ...
private:
    static Pool* pool;
};
```

The function `initwidgetlib` would have to allocate `Widget<T>::pool` for all types `T` such that a `Widget<T>` is used in the program. Unfortunately, it can be difficult or impossible to write code to do that.

12.1.4   Init Checks

Another way that some libraries deal with the static initialization problem is to use init checks. With this approach, whenever we are about to use one of our free-store objects, we first ensure that it has already been allocated:

```
class Widget {
public:
    void* operator new(size_t) {
        new_pool();
        // now we can safely use pool
        // ...
    }
    void operator delete(void*) {
        new_pool();
        // now we can safely use pool
        // ...
    }
    // ...
};
```

Init checks have two disadvantages. First, they can slow down user programs. Fortunately, the number of init checks often can be reduced based on a flow analysis of the library code. For example, if a program that uses

`Widget` is correct, then `Widget::operator delete` will be called only on `Widget` objects that have been constructed with `Widget::operator new`. Hence, we can safely remove the init check from `operator delete`.

If a given init check cannot be eliminated, sometimes it can be moved to where it will be executed less often. For example, suppose that our library contains the following function:

```
Widget* create_widgets(int n) {
    while (--n > 0) {
        Widget* w = new Widget;
        // ...
    }
}
```

Here, the init check is called each time through the loop. Suppose that the class `Widget` is private to the implementation of our library and that there are no calls to `Widget::operator new` other than through the call to `new` in `create_widgets`. Then instead of performing the init check in `Widget::operator new`, we can move the check to `create_widgets`:

```
Widget* create_widgets(int n) {
    Widget::new_pool();  // init check moved to here
    while (--n > 0) {
        Widget* w = new Widget;
        // ...
    }
}
```

Now the init check happens only once per call of `create_widgets`. (To effect this change, we must make `create_widgets` a friend of `Widget`.)

A library implementor who eliminates or moves any init checks based on a flow analysis of library code should document fastidiously each such optimization for future developers and maintainers of the code. Changes to the implementation of the library could invalidate the flow analysis.

The second disadvantage of init checks is that the technique does not help us determine when to delete our objects. In our example, the object pointed to by `Widget::pool` should be deleted after it is no longer needed. Detecting when that is would be nontrivial. In practice, there are libraries that use init checks and never delete certain objects. If, for example, we know that our users will not care if we never delete `Widget::pool`, then we might not bother to delete it. (This approach violates our recommendation of Section 4.5.2 that resources be freed as soon as possible.)

12.1.5   Init Objects

A third way that some libraries deal with static initialization is to use init objects. We shall show how an init object would be used for our Widget example. First, we place the following definitions in *Widget.h*:

Widget.h:

```
class Widgetinit {
    static int counter;
public:
    Widgetinit();
    ~Widgetinit();
};

class Widget {
    friend class Widgetinit;
    // ...
};

static Widgetinit widgetinit;  // the init object
```

Here, widgetinit is the init object. We also declare Widgetinit a friend of Widget. We implement Widgetinit as follows:

Widget.c:

```
int Widgetinit::counter = 0;

Widgetinit::Widgetinit() {
    if (counter++ == 0)
        Widget::new_pool();
}

Widgetinit::~Widgetinit() {
    if (counter-- == 1)
        Widget::delete_pool();
}
```

(In a real library, the init object would initialize and finalize everything Widget needs, not just Widget::pool.)

Let us make the reasonable assumption that anyone who uses Widget, other than just to declare its name, first includes *Widget.h*. Then it will be impossible for a program to use the Pool pointed to by Widget::pool before that object has been allocated. We are guaranteed of this impossibility because the initialization of the init object `widgetinit` in each transla-tion unit will precede the initialization of any nonsimple objects involving `Widget` in that translation unit, and the initialization of `widgetinit` ini-tializes `Widget::pool` if it has not been initialized already.

Init objects have several disadvantages. First, they can increase un-expectedly the code size of user programs. Suppose, for example, that *Widget.h* includes the standard `iostream` header file *iostream.h*. Suppose further that the implementation of `iostreams` our users have, like many im-plementations of `iostreams`, uses an init object. Then every program that uses `Widget` — even programs that do not use any `iostream` functionality — will pull in all the code needed to initialize the `iostream` library. To prevent this undesirable pull-in, we should directly declare the `iostream` classes we need rather than include *iostream.h* (see Section 4.2.1).

Similarly, suppose that the following file appears in our library's imple-mentation:

Widget.c:

```
#include <iostream.h>

void func1() {
    // ...
    cout << "Make it so!";
    // ...
}
void func2() {
    // ...
}
```

The function `func1` uses the `iostream` library, but `func2` does not. When an implementation of `iostream` that relies on init objects is used, any user program that calls `func2`, directly or indirectly, will pull in the `iostream` library initialization code. To prevent this pull-in, we must move `func2` into a file that does not include *iostream.h*.

The second disadvantage of init objects is that they can increase the run time of user programs. Suppose that a program includes *Widget.h* in many translation units (the file *Widget.h* might be included in a header file that is itself included by most of the files in a project). Each such translation unit will contain the definition of a `Widget` init object. These `Widget` init objects probably will be distributed more or less randomly throughout the program's object code. On virtual memory systems, calling all the init object constructors will cause all the pages containing init objects to be faulted into memory at program start-up, causing a noticeable delay.

The third drawback of init objects is that, like init functions, they do not work well with templates. We leave consideration of the details to the reader (see Exercise 12.1).

12.1.6   Double Construction

There are techniques, such as *double construction,* that allow a C++ library to define and use a static object that is both nonsimple and nonlocal, and run only a small risk that a user program will use that object before it is initialized. Suppose that the class `Pool` has a special constructor that is guaranteed to execute no code:

```
class Pool {
public:
    enum Do_nothing_ctor { do_nothing_ctor };
    Pool(Do_nothing_ctor) { /* executes no code */ }
    // ...
};
```

The enum `Do_nothing_ctor` appears solely for the purpose of providing this special constructor — by overloading. The library implementor must also ensure that any constructors implicitly invoked for base classes and data members do nothing.

With our special constructor, instead of moving the nonsimple, nonlocal, static object `Widget::pool` to the free store, we rewrite the function `Widget::new_pool` (first shown in Section 12.1.2) as follows:

```
#include <new.h>

class Widget {
private:
    static void new_pool() {
        static bool first_time = true;
        if (first_time) {
            new(&pool) Pool(sizeof(Widget));
            first_time = false;
        }
    }
    static Pool pool;
    // ...
};
```

Here, we use the placement version of operator **new**. We can now use any of the techniques discussed in Sections 12.1.3 through 12.1.5 to help ensure that `Widget::pool` is initialized before it is used. Note that double construction does not obviate the need for init objects, init functions, or init checks, but it does allow a library to use nonsimple, nonlocal, static objects (and frees the library from having to move such objects to the free store).

A program using `Widget` will construct the object `Widget::pool` twice: once in the first call to `new_pool` and once at `Widget::pool`'s definition site. To render the constructor call from the definition site innocuous (recall that we have no guarantee in which order these calls will occur — which is the crux of the problem), we call the constructor that executes no code:

```
Pool Widget::pool(Pool::do_nothing_ctor);
```

You might consider the double-construction technique inelegant. Some C++ implementations use double construction coupled with an init object to implement the `iostream` library. Nevertheless, we advise against use of double construction in any other library. As explained by Plauger [Pla95], the technique does not eliminate the possibility of a program using a doubly constructed object before it is initialized.

12.2   The Principle of Localized Cost

An important design goal for any reusable code is *localizing cost*. A system has localized cost if only those who use a feature pay for it. Everyday life provides examples of the principle of localized cost: A salad bar priced by weight localizes cost — each diner pays only for what he or she takes. An open bar at a club on New Year's Eve does not localize cost — even those not drinking pay (through the price of admission) for the alcohol consumed by others. Sometimes, costs are distributed deliberately: When we purchase major medical insurance, we all agree to pay a share of the (possibly large) costs that will be incurred by the few who file claims.

The principle of localized cost applies to almost every domain in computer science. In hardware, for example, the goal of reduced instruction set computers (RISC) was to re-establish localized cost in machine instruction sets. Instruction sets had become more and more complex over the years, with the effect that every program was paying — in slower execution — for the presence of highly specialized, infrequently used instructions. Machines can be designed that process each instruction in a simplified instruction set faster. By eliminating the more esoteric instructions, localized cost is restored to the hardware design.

12.2.1 Localized Cost and C++

Many features of C++ were designed with the goal of enabling implementations to localize costs. The idea was that programmers should not have to pay — in increased compile, link, or run time; in increased code size; or in increased complexity of the language — for features they do not use. No language feature can satisfy these constraints perfectly. Any feature thickens the reference manual at least a little, enlarges the compiler at least a little, and gives the standardization committee something more to deliberate. The designer of a language, then, must decide whether the usefulness of a proposed feature justifies its cost.

Consider C++'s virtual functions and localized cost. Virtual functions carry the following costs:

- Each virtual function call requires only two to five more machine instructions, in most implementations of the language, than does a nonvirtual function call.
- Most current implementations cannot inline virtual function calls in certain contexts (see Section 4.4.2).
- Most implementations use tables to determine which instance of a virtual function to call. These tables, and a pointer to a virtual function table in each object of a class with one or more virtual functions, occupy memory in the user's compiled code.
- The presence of a pointer to a virtual function table in class objects renders the object layout link incompatible with C.

Except for the increased complexity of the language, each of these costs is localized — only programs that contain classes with virtual functions incur the costs. Further, execution speed is strongly localized: Programs that use virtual functions pay for them only when a virtual function is invoked.

12.2.2 Localized Cost and Libraries

It is easy to violate localized cost when designing or implementing a C++ library. Library designers should be aware of possible violations of localized cost and strive to avoid them. The pull-in of code to initialize `iostream` init objects discussed in Section 12.1.5 is an example of how a library might, if care is not exercised, violate localized cost.

For another example, consider the following class in some library:

```
class T {
protected:
    inline void f() {
        // ...
    }
    // ...
};
```

The definition of f has been inlined to increase the speed of code that calls f. Suppose, however, that several users of the library report that they want to derive from T and they need to be able to override f. The library providers therefore propose to make f virtual in the next release, as follows:

```
class T {
protected:
    virtual inline void f() {
        // ...
    }
    // ...
};
```

Unfortunately, this change would violate localized cost. As discussed in Section 4.4.2, most current implementations of C++ fail to inline virtual function calls when the compiler cannot easily determine the type of the object for which the function is to be called. Thus, if f becomes virtual, all callers of f will pay — in increased execution time for calling f out-of-line and possibly in the code size of outlined copies of f (see Section 4.3.2) — for the ability of some programs to override f.

On the other hand, not making f virtual can also be considered a violation of localized cost. For the benefit of those users who want a slightly faster f, all users forgo the ability to override f. (See Section 4.4.2 for an analysis of when to inline a function versus when to make it virtual.)

12.3   Endogenous and Exogenous Classes

In this section, we clarify a frequent source of confusion among library designers: the difference between endogenous and exogenous containers. Suppose that List<T> represents a list of values of type T. List can be implemented in either of two ways. An *endogenous* implementation would store the contained values directly in the underlying list nodes, as shown in Figure 12.1.

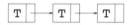

Figure 12.1   Endogenous implementation of a `List`.

An *exogenous* implementation would store the contained values in separate objects, as shown in Figure 12.2.

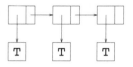

Figure 12.2   Exogenous implementation of a `List`.

The difference between endogenous and exogenous containers is an implementation difference only, not an interface difference. Regardless of how it is implemented, a `List<T>` should behave as a list of values of type T. For example, the equality function

```
template<class T>
bool operator==(const List<T>& l1, const List<T>& l2);
```

should — for either implementation — return `true` if l1 and l2 represent equal lists (that is, if l1 and l2 have the same length and corresponding elements are equal). For example, if `List` is exogenous, the three `List<int>` objects l1, l2, and l3 shown in Figure 12.3 should all test equal. If l1, l2, and l3 are endogenous lists of T*, however, then l1 is equal to l2 but neither l1 nor l2 is equal to l3.

Notice the similarities as well as the differences between an exogenous list of T and an endogenous list of T*. The pictures of these lists look the same, as shown in Figure 12.4. An exogenous list of T and an endogenous list of T* behave differently, however.

A mistake some library designers make is to provide a class that for some operations models an endogenous container of T* and for other operations models an exogenous container of T. Consider the following class and associated function:

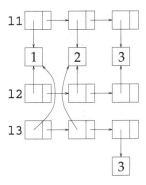

Figure 12.3   Equality of List objects. If List is exogenous, objects
11, 12, and 13 all test equal. If List is endogenous, 11 is
equal to 12 but not to 13.

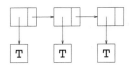

Figure 12.4   Exogenous list of T or endogenous list of T*.

```
template<class T>
class Ptrlist {
public:
    void insert(T* t);
    // ...
};

template<class T>
bool operator==(const Ptrlist<T>& l, const Ptrlist<T>& m);
```

Suppose that this class is documented as follows:

A Ptrlist<T> is a list of pointers to T. The function insert inserts
t at the beginning of the list. The function operator== dereferences
each contained pointer when comparing l and m.

In spite of the first sentence, the designer of `Ptrlist` apparently cannot decide whether a `Ptrlist<T>` models a list of `T*` or a list of `T`. The definitions of the abstraction and the function `insert` assume the former; the definition of `operator==` assumes the latter. Notice, incidentally, that if `Ptrlist` indeed models a list of `T*`, then `operator==` does not have regular semantics (see Section 2.2).

Some readers might argue that users often *want* containers of pointers to have irregular semantics. Library designers who decide to provide irregular classes should clearly and boldly document them as such to avoid introducing insidious errors into the code of users who (quite reasonably) expect all classes to be regular.

12.4   Iterators

Iterators, widely used in conjunction with container classes, deserve special mention because they have semantics that are tricky to define and implement well. Suppose that our library provides a `Map` class (see Section 3.2.2):

```
template<class X, class Y>
class Map {
public:
    void insert(const X& x, const Y& y);
    void remove(const X& x);
    // ...
};
```

Recall that `insert` adds the pair ⟨x, y⟩ to the mapping after removing any pair whose first value is `x`, and `remove` removes any pair whose first value is `x`. (There are other ways to design a `Map` class; see Exercise 4.4.)

Users of `Map` will want a way to iterate over the values in a map. Usually the best way to allow users of a container to iterate over its values is to provide a companion iterator class. Here is an iterator class for `Map`:

```
template<class X, class Y>
class Map_iter {
public:
    Map_iter(const Map<X,Y>& m);
    bool next(X& x, Y& y);
    // ...
};
```

The `Map_iter` constructor creates an iterator over `m`. As long as there are pairs in `m` that have not yet been returned by the iterator, the function `next` assigns another map pair to `x` and `y` and returns `true`; when there are no more pairs, `next` returns `false`. Pairs are returned in an unspecified order. Here is a typical use of `Map_iter`:

```
Map_iter<X,Y> i(m);
X x;
Y y;
while (i.next(x, y)) {
    // (x, y) is the next pair in m
    // ...
}
```

You might have noticed that our definition of the behavior of `Map_iter` is incomplete. What is the behavior, for example, of the following code?

```
Map_iter<X,Y> i(m);
X x;
Y y;
while (i.next(x, y)) {
    m.insert(some_x, some_y);  // line 1
    m.remove(another_x);       // line 2
    // ...
}
```

Here, the user iterates over all the pairs in `m` and, while doing so, tries to insert new pairs into `m` and remove pairs from `m`. What should the semantics of inserting and removing while iterating be? After the insertion on line 1, will the iterator `i` eventually return the newly inserted pair? If, when line 2 is executed, `another_x` has not yet been returned by `i`, will it ever be?

An easy way to deal with a problematic operation is to make it illegal. For example, we could impose the precondition on both `Map::insert` and `Map::remove` that there be no extant iterators on the given map. (The effect of a violation of either of these preconditions could be any of the possibilities described in Section 5.3.) Banning the problematic operations would be easy for users to understand and could be implemented easily and efficiently. This semantics is not, however, what many users will want. Changing a container while iterating through it is a useful operation.

Instead of banning the problematic operation, we could document that it is unspecified whether values added or removed during an iteration over a `Map` are seen eventually in that iteration. This approach is also unattractive. An interface with unspecified behavior is more error prone than a similar interface with fully specified behavior (see Exercise 12.13). Further, if our users are typical, at least some of them will want to write code that relies on fully specified behavior.

Programmers who want fully specified behavior for iteration over a container usually want the following semantics:

1. Values added to a container will be seen by all not yet terminated iterators on the container.
2. Values removed from a container will not be seen by any iterators on the container that have not yet seen those values.

Unfortunately, it is difficult to implement this behavior efficiently.

Suppose that we implement `Map` with a binary search tree (see Section 3.2.1). Every node in the tree holds a pair in the map; pairs are inserted and removed using binary search tree insertion and removal algorithms. The implementation of `Map_iter` will walk the tree, maintaining in the iterator's internal state the path from the root of the tree to the node whose pair was returned by the most recent call to `next`. Now consider the following code:

```
m.insert(x, y);
```

Suppose that when this call to `insert` executes, `x` is not in the domain of `m`. The binary search tree insertion algorithm will therefore insert a new node containing the value `x` into `m`'s tree. Now suppose that the region of the tree into which `x`'s node was inserted has already been visited by some extant iterator `i` on `m`. If `i` just continues walking the tree, it will never see the node containing `x`. This behavior would violate part 1 of the desired semantics.

We might try to solve this problem by having every `Map_iter` make multiple passes over its `Map`'s tree, remembering which nodes the iterator visited on earlier passes and terminating only when a pass reveals no new nodes. This implementation, however, would be slow. Every iteration over a `Map` would require at least two passes over the underlying tree, and every time even a single pair is inserted during a particular pass, another pass would have to be performed over the entire tree.

An efficient way to implement the desired semantics is to add a linear list to the implementation of `Map`. If any iterators are extant on the `Map`, `Map::insert` appends the given value onto the list instead of inserting it into the tree. When an iterator finishes iterating through the binary search tree, it then iterates through the list. Removed values can be handled by marking nodes as deleted. When the last extant iterator on a `Map` is destroyed, the values in its list are merged into the tree and deleted nodes

can be freed. The reader is invited to analyze the resulting efficiency of the
`Map` and `Map_iter` operations.

12.5   Class Coupling

Two classes are *coupled* if either class's interface or implementation uses the
other class. Consider a `Parser` class representing a C++ parser. Because
a parser manipulates many strings, `Parser` probably would be easier to
implement if it uses some `String` class rather than manipulating `char*`
values. `Parser` and `String` would therefore be coupled. Similarly, we
might decide to implement `Parser` using a class `Hashtable`, implementing
a hash table, instead of coding with built-in arrays and pointers.

Some programmers believe that coupling is generally undesirable; others believe that it is usually a good idea. Actually, coupling has both
advantages and disadvantages. As our `Parser` example shows, coupling
can simplify the implementation of a library. Coupling can also simplify
the use of a library. Suppose that the `Parser` constructor needs to take
a list of directories in which to search for included files. The following
interface couples `Parser` with the two classes `List` and `String`:

```
class Parser {
public:
    Parser(const List<String>& directories, /* ... */);
    // ...
};
```

Here, `List` is some class representing lists. Consider how we would have
to design the `Parser` constructor if we were not allowed to couple it
with `String`, `List`, or any other class. We might require that users pass
`Parser` constructor a pointer to a null-terminated array of pointers to null-
terminated strings:

```
class Parser {
public:
    Parser(const char* const* directories, /* ... */);
    // ...
};
```

This interface is not as easy to use and it is certainly more error prone than
the interface that uses `String` and `List`. Constructing a null-terminated
array of pointers to null-terminated strings probably requires more lines of
code than constructing a `List` of `Strings`. Further, users might forget to
end the array with a null pointer.

On the other hand, coupling can render a library more difficult to use. Suppose that we wish to allow users of Parser to specify an initial set of macro definitions. For example, we wish to allow users to create a Parser in the state a parser would have after parsing the following code:

```
#define MACRO1 STUFF
#define NULL_MACRO
```

We might consider using the Map class described in Section 12.4 to provide our desired Parser functionality:

```
class Parser {
public:
    Parser(const List<String>& directories,
        const Map<String,String>& initial_defines,
        /* ... */);
    // ...
};
```

Users would write code like this:

```
Map<String, String> initial_defines;
initial_defines.insert("MACRO1", "STUFF");
initial_defines.insert("NULL_MACRO", "");
// ...
Parser p(directories, initial_defines, /* ... */);
```

To use Parser, users would first have to understand String, List, and Map. Thus, programmers who wish to use Parser would first have to learn three other classes.

An alternative design that uses only two other classes is as follows:

```
class Parser {
public:
    Parser(const List<String>& directories,
        const List<String>& initial_defines, /* ... */);
    // ...
};
```

Users now write something like the following:

```
List<String> initial_defines;
initial_defines.insert("MACRO1=STUFF");
initial_defines.insert("NULL_MACRO=");
// ...
Parser p(directories, initial_defines, /* ... */);
```

Now programmers have to learn only two additional classes, `List` and `String`, to use `Parser`. Thus, the `Parser` interface with less coupling is easier to use.

To understand a class completely, we must understand all the classes used in the interface of that class, all the classes used in the interfaces of those classes, and so on. If a library is highly coupled, users might object to having to pore over the library documentation to understand all the class relationships.

Coupling can have a positive or negative effect on any particular measure of efficiency. For example, if `Hashtable` has been heavily optimized for use in C++ parsers, then decoupling `Parser` from `Hashtable` would probably increase run time. On the other hand, consider the use of `List` in the `Parser` interface. This coupling will require users to compile the definition of `List` and will cause `List`'s implementation to be pulled into the user program. The version of `Parser` that uses an array of pointers instead of `List` has neither of these overheads. The `List` version might be slightly slower than the decoupled version because iterating through all the values in a `List` might be slightly slower than iterating through an array of pointers.

Another disadvantage of coupling is that coupled classes are more difficult to scavenge (see Section 1.1.1) than uncoupled classes. If `Parser` uses `String`, `Hashtable`, `List`, and `Map`, then anyone who wants to scavenge `Parser` from our library will spend valuable time determining what `Parser` uses, directly and indirectly, and scavenging those things too.

Library designers should couple two classes if and only if the advantages of the proposed coupling outweigh the disadvantages.

12.6   Deferring Decisions

Often, the author of a library does not have enough information to make a particular design decision wisely. Sometimes, the author can defer such a decision and allow the user to participate in making it. Suppose, for example, that we are designing a library whose intended users write programs for networked computing environments — that is, environments in which different machines are connected and can communicate with each other.

Suppose that we want to give our users a function `location` that, given the name of a machine in the network, returns the location of that machine. The location will be returned as a value of type `Loc`, which is another class in our library:

```
Loc location(const String& machine_name);
```

The implementation of `location` will depend on the mechanism that a program executing on one machine in the user's network must use to get information from another machine. (Remote procedure call is one possibility.) For some networks, a call of `location` will be slow. For example, if a call to `location` is made by a program executing on a machine in Munich, Germany, and `machine_name` is somewhere in Australia, the call to `location` might take quite a while to complete. Let us therefore try to speed up `location`.

A general technique for speeding up a function is to *memoize* it. When a memoized function is called with a given set of arguments, the function determines whether it has already been called with those arguments. If not, it computes and stores the result in a cache before returning. If the function has already been called with those arguments, it simply returns the cached result. Here is pseudocode for the memoized version of a function `f` taking a single `int` argument:

```
int memoized_f(int n) {
        if (this function has already been called with the value n)
            return the value cached for n
        int result = computation of f(n)
        store result in this function's cache
        return result
}
```

If `f` is truly a function of `n` (and its result does not depend, for example, on the values of global variables), then memoizing `f` preserves its meaning. If `f` is called frequently on the same argument values, memoizing `f` can speed it up, sometimes significantly.

Let us suppose that `location` is called frequently on the same argument values. Because the location of a machine can change, `location` is not truly a function of its `machine_name` argument. Fortunately, machine locations change rarely. Let us suppose further that our users prefer a fast `location` that is sometimes — but only rarely — wrong over a slow `location` that is always right.

To memoize `location`, we need to implement a cache. Because the cache is a mapping from `String`s to `Loc`s, we can use the `Map` class described in Sections 3.2.2 and 12.4:

```
Loc location(const String& machine_name) {
    static Map<String, Loc> cache;
    if (cache.contains(machine_name))
        return cache.valueat(machine_name);
    Loc answer;

    // do the expensive network
    // connection to get the answer

    cache.insert(machine_name, answer);
    return answer;
}
```

(The `Map` function `valueat` returns the second value associated with the given first value.)

Suppose, however, that we have given our users flexibility in the use of maps. In particular, suppose that `Map` in our library is an abstract class with two derived class implementations `Small_map` and `Large_map`; `Small_map` is more efficient than `Large_map` for maps that never contain more than a few pairs. Our declaration of `cache` here would therefore be illegal. We must select either `Small_map` or `Large_map` (or some other class).

Suppose for the sake of argument that it is important that we use a highly efficient cache in `location`. If `location` will be called on only a few different machines, then we should use a `Small_map`; otherwise we should use a `Large_map`. Unfortunately, we probably do not know whether `location` will be called on only a few machines. Let us enlist the user's help in making this decision.

A general technique for enlisting the help of the library user is to provide a template, one or more of whose parameters allow the user to supply information that helps resolve the decision. For our problem, we can turn `location` into a template whose single parameter allows the user to supply the cache's map type:

```
template<template Cache<class X, class Y> >
Loc location(const String& machine_name);
```

(We rely here on a new feature of C++: the argument to a templates can itself be a template.) The implementation of this template is similar to the implementation of the nontemplate version of `location`:

```
template<template Cache<class X, class Y> >
Loc location(const String& machine_name) {
    static Cache<String, Loc> cache;
    // ...
}
```

Now users can say either

```
Loc l1 = location<Small_map>(machine_name1);
```

or

```
Loc l2 = location<Large_map>(machine_name2);
```

If the only legal template arguments to `location` for `Cache` are `Small_map` and `Large_map`, then the library designer should document that template argument restriction (for more on documenting template argument restrictions, see Section 11.4.4).

Enlisting the user's help in making a decision has drawbacks. First, the resulting library interface usually reveals implementation details of the library. For example, our `location` template reveals something about how the function is implemented. Revealing implementation details is generally ill advised and should be avoided wherever possible. The second drawback of enlisting the user's help is that doing so typically renders the library more difficult to use. Writing something like

```
Loc l = location<Small_map>(machine_name);
```

is less convenient than writing

```
Loc l = location(machine_name);
```

Often, we can ameliorate this problem by supplying a template default argument:

```
template<template Cache = Small_map>
Loc location(const String& machine_name);
```

Now users who do not care what type of cache is used can write

```
Loc l = location<>(machine_name);
```

This interface, however, is still slightly more difficult to use than the original (nontemplate) interface. Further, the ability to declare default template arguments is a recent addition to C++. Thus, code that relies on default template arguments will be nonportable for some time.

12.7   Summary

Designers of C++ libraries need to be aware of the static initialization problem. We recommend that libraries not define and use nonsimple, nonlocal, static objects. Instead, libraries should use objects in the free store. To allocate and initialize such objects, libraries can use init functions, init checks, and init objects. Each of these approaches has disadvantages.

Localizing costs is an important consideration for any library design. If a program does not use a feature of a library, it should not incur costs associated with the presence of that feature.

Containers are an important kind of reusable class. Designers of container classes should be careful to make those classes either endogenous or exogenous, but not a hybrid. Designing iterators with the right semantics requires attention and care as well.

Usually, coupling of classes within a library simplifies implementation of the library. Coupling sometimes makes the library easier to use; other times, it makes the library more difficult to use. Library designers must therefore weigh carefully the advantages and disadvantages of any proposed couplings.

Sometimes, making a difficult decision can be avoided by deferring it to users. A common technique for deferring a decision is to allow the user to specify a parameter for a template.

Exercises

12.1   We claimed in Section 12.1.5 that init objects cannot be used to solve the static initialization problem for class templates. Show that rewriting the `Widgetinit` class shown on page 272 as a class template will not enable us to initialize the `Widget` class template shown on page 270.

12.2   Explain why we made the destructor for the `Widgetinit` class of Section 12.1.5 call `Widget::delete_pool` when `Widgetinit::counter` has the value 1.

12.3   Explain why, in the definition of `Widget::pool` on page 268, we did not simply write

```
Pool* Widget::pool = new Pool(sizeof(Widget));
```

12.4   Some people have suggested that one way to deal with the static initialization problem would be to document which functions in a library should not be called during static initialization.

   a.   Which of the functions in the `Widget` class on page 266 should not be called during static initialization?

   b.   A function in a library that does not depend directly on the initialization of a nonsimple, nonlocal, static object might call another function that does depend on such an object. Give an algorithm for identifying the functions in a library to document as functions that should not be called during static initialization.

   c.   What compatibility issues arise with this approach to dealing with the static initialization problem?

   d.   What are the most significant disadvantages of this approach to static initialization?

   e.   How would you rank this approach compared to the three approaches presented in this chapter — init objects, init functions, and init checks?

12.5   (**) Let us define an *initialization order* for a C++ program P to be a linear ordering of the nonsimple, nonlocal, objects defined in P. An initialization order o for a program P is *acceptable* if initializing the nonsimple, nonlocal, objects in P in the order specified by o cannot, in any possible execution of P, result in any object in o being used before it is initialized. Consider the following function:

$$\text{orderable}(P) = \begin{cases} true & \text{if } P \text{ has an acceptable initialization order} \\ false & \text{otherwise} \end{cases}$$

   a.   Prove that the function *orderable* is not computable.

   b.   Discuss the implications of the result of part a for C++ compilation systems.

12.6   (*) Discuss the relationship of each of the three approaches to solving the static initialization problem presented in this chapter — init objects, init functions, and init checks — to the principle of localized cost (see Section 12.2). Which of the three violates localized cost most egregiously? Which best localizes costs? Be sure to consider both execution speed and use of space.

12.7   (∗) With virtual base classes in C++, you can write a class hierarchy
as follows:

```
class Link { /* ... */ };
class Sublist1 : virtual public Link { /* ... */ };
class Sublist2 : virtual public Link { /* ... */ };
class List : public Sublist1,
             public Sublist2 { /* ... */ };
```

Sublist1, Sublist2, and List objects each have one (and only one) instance of their common base class Link. Link therefore cannot occupy the
same position relative to Sublist1, Sublist2, and List in all Sublist1,
Sublist2, and List objects. (If you are not convinced of this, try to draw
an object layout for Sublist1, Sublist2, and List with Link in the same
position relative to Sublist1 and Sublist2 in objects of all three derived
types.)

Virtual base classes are typically implemented via indirection. Every
object that has a virtual base class has a pointer (stored at a fixed offset
relative to the beginning of the object) to the base class subobject. All
accesses to members of a virtual base class are indirect.

   a.   Does this implementation of virtual inheritance satisfy localized
cost with respect to execution speed?

   b.   Does this implementation localize cost with respect to space? (To
answer this question, consider an object as being used for as long as the
program retains it in memory.)

12.8   Suppose that we try to solve the conflict between virtual functions
and inlining, described in Section 12.2.2, by providing two versions of the
problem member function: a nonvirtual version and a virtual version that
simply calls the nonvirtual version. What are the drawbacks of this design?

12.9   Before multiple inheritance was added to C++, the code generated
by many C++ compilers for the virtual function call

```
p->f();
```

was more or less equivalent to this code:

```
(p->vptr[index])(p);
```

This code dereferences p to find the virtual function table for objects of p's
type, indexes that table to find the appropriate function to call, and then
calls the function on the object pointed to by p.

When multiple inheritance was added, the code for the same function call, even in programs that do not use multiple inheritance, became something like this:

```
(p->vptr[index])(p+p->vptr[index].delta);
```

This code finds the appropriate function to call the same way the previous code did, but before it can call the function it looks up a *delta* to apply to the value of p — so that the argument passed to the function will be the address of an object of the appropriate type. (Solve Exercise 12.7, if you have not done so, to understand why applying a delta to p might be necessary.)

    a. How does this implementation violate localized cost with respect to run time?

    b. How does this implementation violate localized cost with respect to memory use?

12.10   Consider an implementation of exception handling in which the object code for every function contains code, executed every time the function is called, to handle the possibility that an invocation of that function might have to be cleaned up from the stack when an exception occurs.

    a. Explain how this implementation fails to localize cost.

    b. Suppose that the user is given the ability to tell the compiler that a particular function will never have to be cleaned up from the stack for an occurrence of an exception. Would the implementation then localize cost?

    c. What are the advantages and disadvantages of an implementation of exception handling that provides the feature mentioned in part b?

12.11   How would providing only a single header file for an entire library consisting of many classes and functions violate localized cost?

12.12   With the `Map_iter` class of Section 12.4, every call to `Map_iter::next` must perform at least one X and one Y assignment operation to return (via the reference arguments) the next pair in the iteration.

    a. Why can we not optimize away those assignments by instead returning a reference to m's internally stored copy of the next pair in the iteration, where m is the Map being iterated over?

    b. We could optimize `next` by having it return a pointer (rather than a reference) to m's internally stored copy of the next pair. What effect would this optimization have on the safety, ease of use, and implementability of `Map_iter`? Would you apply this optimization if you were the designer of `Map_iter`?

12.13   Suppose that we choose semantics for the `Map_iter` class of Section 12.4 in which we do not specify whether values added or removed during an iteration over a `Map` are eventually seen in that iteration. Give an example of an error that users might make using this interface that they would not make if the semantics of iteration were specified fully.

12.14   Suppose that you are developing the `Path` class discussed in Exercises 1.2 and 7.1. Consider the following function, which uses another class `List` in your library:

```
class Path {
public:
    List<Path> expand_wildcards() const;
    // ...
};
```

The function `expand_wildcards` looks at the file system on the machine on which the program is executing and returns the list of files that match (according to some defined set of rules) the given `Path`. What are the tradeoffs of this coupling between `Path` and `List`?

12.15   Exercise 2.9 recalled Kleene's theorem [DW83] (a language is accepted by a finite state acceptor if and only if that language can be expressed as a regular expression). For part a of Exercise 2.9, you were to suppose that your library provides both a class `FSA` modeling finite state acceptors and a class `Regex` modeling regular expressions; you were then to show the classes and functions you would provide to model Kleene's theorem. State two disadvantages of the coupling between classes that your solution to part a of Exercise 2.9 would create.

12.16   In Section 12.6, we discussed two versions of `location`. The first version was slow but always right; the second, memoized, version was fast but sometimes wrong. Show how to design the containing library to give users a way to select the behavior they desire.

12.17   (∗) Give an example that shows that it is ill advised to reveal that `location` is implemented with a `Map` (an implementation detail).

References and Further Reading

The static initialization problem is discussed by Reiser [Rei92] and in Stroustrup's Section 3.11.4 [Str94a]. Buroff and Murray [BM94] discuss the difficulty of implementing global constant objects in the face of the static initialization problem. Plauger [Pla95] further discusses double construction.

Designing a C++ container class and a mechanism for iterating over the objects in that container is a surprisingly difficult problem with no best solution. Koenig [Koe92a, Koe92b] discusses some of the problems involved. Real C++ libraries (for example, Standard Components [UNI92], the National Institutes of Health Library [GOP90], `Tool.h++` [Rog92], the Booch Components [Rat91], and the GNU C++ Library [Fre88]) use a variety of container and iterator styles. Koenig [Koe93b] discusses the class design questions arising from the relation between container classes and truth values. Tarjan [Tar83] discusses endogenous and exogenous containers.

The combined binary search tree and linear list data structure described in Section 12.4 was brought to our attention by Steve Buroff.

Carroll [Car93] discusses coupling further. Weinand, Gamma, and Marty [WGM89] give an example of a well-designed C++ library with much coupling among its classes.

Springer and Friedman's Chapter 11 [SF89] has an excellent discussion of memoizing.

Bibliography

[AHU83] A. Aho, J. Hopcroft, and J. Ullman. *Data Structures and Algorithms*. Addison-Wesley, 1983.

[ANS89] ANSI. American National Standard for Information Systems — Programming Language C. Technical Report X3.159–1989, ANSI, December 1989.

[ANS94] ANSI. Working Paper for Draft Proposed International Standard for Information Systems — Programming Language C++. Technical Report X3J16/94–0158, ANSI, September 1994.

[ASU86] A. Aho, R. Sethi, and J. Ullman. *Compilers: Principles, Techniques, and Tools*. Addison-Wesley, 1986.

[AT&89] AT&T. *System V Interface Definition*. Addison-Wesley, third edition, 1989.

[Baa88] S. Baase. *Computer Algorithms: Introduction to Design and Analysis*. Addison-Wesley, second edition, 1988.

[Bec94] P. Becker. Writing portable C++ code. *The C++ Report*, 6(7), September 1994.

[Ben82] J. Bentley. *Writing Efficient Programs*. Prentice Hall, 1982.

[Ber90] L. Berlin. When objects collide: Experiences with reusing multiple class hierarchies. In *ECOOP/OOPSLA '90 Proceedings*, pages 181–193. ACM, 1990.

[BI94] K. Baclawski and B. Indurkhya. The notion of inheritance in object-orient programming. *Communications of the ACM*, 37(9):118–119, 1994.

[BM94]   S. Buroff and R. Murray. C++ oracle. *The C++ Report*, 6(9), November–December 1994.

[BN94]   J. Barton and L. Nackman. *Scientific and Engineering C++*. Addison-Wesley, 1994.

[BV93]   G. Booch and M. Vilot. Simplifying the Booch Components. *The C++ Report*, 5(5), June 1993.

[Car92a] T. Cargill. *Elements of C++ Programming Style*. Addison-Wesley, 1992.

[Car92b] M. Carroll. Invasive inheritance. *The C++ Report*, 4(8):34–42, October 1992.

[Car93] M. Carroll. Design of the USL Standard Components. *The C++ Report*, 5(5), June 1993.

[Car94] T. Cargill. Exception handling: A false sense of security. *The C++ Report*, 6(9), November–December 1994.

[Car95] M. Carroll. Tradeoffs of run-time parameterization. *The C++ Report*, 7(1), January 1995.

[CHS91] B. Cohen, D. Hahn, and N. Soiffer. Pragmatic issues in the implementation of flexible libraries for C++. In *Usenix C++ Conference Proceedings*, pages 193–202, April 1991.

[CL95]   M. Cline and G. Lomow. *C++ FAQs: Frequently Asked Questions*. Addison-Wesley, 1995.

[Cli90] W. D. Clinger. How to read floating point numbers accurately. In *ACM SIGPLAN '90 Conference on Programming Language Design and Implementation*, June 1990. SIGPLAN Notices, 25(6).

[CLR90] T. Cormen, C. Leiserson, and R. Rivest. *Introduction to Algorithms*. The MIT Press, 1990.

[Cog90] J. Coggins. Design criteria for C++ class libraries. In *Usenix C++ Conference Proceedings*, pages 25–35, April 1990.

[Cop92] J. Coplien. *Advanced C++ Programming Styles and Idioms*. Addison-Wesley, 1992.

[DR90]   N. Dershowitz and E. Reingold. Calendrical calculations. *Software Practice and Experience*, 20(9):899–928, September 1990.

[DSS90]   S. Dorward, R. Sethi, and J. Shopiro.   Adding new code to a running C++ program. In *Usenix C++ Conference Proceedings*, pages 279–292, April 1990.

[Dup95]   L. Dupré. *BUGS in Writing: A Guide to Debugging Your Prose.* Addison-Wesley, 1995.

[DW83]   M. Davis and E. Weyuker. *Computability, Complexity, and Languages.* Academic Press, 1983.

[Ede92]   D. R. Edelson. Smart pointers: They're smart, but they're not pointers.   In *Usenix C++ Conference Proceedings*, pages 1–19, August 1992.

[ES90]   M. Ellis and B. Stroustrup. *The Annotated C++ Reference Manual.* Addison-Wesley, 1990.

[Faf94]   D. Fafchamps. Organizational factors and reuse. *IEEE Software*, 11(5):31–41, September 1994.

[FN91]   M. Fontana and M. Neath. Checked out and long overdue: Experiences in the design of a C++ class library. In *Usenix C++ Conference Proceedings*, pages 179–191, April 1991.

[Fre88]   The Free Software Foundation, Cambridge MA. *The GNU C++ Library*, February 1988.

[GOP90]   K. Gorlen, S. Orlow, and P. Plexico. *Data Abstraction and Object-Oriented Programming.* John Wiley and Sons, 1990.

[HO87]   D. Halbert and P. O'Brien. Using type and inheritance in object-oriented programming. *IEEE Transactions on Software Engineering*, 4:71–79, 1987.

[HS91]   S. Harbison and G. Steele. *C, A Reference Manual.* Prentice Hall, third edition, 1991.

[HU79]   J. Hopcroft and J. Ullman. *Introduction to Automata Theory, Languages, and Computation.* Addison-Wesley, 1979.

[HW67]   J. Hodges and M. Whitten. *Harbrace College Handbook.* Harcourt Brace &World, sixth edition, 1967.

[IBM]   *The IBM Systems Journal.* 32(4), 1993.

[IEE90] IEEE. Information technology — portable operating system interface (POSIX) part 1: System appolication program interface (API) [C language]. Technical Report 1003.1–1990, IEEE, December 1990.

[JR92] P. Johnson and C. Rees. Reusability through fine-grain inheritance. *Software Practice and Experience*, 22(12):1049–1068, December 1992.

[KA94] S. Kendall and G. Allin. Sharing between translation units in C++ program databases. In *Usenix C++ Conference Proceedings*, pages 247–264, April 1994.

[Kef93] T. Keffer. The design and architecture of Tools.h++. *The C++ Report*, 5(5), June 1993.

[KL92] G. Kiczales and J. Lamping. Issues in the design and specification of class libraries. In *OOPSLA '92*, pages 435–451, 1992.

[Kni93] A. Knight. Copying. *The Smalltalk Report*, 2(5), February 1993.

[Knu89] D. Knuth. The errors of TEX. *Software Practice and Experience*, 19(7):607–685, July 1989.

[Koe91] A. Koenig. Library design is language design. *The Journal of Object-Oriented Programming*, June 1991.

[Koe92a] A. Koenig. Accessing C++ container elements. *The Journal of Object-Oriented Programming*, July 1992.

[Koe92b] A. Koenig. Designing a C++ container class. *The Journal of Object-Oriented Programming*, February 1992.

[Koe92c] A. Koenig. Space-efficient trees in C++. In *Usenix C++ Conference Proceedings*, August 1992.

[Koe93a] A. Koenig. Functions that return references. *The C++ Report*, 5(8), October 1993.

[Koe93b] A. Koenig. Truth and equality in C++. *The C++ Report*, 5(7), September 1993.

[Lap87] J. Lapin. *Portable C and UNIX System Programming*. Prentice Hall, 1987.

[Lea93] D. Lea. The GNU C++ library. *The C++ Report*, 5(5), June 1993.

[LG86] B. Liskov and J. Guttag. *Abstraction and Specification in Program Development.* McGraw-Hill, 1986.

[Lim94] W. C. Lim. Effects of reuse on quality, productivity, and economics. *IEEE Software*, 11(5):23–30, September 1994.

[Lin92] M. Linton. Encapsulating a C++ library. In *Usenix C++ Conference Proceedings*, pages 57–66, August 1992.

[Lip91] S. Lippman. *C++ Primer.* Addison-Wesley, second edition, 1991.

[LP94] M. Linton and D. Pan. Interface translation and implementation filtering. In *Usenix C++ Conference Proceedings*, pages 227–236, April 1994.

[LS93] M. Lee and A. Stepanov. The science of C++ programming. Invited lecture, ANSI C++ meeting, San Jose, CA, November 1993.

[Mar91] B. Martin. The separation of interface and implementation in C++. In *Usenix C++ Conference Proceedings*, pages 51–64, April 1991.

[Mey88] B. Meyer. *Object-oriented Software Construction.* Prentice Hall, 1988.

[Mey92a] B. Meyer. *Eiffel: The Language.* Prentice Hall, 1992.

[Mey92b] S. Meyers. *Effective C++: 50 Specific Ways to Improve Your Programs and Designs.* Addison-Wesley, 1992.

[Mey92c] S. Meyers. Using C++ effectively: Approaches to effectiveness. *The C++ Report*, 4(6), July–August 1992.

[Mey93a] N. Meyers. Memory management in C++ (part 1). *The C++ Report*, 5(6), July–August 1993.

[Mey93b] N. Meyers. Memory management in C++ (part 2). *The C++ Report*, 5(9), November–December 1993.

[Mey94a] S. Meyers. Code reuse, concrete classes, and inheritance. *The C++ Report*, 6(6), July–August 1994.

[Mey94b] S. Meyers. `operator=`: The readers fight back. *The C++ Report*, 6(9), November–December 1994.

[Mey94c] S. Meyers. Our friend, the assignment operator. *The C++ Report*, 6(4), May 1994.

[MM92]   G. McCluskey and R. Murray. Template instantiation for C++. *ACM SIGPLAN Notices*, 27(12):47–56, December 1992.

[MS94]   D. Musser and A. Stepanov. Algorithm-oriented generic libraries. *Software Practice and Experience*, 24(7):623–642, July 1994.

[Mur88]   R. Murray. Building well-behaved type relationships in C++. In *Usenix C++ Conference Proceedings*, pages 19–30, October 1988.

[Mur93]   R. Murray. *C++ Strategies and Tactics*. Addison-Wesley, 1993.

[NB94]   L. Nackman and J. Barton. Base-class composition with multiple derivation and virtual bases. In *Usenix C++ Conference Proceedings*, pages 57–72, April 1994.

[Nov92]   Novell, Inc. *C++ Language System Release 3.1 Manual, Selected Readings*, 1992.

[Pla93]   P. Plauger. Reusability myths. *Computer Language*, 10(5):25–29, May 1993.

[Pla95]   P. Plauger. *The Draft C++ Library*. Prentice Hall, 1995.

[Rat91]   Rational. *The C++ Booch Components*, 1991.

[RC90]   A. Riel and J. Carter. Towards a minimal public interface for C++ classes. *The C++ Insider*, 1(1), 1990.

[RDC93]   E. Reingold, N. Dershowitz, and S. Clamen. Calendrical calculations, II: Three historical calendars. *Software Practice and Experience*, 23(4):383–404, April 1993.

[Rei92]   J. Reiser. Static initializers: Reducing the value-added tax on programs. In *Usenix C++ Conference Proceedings*, August 1992.

[Rog92]   Rogue Wave Software. *Tools.h++ Class Library*, 1992.

[Sch90]   J. Schwarz. C++ is not an object-oriented language. *The C++ Journal*, Fall, 1990.

[SF89]   G. Springer and D. Friedman. *Scheme and the Art of Programming*. The MIT Press, 1989.

[SM77]   D. Stanat and D. McAllister. *Discrete Mathematics in Computer Science*. Prentice Hall, 1977.

[Spr93]   R. Sprowl. Abbreviated objects. *The C++ Report*, 5(9), November–December 1993.

[Sta94]   W. Staringer. Constructing applications from reusable components. *IEEE Software*, 11(5):61–68, September 1994.

[Ste92]   W. Stevens. *Advanced Programming in the UNIX Environment.* Addison-Wesley, 1992.

[Str91]   B. Stroustrup. *The C++ Programming Language.* Addison-Wesley, second edition, 1991.

[Str93]   B. Stroustrup. Library design using C++. *The C++ Report*, 5(5), June 1993.

[Str94a] B. Stroustrup. *The Design and Evolution of C++.* Addison-Wesley, 1994.

[Str94b] B. Stroustrup. Making a vector fit for a standard. *The C++ Report*, 6(8), October 1994.

[SW79]   W. Strunk and E. White. *The Elements of Style.* Macmillan Publishing Co., 1979.

[SW90]   G. Steele and J. L. White. How to print floating point numbers accurately. In *ACM SIGPLAN '90 Conference on Programming Language Design and Implementation*, June 1990. SIGPLAN Notices, 25(6).

[Tar83]   R. Tarjan. *Data Structures and Network Algorithms.* Society for Industrial and Applied Mathematics, 1983.

[Tea93]   S. Teale. *C++ IOStreams Handbook.* Addison-Wesley, 1993.

[Tra88]   W. Tracz. Software reuse myths. *Software Engineering Notes (ACM SIGSOFT)*, 13(1):17–20, January 1988.

[UNI92]   UNIX System Laboratories. *C++ Standard Components Programmer's Reference*, 1992.

[Vil94]   M. Vilot. An introduction to the STL library. *The C++ Report*, 6(8), October 1994.

[Vil95]   M. Vilot. The C++ standard library. *The C++ Report*, 7(2), February 1995.

[WBF91]   C. Will, J. Baldo, and D. Fife. *Proceedings of the Workshop on Legal Issues in Software Reuse.* Technical report, Strategic Defense Initiative Organization, July 1991. Published by Institute for Defense Analyses, IDA Document D–1004.

[Weg93]   I. Wegener. BOTTOM-UP-HEAPSORT, a new variant of HEAPSORT beating, on an average, QUICKSORT (if n is not very small). *Theoretical Computer Science*, (118):81–98, 1993.

[WGM89]   A. Weinand, E. Gamma, and R. Marty. Design and implementation of ET++, a seamless object-oriented application framework. *Structured Programming*, 10(2):63–87, 1989.

[Wik87]   Å Wikström. *Functional Programming Using Standard ML*. Prentice Hall, 1987.

[WOS94]   B. S. Weide, W. F. Ogden, and M. Sitaraman. Recasting algorithms to encourage reuse. *IEEE Software*, 11(5):80–88, September 1994.

Index

A

abort, handling errors by exit or, 117

abstract

base class, 66

base class; *See also* interface class.

`const`, 35–38

abstraction, 13–14

documenting class, 14, 255

documenting in terms of, 248

access protection and name lookup, order of, 160

acquisition

is initialization technique, resource, 129

of externally reused library, 235

`added` example, 159

adding member function, source compatibility of, 159

alignment restrictions, portability and, 208

alternative version of `new` and `delete`, 122

Annotated C++ Reference Manual. See ARM.

ANSI/ISO

behavior of `new`, 125

conformant code, nonportability of, 206

definition of C++, v–vi, 205–207

run-time library. *See* run-time library.

Standard Template Library, 231

archive

definition of, 3

partitioning, 87

argument evaluation, unspecified order of, 212

ARM, 205

and `cfront`, differences between, 206

`Array` example, 17

assignment

operator not in minimal standard interface, 20–21

problem, derived, 66–69

problem solved with interface class, derived, 69

associative array, 51

automatically generated member function, documenting, 256–257

automatic template instantiation, 216–220; *See also* template instantiation.

`AVLTree` example, 52

B

backward compatibility, definition of, 157

`Bag` example, 27

base class, nontemplate, 80–81

binary compatibility. *See* link compatibility.

binary search tree, 282; *See also* `BSTree`, red-black tree.

bit `const`, 35–36

`BSTree`; *See also* binary search tree.

example, 49–51, 66–69, 79–82, 86, 92

`BSTreebase` example, 80–81, 86

`BSTree_int` example, 49–50

build

procedures, portability of, 205, 226

sequence, 158

build-time efficiency, 76–85

`bzero` example, 204

303

C

C run-time library, 224–225

C++

ANSI/ISO definition of, v–vi, 205–207

extensions, nonportability and nonstandard, 207

implementation details, nonportability and, 213

language definition changing, v–vi

language definition, nonportability caused by changing, 205–207

run-time library, 223–225

`Cache` example, 287–288

`Car` example, 14

casting

away `const`, 37

in pointer containers, safe, 83

CED example, 181–192

`CED_factory` example, 185–187

`CED_int` example, 182–184

cfront, 206

differences between ARM and, 206

`char`, implementation-defined signedness of, 211

Cheshire-cat class. *See* handle class.

City on the Edge of Forever, 113

class; *See also* interface class.

abstraction, documenting, 14, 255

conversions required by special-purpose, 106

definition of exception safety of, 128

definition of nice, 18

definitions, one-definition rule for, 139–140

depth of, 177

documenting syntactic interface of, 256–258

fanout of, 177

nice, 16–18

root, 177

special-purpose, 104–107

class design, 13–41; *See also* `const`, interface consistency, minimal standard interface.

rules, summary of, 41

clean library, 152–153

code size, 85–88

definition of, 85

effective, 90

function definition and, 90

inlining vs., 90

run time, and inlining, relation among, 89–91

template specialization, 88

commands, nonportability and system, 226

`Companyxyz_libabc_widget` example, 143

compatibility, 157–169; *See also* build sequence, deprecated features, incompatibility, release synchronization.

definition of backward, 157

definition of forward, 157

documenting, 238

forms of, 158–159

in practice, definition of, 159

in theory, definition of, 159

of changing undocumented property, 167–168

compilation unit. *See* translation unit.

`compile` example, 97

compile-time efficiency, 76–78

compile-time template instantiation, 217; *See also* template instantiation.

compiling with exceptions turned off, 119

`Complete_bstree` example, 49–50

`Complex` example, 32–33

complexity class, 43

conceptual template parameter independence, 81

concrete class, definition of, 66

conflict, 137–154; *See also* clean library, good-citizen library, naming conventions.

created by external reuse, 236

definition of, 137

environmental name, 151–152

global name, 137–146

header file name, 151

macro name, 146–151

prevention via `namespace` construct, 145–146

conformant code, nonportability of ANSI/ISO, 206

consistency. *See* interface consistency.

consistent state. *See* exception safety.

`const`, 35–41; *See also* class design.

abstract, 35–38

bit, 35–36

casting away, 37

Credits

Epigraph Credits
For Preface, reprinted with permission of W. W. Norton Publishing Co. from *The Greek Way* by Edith Hamilton, copyright 1930. For Chapter 2, from a cartoon appearing in *The Times* (London), Time Newspapers Ltd., 1976. For Chapter 4, used with permission of the author Wm. A. Wulf. For Chapter 6, used with permission of Jerry Schwarz. For Chapter 7, used with permission of Robert Murray. For Chapter 12, reprinted with permission of Scribner, an imprint of Simon & Schuster, Inc. from *End of the Chapter* by John Galsworthy. Copyright 1934 by Charles Scribner's Sons; copyright renewed.

Portions of material on localized cost; handle, interface, and container classes; self-contained libraries; fine-grained inheritance; error handling; and efficiency have appeared in previous editions of *The C++ Report*.

Current Titles in C++ from Addison-Wesley

Barton/Nackman, *Scientific and Engineering C++: An Introduction with Advanced Techniques and Examples* © 1994

Budd, *Classic Data Structures in C++* © 1993

Buzzi-Ferraris, *Scientific C++: Building Numerical Libraries the Object-Oriented Way* © 1993

Cline/Lomow, *C++ FAQs: Frequently Asked Questions* © 1995

Coplien, *Advanced C++: Programming Styles and Idioms* © 1992

Ellis/Stroustrup, *The Annotated C++ Reference Manual* © 1990

Friedman/Koffman, *Problem Solving, Abstraction, and Design Using C++* © 1994

Lippman, *C++ Primer, Second Edition* © 1991

Soukup, *Taming C++: Pattern Classes and Persistence for Large Projects* © 1994

Stroustrup, *The C++ Programming Language, Second Edition* © 1991

Stroustrup, *The Design and Evolution of C++* © 1994

Teale, *C++ IOStreams Handbook* © 1993

Winston, *On to C++* © 1994